Collaborating for English Learners

Second Edition

We dedicate this book to all educators who are committed to working with English learners. We also dedicate this book to our respective families, who are our daily inspirations: Howie, Benjamin, Jacob, and Noah; Tim, Dave, Jason, Sara, Meadow, Gavin, and Rohnan.

Collaborating for English Learners

A Foundational Guide to Integrated Practices

Second Edition

Andrea Honigsfeld

Maria G. Dove

FOR INFORMATION:

Corwin

A SAGE Company

2455 Teller Road

Thousand Oaks, California 91320

(800) 233-9936

www.corwin.com

SAGE Publications Ltd.

1 Oliver's Yard

55 City Road

London EC1Y 1SP

United Kingdom

SAGE Publications India Pvt. Ltd.

B 1/I 1 Mohan Cooperative Industrial Area

Mathura Road, New Delhi 110 044

India

SAGE Publications Asia-Pacific Pte. Ltd.

18 Cross Street #10-10/11/12

China Square Central

Singapore 048423

Program Director and Publisher: Dan Alpert

Content Development Editor: Lucas Schleicher

Senior Editorial Assistant: Mia Rodriguez

Production Editor: Amy Schroller

Copy Editor: Colleen Brennan

Typesetter: C&M Digitals (P) Ltd.

Proofreader: Dennis Webb

Indexer: Jeanne Busemeyer

Cover Designer: Scott Van Atta

Marketing Manager: Sharon Pendergast

Printed in the United States of America

ISBN 978-1-5443-4003-6

This book is printed on acid-free paper.

19 20 21 22 23 10 9 8 7 6 5 4 3 2 1

Contents

Note From the Publisher: The authors have provided video and web content throughout the book that is available to you through QR (quick response) codes. To read a QR code, you must have a smartphone or tablet with a camera. We recommend that you download a QR code reader app that is made specifically for your phone or tablet brand.

 Videos may also be accessed at resources.corwin.com/CollaboratingforELs.

Preface

I am just a child who has never grown up. I still keep asking these "how" and "why" questions. Occasionally, I find an answer.

—Stephen Hawking

Questions about collaboration for the sake of English learners—a collection of candid, genuine queries we gathered over a number of years from our professional learning workshop participants—have been not only the guidepost for the direction of our work but also the driving force behind our investigation into collaborative practices well before the first edition of this book was published in 2010. Almost ten years later, we are still traveling along this journey, amassing more questions not only from teachers and school leaders in the field but also from our ongoing research. Like the quote from Stephen Hawking, we sometimes find we have more questions than answers as we continue to investigate collaboration for the sake of English learners.

We started our own journeys of collaboration at the onset of our teaching careers about thirty years ago. We have been exploring the *Whos, Whats, Whens, Wheres, Whys,* and *Hows* of teacher collaboration and co-teaching for the sake of our English learners ever since then. Since 2010, when the first edition of this book was published, we have been fortunate to support schools across the country to develop integrated, collaborative service delivery models for English learners in Colorado, Florida, Georgia, Hawaii, Idaho, Illinois, Indiana, Iowa, Kentucky, Maryland, Massachusetts, Michigan, Minnesota, Missouri, New Hampshire, New Jersey, North Carolina, Oregon, Pennsylvania, Rhode Island, South Carolina, Tennessee, Texas, Vermont, Virginia, Washington, Wisconsin, and our hometown state, New York. We have also witnessed and documented how many school districts have moved in this direction. We have written this second edition with these promising programs in mind, and we have made every effort to provide our readers with updated information via research, frameworks for implementation, and authentic documentation of collaborative practices in the field. To this end, we have included the following in this second edition:

- The latest research and literature to support collaboration for English learners as well as new evidence that identifies the positive effects of teacher collaboration
- Authentic voices from teachers in the field throughout the United States who share their collaborative experiences

- A detailed analysis of the six principles for the exemplary teaching of English learners (TESOL International Association, 2018) and how collaboration is a key factor in meeting the challenges of these principles
- The critical role of emphasizing and maintaining an asset-based mindset when working in cooperation with other teachers for the sake of English learners
- Expanded information regarding noninstructional collaborative activities and how to make them a success
- Sample frameworks for creating and sustaining collaborative teams
- New ideas for developing virtual meeting spaces via technology
- Enhanced guidance for reflective practices
- New evidence from multiple schools via a series of case studies, in which practitioners identify the challenges and successes of their collaborative practices and provide their own words of wisdom
- Updated key resources for further investigation

We have written this second edition with the most up-to-date information about teacher collaboration in mind, recognizing that

- "the long-standing culture of teacher isolation and individualism, together with teachers' preference to preserve their individual autonomy, may hinder deep-level collaboration to occur" (Vangrieken, Dochy, Raes, & Kyndt, 2015, p. 36);
- research on teacher collaboration and co-teaching is expanding (Kuusisaari, 2014); and
- collaborative practices, including co-teaching, for the sake of ELs are growing (Beninghof & Leensvaart, 2016; Honigsfeld & Dove, 2017; Honigsfeld, McDermott, & Cordeiro, 2017; Martin-Beltrán & Madigan Peercy, 2014; Pappamihiel, 2012; Peercy, Ditter, & Destefano, 2017).

As we mentioned previously, we have been collecting questions during our professional-development sessions for many years. The difference is the medium we use today—whereas in previous years we might have collected hundreds of questions on index cards, Post-it notes, and chart-paper designated as "parking lots," we now use Padlet as a tool to gauge educators' interest in and challenges with the topic of teacher collaboration and co-teaching for the sake of ELs. From the more than 5,000 questions collected on our various Padlet sites, we continue to see some recurring questions:

- How do you successfully plan with the English language development/English language learner (ELD/ELL) teacher? Do other districts have common planning time scheduled for collaboration?
- How could the administration best support teacher collaboration?
- How do we get through the curriculum with such diverse student needs among ELs?
- How can we facilitate communication with parents?
- What are key factors to consider when grouping ELs?

- How do we support all teachers of ELs when not co-teaching?
- How does this work for paraeducators? What is their role in the co-taught classroom?
- What should teachers consider when selecting a co-teaching model?

The questions we receive range from novice-level, sincere inquires, such as *Who should collaborate?* to more complex, building-wide concerns such as *How might administrators support teacher collaboration more effectively?* We find a similar pattern of questions each time we work with teachers on collaborative strategies and co-teaching. Our answers grow out of our investigations of authentic collaborative practices in the field. The more questions we answer, the more questions we raise. Each person we encounter has a unique perspective on what educators could and should do to help ELs.

Do you have a few questions? If you are reading these pages, you probably do, and this updated edition of our book was written just for that purpose. The concepts of teacher collaboration, collaborative schools, and co-teaching are not new; however, our invitation to all teachers (general-education, content-area, and ELD/ELL specialists alike) to set out on a journey from collaboration to co-teaching may still be new in many schools. Enjoy your trip through the following nine chapters, each centered on an essential question.

Chapter 1 establishes the framework for the rest of the book ("What Is This Book About?"). Chapter 2 explores the importance of teacher collaboration and offers a rationale for collaborative practices and co-teaching ("Why Is Collaboration Needed?"). Chapter 3 identifies all stakeholders in a multilingual educational community and describes their unique roles and responsibilities in developing a school culture that fosters teacher collaboration and co-teaching for the benefit of English learners ("Who Does Teacher Collaboration and Co-Teaching for ELs Concern?"). Chapter 4 highlights the collaborative practices that teachers participate in ("What Are the Essential Components of an Integrated, Collaborative Service Delivery for ELs?). Chapter 5 identifies the nuts and bolts of collaborative and co-teaching practices ("How Do Teachers Plan, Instruct, Assess, and Reflect Collaboratively?"). Chapter 6 explores the time frames available for collaborations ("When Do Teachers Collaborate and Co-Teach?"). Chapter 7 describes the different physical and virtual environments that teachers use to enhance their collaborative processes ("Where Do Teachers Collaborate and Co-Teach?"). Chapter 8 promotes reflective practices and presents informal assessment and evaluation techniques ("What Next? Reviewing and Evaluating Integrated, Collaborative Service Delivery for ELs). Finally, Chapter 9 introduces seven authentic case studies of collaboration and co-teaching across the United States and across grade levels representing a range of contexts ("Portraits of Collaboration").

We hope you enjoy your journey exploring the possibilities that teacher collaboration holds for ELD/ELL programs and the education of English learners. In addition, it is our wish that the information and personal stories we have shared regarding co-teaching and inclusive programs to benefit ELs may inspire you to devise, experiment with, and evaluate innovative programs for this special student population.

Acknowledgments

We extend a special thank-you to all the teachers and administrators who—directly or indirectly—supported the development or inclusion of the case studies, classroom examples, and authentic snapshots presented in this book: Sarita Amaya, Karen Buckles, Yanick Chery-Frederic, Joyce Dallas, Melissa Eddington, Molly Fuentealba, Susan Dorkings, Alla Gonzalez Del Castillo, Pam Hardy, Carlota Holder, Angela Hudson, Tan Huynh, Natasa Karac, Toshiko Maurizio, Lucia Posillico, Katie Toppel, Jennifer Visalli, and Jennifer Wolf.

We appreciate the willingness of all the teachers featured in Chapter 9—who also served as co-authors of their case studies—to share their collaborative experiences: Patricia Beltran, Ashley Blackley, Andrea Calabrese, Allyson Caudill, John Cox, Nick DiBenedetto, Ashley DeKoch, Nicole Fernandez, Mike Garguilo, Rachel Ogimachi, Brittany Schmidt, Faith Tripp, Thad Williams, and Danielle Youngs.

We would also like to acknowledge the technical assistance offered by several Molloy College doctoral research assistants—Donna Cempa-Danziger, Jennifer Delahunt, Nadia Khan-Roopnarine, and Shalinie Sarju.

We thank Dan Alpert for being the most insightful and encouraging editor we could have asked for. We would like to express our gratitude to Dan publicly for believing in this project from the beginning and for supporting it ever since. Our sincere appreciation goes to the entire Corwin team, especially to Mia Rodriguez, Lucas Schleicher, Maura Sullivan, Amy Schroller, and Colleen Brennan, for their work on the manuscript preparation and production process.

We would like to thank all the teachers and professors with whom we co-taught and who helped us develop our own collaborative practices, in particular, Nancy Bart, Dr. Audrey Cohan, Dolly Ging, Eileen Haydock, Dr. Mark James, Joanne Lufrano, Alison Roberts, Dr. Allison Roda, Sandy Rubin, Sandy Schlaff, and Joyce Smithok.

The richness of the content and variety of ideas could not have been possible without the generous input and feedback of those who have attended professional-development trainings with us or participated in our research projects. We also wish to acknowledge individuals who have encouraged us to pursue this project, including all colleagues at Molloy College, Rockville Centre, New York.

Last but not least, without the ongoing support of our immediate and extended families and friends, this book could not have happened. You know who you are, and we love you!

About the Authors

Andrea Honigsfeld, EdD, is Associate Dean and Professor in the Division of Education at Molloy College, Rockville Centre, New York. She directs a doctoral program in Educational Leadership for Diverse Learning Communities. Before entering the field of teacher education, she was an English-as-a-foreign-language teacher in Hungary (Grades 5–8 and adult) and an English-as-a-second-language teacher in New York City (Grades K–3 and adult). She also taught Hungarian at New York University.

She was the recipient of a doctoral fellowship at St. John's University, New York, where she conducted research on individualized instruction and learning styles. She has published extensively on working with English language learners and providing individualized instruction based on learning style preferences. She received a Fulbright Award to lecture in Iceland in the fall of 2002. In the past twelve years, she has been presenting at conferences across the United States, Great Britain, Denmark, Sweden, the Philippines, and the United Arab Emirates. She frequently offers staff development, primarily focusing on effective differentiated strategies and collaborative practices for English-as-a-second-language and general-education teachers. She co-authored *Differentiated Instruction for At-Risk Students* (2009) and co-edited the five-volume *Breaking the Mold of Education* series (2010–2013), published by Rowman and Littlefield. She is also the co-author of *Core Instructional Routines: Go-To Structures for Effective Literacy Teaching, K–5* (2014) and *Core Instructional Routines: Go-To Structures for the 6–12 Classroom* (2016), published by Heinemann. With Maria Dove, she co-edited *Coteaching and Other Collaborative Practices in the EFL/ESL Classroom: Rationale, Research, Reflections, and Recommendations* (2012) and co-authored *Collaboration and Co-Teaching: Strategies for English Learners* (2010), *Common Core for the Not-So-Common Learner, Grades K–5: English Language Arts Strategies* (2013), *Common Core for the Not-So-Common Learner, Grades 6–12: English Language Arts Strategies* (2013), *Beyond Core Expectations: A Schoolwide Framework for Serving the Not-So-Common Learner* (2014), *Collaboration and Co-Teaching: A Leader's Guide* (2015), *Co-Teaching for English Learners: A Guide to Collaborative Planning, Instruction, Assessment, and Reflection* (2018), five of which are Corwin bestsellers.

Maria G. Dove, EdD, is Associate Professor in the Division of Education at Molloy College, Rockville Centre, New York, where she teaches preservice and inservice teachers about the research and best practices for developing effective programs and school policies for English learners. Before entering the field of higher education, she worked for over thirty years as an English-as-a-second-language teacher in public school settings (Grades K–12) and in adult English language programs in Nassau County, New York.

In 2010, she received the Outstanding ESOL Educator Award from New York State Teachers of English to Speakers of Other Languages (NYS TESOL). She frequently provides professional development for educators throughout the United States on the teaching of diverse students. She also serves as a mentor for new ESOL teachers as well as an instructional coach for general-education teachers and literacy specialists. She has published articles and book chapters on collaborative teaching practices, instructional leadership, and collaborative coaching. With Andrea Honigsfeld, she co-authored five best-selling Corwin books: *Collaboration and Co-Teaching: Strategies for English Learners* (2010), *Common Core for the Not-So-Common Learner, Grades K–5: English Language Arts Strategies* (2013), and *Common Core for the Not-So-Common Learner, Grades 6–12: English Language Arts Strategies* (2013), *Collaboration and Co-Teaching: A Leader's Guide* (2015), and *Co-Teaching for English Learners: A Guide to Collaborative Planning, Instruction, Assessment, and Reflection* (2018). The same writing team also co-edited *Coteaching and Other Collaborative Practices in the EFL/ESL Classroom: Rationale, Research, Reflections, and Recommendations* (2012), published by Information Age. With Andrea Honigsfeld and Audrey Cohan, she co-authored *Beyond Core Expectations: A Schoolwide Framework for Serving the Not-So-Common Learner* (2014).

What Is This Book About?

That is what learning is. You suddenly understand something you've understood all your life, but in a new way.

—Doris Lessing

OVERVIEW

The goals of this chapter are to offer a rationale for this book and to provide insight into its purpose and organization. We offer important background information on demographic trends for English learners (ELs) and compare various program models serving ELs across the United States. We examine how to benefit ELs through a framework of collaborative teaching practices and define key concepts related to teacher collaboration and co-teaching for the benefit of ELs. After we describe various current program models to support ELs and present a historical perspective on teacher collaboration, we make a claim for teacher collaboration for the sake of ELs in today's schools.

Student Snapshots

Kaman and her younger sister Feng arrived with their family from Shanghai just two weeks before the school year began. They hardly had settled into their American home when, filled with a strange mix of concern and excitement, they entered their new school. Kaman, a sixth grader, and Feng, a second-grade student, spoke little English, although Kaman had some facility with understanding and reading the language.

(Continued)

(Continued)

When Feng reached her classroom, her eyes opened wide and a huge smile appeared across her petite face. She was amazed to see others who looked just like her as there were many Asian families in the neighborhood. When the teacher led her by the hand to her seat, she seemed undisturbed by the unfamiliar words she heard everyone speaking. Feng was undaunted by her lack of English language skills. She clearly made her thoughts known to her classmates and her teacher by using simple gestures and pointing to the things she needed. Several of her classmates taught her some new words like "water," "lunch," and "bathroom," which she had trouble pronouncing, but she felt wholly satisfied with her newfound understanding and word approximations. And when it came time for math, Feng not only was able to understand the lesson, she provided one of her new friends the answers to some of the number problems. Feng was having a great first day at her new school.

In contrast, Kaman's day was filled with intermittent waves of anxiety and fear. When she entered her new classroom, the teacher was busy, organizing science textbooks that had just arrived, and her new classmates seemed to ignore her. Kaman stood for some time in the back of the room waiting for all the desks to fill before she chose one for herself. She was disturbed and distracted by all the foreign sights, sounds, and smells around her. Kaman tried to learn what was expected of her by observing her fellow students, but she felt as if she was always one step behind the others. She copied everything the teacher wrote on the board, although the teacher said so many things he did not write, and Kaman was unable to understand him. She also did not understand all of the abbreviations the teacher used when writing the homework assignments. Surprisingly, no one seemed to address Kaman's emerging English skills on her first day in her new school, but as the day ended, Kaman dreaded the thought of what might happen when she was found out.

Consider This

Although Kaman and Feng come from the same household, their psychological and emotional needs differ greatly. On occasion, older siblings, in spite of their better facility with the English language, have more difficulty adjusting than their younger brothers and sisters. Attending the same school may end up being a very different experience for children coming from the same family. What we advocate for is a collaborative approach to serving ELs and their families that invites all stakeholders to the table.

When complex learning environments are as diverse as they tend to be in classrooms across the United States, curricular and instructional decisions must be made carefully and intentionally. Heidi Hayes Jacobs and Marie Hubley Alcock (2017) suggest that we create "quests for our children and young people as we design personalized learning opportunities" (p. 64). Jacobs and Alcock contend that in order to explore the diverse needs of students, teachers and administrators must be mindful of the distinct challenges of students along with their various individual needs. In the best interest of the students, educators must collaborate and develop innovative strategies to design classroom instruction.

WHAT GUIDED US WHEN WE WROTE THIS BOOK?

When we wrote the first edition of this book, *Collaboration and Co-Teaching: Strategies for English Learners*, we invited our readers to explore the many possibilities of teacher collaboration for the benefit of ELs. In the same way, whether you have earned an English for Speakers of Other Languages (ESOL) teaching license, an endorsement from your state, work with ELs in a sheltered-content class, or are a general-education teacher perhaps without formal EL training, all educators must have shared goals in common when it comes to the teaching and learning of ELs. Through our many years of talking with educators, visiting classrooms, and guiding teachers for the sake of this population of students, we have noted that the most successful programs are created when all service providers strive to deliver the rigorous, engaging instruction to ELs collaboratively and in alignment with grade-appropriate standards.

We updated this book to be a valuable resource that assists both novice and experienced teachers in their endeavors to initiate or continue to provide effective *integrated, collaborative* instruction for ELs. We define this approach to serving ELs as one that has the following characteristics:

- The core content curriculum is integrated with language and literacy development goals.
- Daily instruction intentionally includes language and literacy development targets across all content areas.
- Support services are fully integrated into the regular school schedule.
- Educators plan, deliver, and assess instruction in collaboration with each other.
- All children have a strong sense of belonging in the class and school community.

Why is this type of instruction necessary, and how can it be done? This new edition will provide extensive evidence for the success of *integrated, collaborative* instruction for ELs and practical strategies on how to implement it.

Much has been written about the cognitive, academic, and linguistic needs of ELs (García & Kleifgen, 2018; Nieto & Bode, 2012). Many guidebooks and professional-development materials have been produced on teacher collaboration and co-teaching for inclusive classrooms (Dove & Honigsfeld, 2018; Friend & Cook, 2013; Honigsfeld & Dove, 2015; Murawski & Lochner, 2017; Stein, 2016, 2017; Villa & Thousand, 2016; Villa, Thousand, & Nevin, 2013). Much has been published about effective strategies general-education teachers can use to offer more culturally and linguistically responsive instruction for ELs (Calderón & Slakk, 2018; Ferlazzo & Hull Sypnieski, 2018; Gibbons, 2015; Singer, 2018; Staehr Fenner & Snyder, 2017). However, very few resources are available to help general-education teachers and English language development/English language learner (ELD/ELL) specialists collaborate effectively on all grade levels. Our goal is to fill that gap by offering a user-friendly and comprehensive guide that considers all types and levels of collaboration.

We recognize the variety of ELD program models, diverse local needs, and considerable regional differences that exist in services for ELs. We also acknowledge that each student is unique, as is every educator reading this book. For this reason, we respond to this diversity by addressing the spectrum of current, collaborative practices. These range from informal and occasional exchanges of teaching ideas, to systemic and formal initiatives such as curriculum alignment and parallel teaching, to the most complex form of collaboration, which is co-teaching embedded in the context of a vibrant professional learning community (Mattos, DuFour, DuFour, Eaker, & Many, 2016).

With increasing numbers of ELs in the general-education classrooms, there are a number of program models available to ELD/ELL service providers. Schools need to examine all available program models and instructional delivery systems to be able to provide the best services for a growing population of ELs. There is a documented need for teachers to work together formally and informally, inside and outside the classroom, and during academic learning time or instructional time and professional-development time. Our book offers a vehicle to explore the world of collaboration by answering essential questions that we used as chapter titles. Additionally, we define the role school administrators play in collaboration, offer comprehensive guidelines on conducting collaborative program evaluations, and outline how the book can be used as a professional-development tool to help build professional learning communities that focus on ELs' needs.

THE PURPOSE

The purpose of this book is manifold and as follows:

1. To define teacher collaboration, collaborative team teaching, and co-teaching in the context of English language development

2. To explore how teacher collaboration and co-teaching can provide an effective framework for integrated ELD practices to accommodate the academic, sociocultural, and linguistic needs of diverse English learners

3. To establish a vehicle for professional development toward creative collaboration between ELD/ELL specialists and general-education teachers

4. To offer a framework for implementing an effective co-teaching model to differentiate instruction for all learners

5. To recount real-life vignettes that depict challenges and successes teachers experienced in collaborative partnerships

6. To share extensive case studies of ELD/ELL teachers' collaborative experiences at the elementary, middle, and high school levels

7. To offer guidelines to school district administrators on how to create a collaborative instructional model to support ELs

8. To provide insight into areas of best practice where further research is needed

STRUCTURE AND ORGANIZATION OF THE BOOK

Our second edition title reflects a broad perspective: *Collaborating for English Learners: A Foundational Guide to Integrated Practices.* We invite you to take your own journey and encourage you to choose your own collaborative paths, using this book as a roadmap. We also recognize that different educational institutions may have teachers committed to certain formal collaborative activities in the form of grade-level, department, or general faculty meetings. For this reason, each chapter examines both formal and informal teacher collaboration practices as well as co-teaching with the ELD/ELL specialist. The chapters are structured in a similar fashion for consistency. Recurring features are intended to provide easy access to the content of the book.

Overview: We offer a descriptive preview of the entire chapter by highlighting the key ideas that are included.

Voices From the Field: We present a short, authentic vignette shared by different teachers from around the country at the elementary, middle, or high school level in each chapter. Their personal and professional experiences are directly connected to the content of the chapter. We periodically revisit their stories as they relate to our discussion of the dilemmas, challenges, and successes discussed in the chapter.

Following the two introductory features, the main body of each chapter addresses both general collaborative practices and specific co-teaching experiences with ELD/ELL specialists. Chapters 2 through 8 end with the following recurring features:

Administrators' Roles: We recognize that teacher collaboration and co-teaching practices have sometimes developed as grassroots initiatives—teachers, through their own leadership and action, created opportunities for collaboration to occur without administrative directives. We have both been involved in such pioneering experiences. We also recognize that collaboration goes beyond what individual teachers do; it involves school and district level administrators, support staff, the entire school faculty, and the larger educational community. Building a professional learning community—in which a culture of collaboration is the norm and co-teaching is instructionally and logistically supported—requires administrators' full support. In each chapter, we address the role of school leadership and offer key points to be considered when creating an integrated, collaborative model of ELD services.

Summary: At the conclusion of each chapter, we briefly synthesize the main ideas and their implications for teachers working in diverse contexts.

Discussion Questions: We anticipate that our book will be useful in both preservice teacher education courses and inservice professional-development situations. We invite you to continue exploring the topics presented in each chapter. The end-of-chapter questions are designed to prompt further reflections for the individual reader and to initiate group discussions and collaborative inquiry for teacher groups.

Key Online Resources: We offer a list of online resources at the end of each chapter that allows you to search for more information on the topic.

Chapter 9 stands apart from the first eight chapters. Instead of following the previously established template, it exhibits seven case studies to demonstrate the variety of collaborative experiences in elementary, middle, and high school contexts. This final chapter is designed to aid in the synthesis of the ideas in the book in a cohesive and authentic way.

We wish to emphasize that teacher collaboration is a vehicle for ongoing, site-based professional development through mentoring (for novice teachers), peer coaching (for midcareer teachers), and establishing teacher leadership roles (for more experienced teachers). Thus, our book is designed to further ideas on how to engage in a collaborative inquiry process, in a collegial circle, or a teacher study circle.

THE ENGLISH LEARNER POPULATION

The population of English learners in the United States continues to rise. According to Joel McFarland and colleagues (2017), the population of students designated as English language learners (ELLs) increased from 4.3 million in 2004–2005 to 4.6 million in 2014–2015. All except 15 states reported increases in students needing support services for English language assistance programs.

> In 2014–15, the percentage of public school students who were ELLs was 10.0 percent or more in the District of Columbia and seven states. These states, most of which are located in the West, were Alaska, California, Colorado, Illinois, Nevada, New Mexico, and Texas. California reported the highest percentage of ELLs among its public school students, at 22.4 percent, followed by Nevada at 17.0 percent . . . with the largest percentage-point increase occurring in Maryland (4.4 percentage points). (pp. 106–107)

Various school districts as well as adult programs use different labels to identify students who are learning English; these include English learners (ELs), English language learners (ELLs), emergent bilinguals (EBs), multilingual learners (MLLs), and others. In this book, we have chosen to use the acronym EL as it is the most commonly used reference in the United States and internationally.

COLLABORATION

The concepts of teacher collaboration and collaborative schools are not new; however, our invitation to all teachers (general-education, content area, and ELD/ELL specialists alike) to set out on a journey beginning with collaboration and moving toward co-teaching *for the sake of English learners* may be new in many schools.

The word *collaboration* comes from "co-labor," or "work together." According to *Merriam-Webster's Collegiate Dictionary*, *to collaborate* means "to work jointly with others or together especially in an intellectual endeavour."

In the *Merriam-Webster Thesaurus* (online), *collaboration* is defined two ways:

1. The state of having shared interests or efforts (association)
2. The work and activity of a number of persons who individually contribute toward the efficiency of the whole (teamwork)

Several educational researchers and practitioners have offered their definitions and descriptions of collaboration. Many others emphasize the importance of collaboration as an essential skill for bringing about much-needed educational and social change. Finally, some seminal as well as current research indicates that collaboration may hold the answer to improved teacher and student learning.

- As early as 1990, Stuart Smith and James Scott claimed that "collaboration depends inherently on the voluntary effort of professional educators to improve their schools and their own teaching through teamwork" (p. 2). They confirmed Ann Lieberman and Lynne Miller's (1984) position that the norm continues to be "self-imposed, professionally sanctioned teacher isolation" (p. 11).

- Linda Darling-Hammond and Dion Burns (2014) report that "more than any other policy area, actions that support collaborative learning among teachers appear to hold promise for improving the quality of teaching" (p. v), thus confirming that teacher collaboration is an important dimension of teacher effectiveness.

- Ben Jensen and his colleagues (2016) note that as adult learners, teachers learn "not simply from reading and observing others work, but from combining these passive activities with active collaboration and learning-by-doing" (p. 8).

- Les Foltos (2018) blogs about ways teachers learn together through collaboration, reminding us that "reducing the isolation starts with the recognition that collaboration is a learned skill" (para. 2).

- In *What Works Best in Education*, John Hattie (2015) synthesizes some key understandings about collaboration:

> Collaboration is based on cooperativeness, learning from errors, seeking feedback about progress and enjoying venturing into the "pit of not knowing" together with expert help that provides safety nets and, ultimately, ways out of the pit. Creative collaboration involves bringing together two or more seemingly unrelated ideas, and this highlights again the importance of having safe and trusting places to explore ideas, to make and to learn from errors and to use expertise to maximise successful learning. (p. 27)

Many definitions and accounts of successful teacher collaboration yield common themes, including an emphasis on building trust; sharing expertise; having a common goal (e.g., enhancing instruction for students, school improvement); participating in supportive, interdisciplinary endeavors; and finding multiple creative solutions while keeping it manageable.

Although it has been recognized that "the long-standing culture of teacher isolation and individualism, together with teachers' preference to preserve their individual autonomy, may hinder deep-level collaboration to occur" (Vangrieken, Dochy, Raes, & Kyndt, 2015, p. 36), teacher collaboration has been an integral part of many schools and institutions of higher education; it has been thoroughly researched and conceptually connected to various theoretical frameworks (Kuusisaari, 2014).

Inclusive pedagogy is based on the premise that teachers recognize and respond to all students' needs and extend what is available to some students and make it accessible to all:

> Human diversity is seen within the model of inclusive pedagogy as a strength, rather than a problem, as children work together, sharing ideas and learning from their interactions with each other. The inclusive pedagogical approach fosters an open-ended view of each child's potential to learn. (Spratt & Florian, 2013, p. 135)

While the notion of inclusive pedagogy is closely tied to instructional practices in the preK–12 special-education context, it provides a helpful framework for working with ELs in a collaborative, integrated program as well. At the core of successful inclusive pedagogy is teacher collaboration, often including or centering on co-teaching practices that allow two or more educators to plan, deliver, and assess instruction for the sake of special populations while also setting challenging educational goals and delivering differentiated instruction for all students.

Co-Teaching as a Unique Form of Teacher Collaboration

Co-teaching is traditionally defined as the collaboration between general- and special-education teachers on all of the teaching responsibilities for all of the students assigned to a classroom (Gately & Gately, 2001). This definition has frequently been expanded to allow the collaborative partnership between a general-education teacher and a service provider or specialist other than a special-education teacher, such as a math intervention teacher, a reading specialist, a teacher of the gifted and talented, a speech-language pathologist, and, more recently, the ELD/ELL specialist.

Richard Villa et al. (2008) suggest that "co-teaching involves the distribution of responsibility among people for planning, instruction, and evaluation for a classroom of students" (p. 50). It is a unique professional relationship in which "partners must establish trust, develop and work on communication, share chores, celebrate, work together creatively to overcome the inevitable challenges and problems, and anticipate conflict and handle it in a constructive way" (p. 5). Often, educators working with ELs look to borrow, adapt, and synthesize information and ideas from a related field. Thus, resources such as Richard DuFour and colleagues' (2016) work on professional learning communities, Richard Villa and colleagues' (2008, 2013, 2016) contributions, and Marilyn Friend's (2005, 2008, 2013, 2017) publications on co-teaching in the inclusive setting have been influential among ELD/ELL specialists.

In the past ten years, research on collaboration and co-teaching for English learners has expanded. Early research documented the challenges of developing effective collaborative relationships and co-teaching practices (Davison, 2006; DelliCarpini, 2008, 2009; Hurst & Davison, 2005). Documentary accounts of successful collaborative and co-teaching practices have also surfaced (Kaufman & Crandall, 2005). More recent, emerging research has documented that ELD/ELL specialists and their general-education co-teachers continue to struggle with establishing an equitable partnership (Fogel & Moser, 2017) or with defining their roles when it comes to content and language integration (Martin-Beltrán & Madigan Peercy, 2012, 2014; Norton, 2016; Peercy & Martin-Beltrán, 2011).

To explore what makes co-teaching successful for language learners, we conducted a multicase study that included surveying and interviewing secondary co-teaching partners about their experiences (Honigsfeld & Dove, 2017). Our sampling was strategically aligned with the research goal of documenting successful practices, so we systematically sought out co-teachers who had built strong partnerships and began to achieve high levels of effectiveness with learners through a collaborative, integrated approach to instruction.

We found that when co-teachers achieve a state of flow—when one is deeply involved, energized, and present in an activity (Csikszentmihalyi, 1990)—they engage in risk taking, open-mindedness, and professional learning in planning and teaching. Highly developed co-teaching teams provide integrated classes via predictable routines, methods, and techniques that create an environment for learning in which ELs develop English language proficiency along with content-area skills in a safe, highly engaging learning environment.

Effective Teacher Collaboration

Our belief that effective collaboration benefits students (and teachers alike) is affirmed by the well-deserved attention it receives in the educational community. We build on several available collaborative frameworks by synthesizing their essential dimensions and adapting them to the context of culturally and linguistically diverse schools. We take a broad look at what exemplifies effective teacher collaboration, what essential frameworks need to be established in order for ELD/ELL and general-education teachers to work together effectively, and how integrated approaches to ELD services benefit all stakeholders.

PROGRAM MODELS SERVING ENGLISH LEARNERS

Have you wondered about all the different types of program models available across the United States to respond to the growing needs of English learners? Let's take a quick look at the ELD and bilingual education landscape.

After students are classified as English learners, several program models are available in some schools, whereas in other schools only one type of support service or program is available. Depending on what source you consult, program models or service delivery approaches are categorized in numerous ways ranging from three main models (Rossell, 2003), four models (Valentino & Reardon, 2014), to as many as six or more (Genesee, 1999).

To help navigate the maze of programs, let's focus on the following three most common program models:

1. English language development programs

2. Bilingual education (transitional or maintenance)

3. Dual-language or two-way enrichment bilingual programs

English Language Development (ELD) Programs

In an ELD program, students who are identified as ELs receive specially designed language and academic instruction for the entire school day, or some part of it, offered by an ELD specialist. The more proficient students are, the less time they tend to spend with the ELD teachers. In some states, education departments have developed closely monitored guidelines for the number of and type of periods each EL is entitled to receive ELD services. In some cases, collaborative, integrated services are policy-endorsed. For example, in New York State, entering and emerging students are required to receive stand-alone English as a new language (ENL) services and all students participate in integrated services described as follows:

> Students receive core content area and English language development instruction, including the use of the home/primary language as support and appropriate instructional supports to enrich comprehension. Integrated ENL classes are taught by a teacher dually certified in the content area and ENL or are co-taught by a certified content area teacher and a certified ENL teacher. In a stand-alone ENL class, students receive English language development instruction taught by a NYS-certified teacher of English to Speakers of Other Languages (ESOL) in order to acquire the English language needed for success in core content areas. This program typically serves ELL students from many different home/primary language backgrounds whose only common language is English and therefore cannot participate in a bilingual program. (New York State Education Department, 2018, p. 4)

Most other state education departments post their own guidelines on their websites to offer a framework for required services. Depending on your location, make sure you carefully consult state and local guidelines regarding service options for ELs.

Types of ELD Services

ELD programs take several alternative forms. Many schools implement either stand-alone or collaborative, integrated instruction, or a combination of both. Whereas in our previous edition we referred to these programs as *pull-out* and *push-in* models, we no longer use this terminology. As indicated by these traditionally used names, the specialist either (a) provides ELD/ELL services in a designated area outside the classroom (usually in a specially equipped ELD/ELL classroom), thus the name *pull-out*, or (b) he or she offers language support in the general-education classroom, also referred to by some as *push-in* ELD. We argue that these labels are deeply troubling and need to be replaced permanently with more accurate and equitable terms. Pushing in suggests one teacher invading or at least entering the territory of another with force, whereas pulling out indicates that the children may not remain in the classroom since they do not belong there—they have to leave to learn—and their classroom teachers would not know how to work with them if they remained.

Stand-Alone ELD Programs

Stand-alone programs may also be referred to as self-standing ELD instruction. The ELD specialist either follows a specially designed curriculum that is based on the participating students' individual language and academic needs, or the specialist develops a curriculum closely aligned with the general-education curriculum. Within the stand-alone setting, ELs benefit from small-group instruction and the unique adaptations to the general-education curriculum that the ELD specialist is able to offer, yet there are dangers in segregating ELs from their peers for extended periods of time.

Integrated ELD Programs

If the ELD specialist provides instruction in the general-education classroom, there are a few additional considerations:

1. Will the ELD/ELL teacher pull ELs aside to a learning center or a designated area in the classroom and teach a stand-alone ELD curriculum? (We strongly caution against this approach, as it is de facto segregation as well as a very distracting set-up.)

2. Will the ELD/ELL teacher pull ELs aside to a learning center or a designated area in the classroom and support the general-education curriculum by following the lesson conducted by the classroom teacher? (A little better, but the students are still not integrated into the classroom, even though the curriculum may be.)

3. Will the ELD/ELL teacher and the general-education teacher collaboratively plan and carry out the instruction following one of several possible co-teaching models? (For implementation of teacher collaborations, see Chapters 4–7 and Honigsfeld & Dove, 2015; Dove & Honigsfeld, 2018.)

In California (and elsewhere) the term *integrated ELD* may have a different meaning. In California, *designated ELD* is essentially a pull-out or stand-alone period, typically 30 minutes of a student's day, devoted for targeted English language development. *Integrated* refers to deliberate efforts on the part of general-classroom teachers (or content teachers) to promote ELD in the context of teaching content. Typically, ELD teachers don't participate in integrated ELD since it is typically strictly the responsibility of the content teacher. Our hope is that the integrated ELD period may also be supported through collaborative planning, joint professional development, or additional sustained opportunities for collaboration.

Newcomer Schools and Classes

When the EL population is large enough, self-contained ELD classes may be serviced by teachers certified both in ESOL and a content specialty. Newcomer schools or classes may be established in school communities with large recent immigrant groups. Deborah Short and Beverly Boyson (2012) conducted a three-year multicase study on newcomer programs at the middle and high school level located in urban, suburban, and rural settings. They reported on three types of programs that varied according to location—those within a school, those at a separate location, and whole-school programs. Despite the huge variation among these programs, Short and Boyson (2012) conclude that many programs share the following characteristics:

- Flexible scheduling of courses and students
- Careful staffing plus targeted professional development

- Basic literacy development materials for adolescents and reading interventions adapted for English language learners
- Content-area instruction to fill gaps in educational backgrounds
- Extended time for instruction and support (e.g., after-school, Saturday, and summer programs)
- Connections with families and social services
- Diagnostics and monitoring of student data
- Transition measures to ease newcomers into the regular school programs or beyond high school (p. vi)

ELD programs across the United States tend to follow either the WIDA standards (39 states and more than 200 international schools), the English Language Proficiency Assessment (ELPA) standards (7 states), or state-mandated language development standards (the remaining states). All standards-related documents we reviewed share several essential elements. The ELD standards are organized by grade level or grade cluster, recognizing age-appropriate goals in language and literacy acquisition. They typically address the four language domains: listening, speaking, reading, and writing. There is some variation in whether standards address the four main content areas— English language arts (ELA), social studies, math, and science—or merely focus on social and instructional language and literacy skills. The California ELD standards are intentionally designed to be used as a complement to the Common Core State Standards (CCSS) ELA standards. They're organized by three major parts: "Interacting in Meaningful Ways," "Learning About How English Works," and "Using Foundational Literacy Skills." Similarly, in New York State, the Next Generation Learning Standards in ELA (the locally revised version of the CCSS) offer a foundation for the Bilingual Common Core Progressions that support home language and English as a new language (ENL) development.

Bilingual Education (Transitional or Developmental)

Bilingual education has been at the center of political and educational debates for decades (Krashen, 1999). Carefully designed, longitudinal research studies showing the effectiveness of these program models cannot, and should not, be ignored (Collier & Thomas, 2002, 2007). The two main subtypes of bilingual education focus on the ultimate outcome of the program:

1. Is it to help students exit the bilingual classroom and enter the general-education, "English only" setting as soon as possible? or

2. Is it to maintain and further enhance students' native language and literacy skills while simultaneously assuring they develop English language proficiency and literacy?

The first is often referred to as transitional bilingual education, whereas the second may be labeled as maintenance, developmental, or late-exit bilingual education and may also be considered for use as an enrichment program and identified as a dual-language program. Within each program model, there are several other factors to consider. The most prevalent feature is the amount of time spent on each of the target languages. When Wayne Thomas and Virginia Collier (2002) examined various bilingual-education programs, they described one-way bilingual programs (both the transitional and developmental) as either following a 90/10 or a 50/50 model. In the 90/10 model, students initially receive 90 percent of instruction in their native language, which is then gradually reduced to about 50 percent by the fifth grade. In the 50/50 model, one or two teachers use both the native language and English for an approximately equal amount of time for instructional purposes throughout the implementation process.

Dual-Language Program: One-Way or Two-Way Programs

Dual-language models are among emerging program initiatives focusing on enrichment for both native and nonnative speakers of English. According to Elizabeth R. Howard and colleagues (2018), a dual-language program "provides literacy and content instruction to all students through two languages and that promotes bilingualism and biliteracy, grade-level academic achievement, and sociocultural competence—a term encompassing identity development, cross-cultural competence, and multicultural appreciation—for all students" (p. 3). Dual-language programs used in the United States tend to fall into one of two categories:

1. One-way programs tend to enroll only English learners who speak the same primary or home language and who aim to develop biliteracy.

2. Two-way programs serve an approximately even number of students, who, at the onset of the program, are dominant either in English or in their primary language (also called the partner language).

What Works Best?

You might be wondering which of the previously discussed program types is the best program model for English language learners. If we believe and agree that one size does *not* fit all, there cannot be *one* right answer to this question. Each model has its merits; each model has numerous documented success stories and its own share of challenges, the discussion of which goes beyond the scope of this book.

What Edward Zigler and Carol H. Weiss noted in 1985 still holds true: Research on program effectiveness must "go beyond the question of whether or not a program 'works' to ask *what works, for whom, how, when, and why*" (p. 199, emphasis added). Their message is still valid, though the educational context has changed considerably since the 1980s. We live in an age of increased accountability and standardized assessments.

We also concur with James Crawford (2008), who states that "decisions on how to teach English learners are being made not in the classroom, but in legislative chambers and voting booths; not on the basis of educational research data, but on the basis of public opinion, often passionate but rarely informed" (p. 59). Our commitment is to take on a pronounced role of advocacy to help schools and communities learn about the needs of ELs and the organizational, curricular, and instructional options we can offer them. All stakeholders engaged in a local decision-making process collaboratively may be able to come to a resolution on what program models to use for which students, how to initially pilot new programs, when to maintain existing programs, and why and how to revise them.

Program Decisions for Feng and Kamen

Which ELD or bilingual program might be best for Feng or Kaman? Are some programs better for entering-level students? Should the age of the youngster be considered? Does the child's prior schooling matter? Each program designed for ELs provides valuable assistance and essential instruction to ensure academic growth and language development, and schools often have more than one model of instruction to meet students' individual needs. Feng may thrive in an integrated, collaborative program due to her young age and relaxed disposition in the general-education classroom. However, Kaman may not wish to stand out in her class, afraid of being embarrassed, and her psychological needs might best be served initially in a stand-alone class.

Administrative Decision Making About ELD/ELL Program Models

The U.S. Department of Education published an updated *English Learner Tool Kit* in 2017 offering some overarching guidelines about selecting programs or services for ELs. The key considerations include students'

1. English proficiency level,

2. Grade level,

3. Educational background,

4. Language background for bilingual programs,

5. Native-language literacy,

6. Acculturation into U.S. society, and

7. Age of arrival in the United States. (Chapter 2, p. 2)

To guide schools and districts, the U.S. Department of Education (2017) offers some questions to consider when deciding on the most appropriate program or service model. Here is a shortened, adapted list highlighting some key questions. (For the full list of questions, see https://ncela.ed.gov/files/english_learner_toolkit/2-OELA_2017_language_assist_508C.pdf.)

- On which educational theory are the EL services and program options based?
- What are the resources needed to effectively implement the chosen program?
- Does the school have qualified staff to implement the chosen program?
- How are placement in a particular EL program and the provision of EL services informed by a student's English proficiency level, grade level, and educational and language backgrounds?
- Are EL services and programs provided to all eligible ELs, regardless of scheduling conflicts, grade, disability, or native language?
- Does the chosen EL program include instruction aligned to the state ELP [English language proficiency] standards and grade-level content standards? (Chapter 2, p. 2)

This list is especially helpful when a school or district is considering a more collaborative, integrated approach to serving ELs, whether in ELD or bilingual programs. We further suggest reflecting on how the following factors may each contribute to the decision-making process:

1. Number of ELs on each grade level (Should ELs be clustered or distributed evenly across the classes?)

2. Availability of ELD/ELL support personnel (Are there highly qualified and certified ELD/ELL teachers and teaching assistants?)

3. Classroom space (Is there a separate ELD classroom for stand-alone services, or is there a shortage of classroom space such as in some large urban schools?)

4. The instructional philosophy of the district or school (Are general-education teachers and ELD/ELL specialists encouraged to collaborate? Are they given common preparation periods to plan together?)

WHAT CAN WE LEARN FROM THE HISTORY AND RESEARCH ON COLLABORATIVE PRACTICES?

Dan Lortie's *Schoolteacher: A Sociological Study*, published in 1975, was first to call attention to teacher isolation as a major obstacle to improvement in American schools. As Lortie describes the day-to-day lives of teachers, he frequently points out the lack of extensive opportunities or well-defined structures for collaboration among teachers. He observes that "mutual isolation during most of the day is the rule in many schools" (p. xi), which undoubtedly results in the loss of valuable knowledge. He also notes that "those in professional development help when they bring teachers together, and principals are also in a position to increase opportunities for teachers to work together and to share know-how" (p. xi).

Teacher isolation continues to prevail, as Jeffrey Mirel and Simona Goldin (2012) report that teachers in the United States spend only about 3% of their teaching day in collaboration with colleagues. A lot of American teachers continue to plan their lessons, teach their classes, and reflect on their teaching and assess their students' work alone. "In other countries, such as Finland and Japan, where students outperform those in the US . . . collaboration among teachers is an essential aspect of instructional improvement" (Mirel & Goldin, 2012, para. 4).

Close to four decades ago, Judith Warren Little (1982) examined the differences between more and less effective schools and found that the more effective ones had a greater degree of collegiality. She discusses unique characteristics of collegiality (or collaboration) in schools where teachers participate in the following activities:

1. Teachers engage in frequent, continuous, and increasingly concrete and precise talk about teaching practice.

2. Teachers are frequently observed and provided with useful critiques of their teaching.

3. Teachers plan, design, evaluate, and prepare teaching materials together.

4. Teachers teach each other the practice of teaching. (pp. 331–332)

We translated Little's (1982) frequently quoted four key ideas into a framework of four Cs, in which *collaborative* serves as a defining adjective, followed by a key dimension of behavior that teachers engage in collaboratively:

1. Collaborative Conversations: Enhanced communication among all teachers

2. Collaborative Coaching: A climate that allows for critical feedback

3. Collaborative Curriculum: Curriculum and materials alignment

4. Collaborative Craftsmanship: Continuous improvement of the craft of teaching, while coordinating time, resources, and support for each other

Table 1.1 reveals how we co-constructed meaning from Little's original findings and transferred the concept of collegiality to the linguistically and culturally diverse school context that we see in the twenty-first century.

Table 1.1   The Four Cs of Collaboration

Collaborative Conversations	**Collaborative Coaching**
Talk about	*Engage in peer coaching to improve*
<ul><li>Students' needs</li><li>Students' lives</li><li>Students' work</li><li>Curriculum</li><li>Instruction</li><li>Teachers' own struggles</li><li>Teachers' own successes</li><li>What matters to you, the teacher</li></ul>	<ul><li>Lesson planning</li><li>Lesson delivery</li><li>Unit design</li><li>Use of supplementary materials</li><li>Adapted content</li><li>Modified instruction</li><li>Assessment</li></ul>
Collaborative Curriculum	**Collaborative Craftsmanship**
Align	*Explore*
<ul><li>Lesson objectives (language objectives and content objectives)</li><li>Unit goals</li><li>Curriculum maps</li><li>Supplementary materials</li><li>Resources</li><li>Adapted texts and materials</li></ul>	<ul><li>ELs' background knowledge</li><li>ELs' prior learning</li><li>Peer coaching</li><li>Planning instruction collaboratively or in the context of co-teaching</li><li>Effective methods for aligning curriculum and objectives</li><li>Using time more effectively</li><li>Making the most of collaborative efforts</li></ul>

TEACHER COLLABORATION IN TODAY'S SCHOOLS

Collaboration may start out as a small, grassroots effort, involving only two or three teachers who share the responsibility for some of the same ELs and are concerned about their students' progress. It may involve an entire grade level. Some examples include grade clusters working together to develop or enhance curricula in elementary schools, an interdisciplinary team of math, science, social studies, English, and ELD/ELL teachers (sharing responsibility for a cluster of classes in middle schools), or a discipline-specific department (focusing on preparing all students to meet graduation requirements of high schools).

When we ask teachers if they collaborate, we receive reassuring responses and critical insights into what is happening in schools. When we further probe what they do when they "collaborate," the answers range from talking to each other in the teachers' lounge about students to co-teaching on a daily basis, with a wide variety of activities in between. Some teachers serve on child study teams, others supervise students during arrival and dismissal; some co-plan lessons, some make joint decisions about new textbooks or other instructional materials. Many schools invite tenured teachers to participate in research and development teams or to conduct collaborative lesson studies in place of formal observations.

Collaboration efforts are further refined when teachers enter into a co-teaching arrangement. Co-teaching for English language learners is a means of reducing teacher isolation without eliminating teacher autonomy. When co-teaching teams plan lessons for ELs, they have team-teaching autonomy, the ability and freedom to guide instruction together to meet the needs of a particular group of learners. With the development of trust over time, co-teaching team members have the power to influence how curriculum is presented to all students and to create opportunities for new ideas and strategies that can be undertaken with ELs in mind.

Ten years ago when we wrote the first edition of this book, we noted that we were at an interesting turning point in education. Since then, collaborative practices have expanded substantially. The old mores and the physical realities of schools built in the mid- to late-twentieth century still continue to reinforce teacher autonomy and isolation. At the same time, there is an exceedingly growing trend of and need for collaboration in both instructional and noninstructional activities and through a variety of professional-development models. To best respond to the demands of today's schools, we propose a collaborative, integrated approach to ELD services, which is outlined in the following chapters.

Summary

Teacher collaboration must have intrigued educators ever since the Little Red School House expanded to include more than one teacher. Most schools still follow the early twentieth-century model of "Cells and Bells" (Nair & Fielding, 2005), with many teachers working in isolation in their own classrooms. We believe that for the sake of ELs, there is a place and time for creative collaboration among all teachers in every school that serves ELs. This book was born out of our strong conviction regarding the benefits of, and even stronger commitment to, helping everyone find a shared learning and teaching experience. No doubt, our ELs need us to work together.

Discussion Questions

VIDEO 1.1

Introduction

VIDEO 1.2

The Collaborative Instructional Cycle

VIDEO 1.3

The Four Cs of Collaboration

http://www.resources
.corwin.com/
CollaboratingforELs

1. In Video 1.1, Andrea and Maria share how they began to work together. What is the significance of teachers' questions for Andrea and Maria in their roles as authors? In Video 1.2, how do they define integrated service delivery? Based on Judith Warren Little's work, what do Andrea and Maria say are the four Cs of collaboration?

2. Examine how teacher collaboration might impact instruction for ELs in your school.

3. What factors determine the ELD delivery service models in your district?

4. In 1975, Lortie stated,

> Official curricula are accepted as blueprints for instruction, but when teachers seek advice, they are considerably more likely to turn to each other than to administrators; at the same time . . . in considering whether to adopt new ways of teaching they frame any such decision in terms of its match with their own personalities. (pp. xiv–xv)

   Would Dan Lortie observe the same today? What would a sociologist say about our professional lives? How far have we come? What should we still be working on?

5. Engage your colleagues in a shared-reflection session using the conclusions of Little's (1982) study. Is there still a lesson to be learned from her work? What do the findings mean for today's ELD/ELL and general-education teachers in your school? What ideas would you add to Table 1.1?

Key Online Resources

Learning Forward: The Professional Learning Association
www.learningforward.org

National Clearinghouse for English Language Acquisition (NCELA)
www.ncela.us

The Partnership for 21st Century Learning
www.p21.org

WIDA
www.wida.us

2

Why Is Collaboration Needed?

It takes two flints to make a fire.

—Louisa May Alcott

OVERVIEW

This chapter underscores the benefits of collaboration, which supports all regular classroom responsibilities, as well as various school activities such as curriculum committees, faculty conferences, and parent–teacher meetings. Each undertaking has a definite focus and meaningful purpose to which teachers subscribe. This chapter will guide educators to embrace the importance of teacher collaboration and understand the reasons why it must be an integral part in planning and delivering instruction for English learners (ELs). While maintaining an asset-based philosophy at the core of our explorations, we will review the challenges ELs, their teachers, and school administrators face and why collaboration may be an answer to the demands placed on them. We will emphasize that the research base for collective teacher efficacy, collaborative teacher learning, teacher collaboration, and co-teaching is well established, and we will present arguments for developing a site-based professional learning community for the benefit of ELs.

Voices From the Field

Katie Toppel, a K–5 ELD specialist in Portland, Oregon, describes colleagues' reactions to leadership's request for greater connection between English language instruction and core instruction.

At a recent meeting, my English language development (ELD) specialist colleagues and I received information from leadership about the district's vision for "Connected ELD." This vision emphasized the need to create more continuity for English learners due to the number of disruptions they often experience, in both their schedule and the instruction they receive, when removed from their regular classrooms for English language development classes. Despite the intention to create more instructional continuity for these students, who are often also adjusting to new cultural and school norms in addition to learning English, the vision did not involve changing the current pull-out service delivery model. Instead, the presentation emphasized the desire to create an ELD experience that would be connected to core instruction as well as the need for classroom teachers to use specific oral language practice routines so that ELs would have language instruction outside of their designated pull-out time.

    Many of us immediately became concerned about the impending shift from being able to choose our own content for language instruction to being expected to align our instruction with what students would be learning in their core classes. I overheard several teachers complaining about having to collaborate with classroom teachers in order to know what content they were working on. We were concerned about the logistics involved because classroom teachers often have different schedules and grade-level teams don't necessarily cover the same content at the same time, which would make it challenging to plan our ELD lessons involving students from all of the different classrooms. Toward the end of the meeting, some teachers began to disagree over which content area would be the best for ELD to align with in order to provide the best support for ELs. Most of us left the meeting feeling confused, frustrated, and overwhelmed.

Vignette Reflection

Katie's story highlights the concerns and challenges that surround initiating a shift in service delivery options and the initial apprehension and frustration teachers face when they need to find ways to align ELD curriculum and instruction to core content requirements. On the one hand, the ELD specialists were apprehensive about planning lessons that correlate to the needs of children pulled from multiple classes, and the classroom teachers reacted to yet another instructional change whose tenets were not presented for consistent implementation.

UNDERSTANDING ENGLISH LEARNERS

Whether newly arrived or U.S. born, English learners must leap over the many hurdles they encounter along the road to becoming English proficient and academically successful. Take into account, for example, that some of our youngest learners and those with interrupted formal schooling also must negotiate acquiring literacy skills along with a new language and academic content. The challenge for many of these students is great and for some, the time they have to acquire needed skills is short. Thus, developing a shared appreciation for the assets and rich funds of knowledge ELs bring to school as well as understanding the complex sociocultural, socioeconomic, affective, linguistic, and academic challenges they face are key to their success.

In light of these complex issues, TESOL International Association (2018) identified a core set of six principles that define exemplary teaching for English learners. Unlike standards, these principles offer universal guidelines that may be applicable to any kind of approach to English language instruction. They are built on substantial research in language acquisition theory and language education. In the next section we will make a strong case that teacher collaboration further enhances the impact of these core principles in achieving excellence in EL education.

Principle 1: Know Your Learners

Consider these two student stories, and reflect on why it is essential to get to know your students and better understand their unique backgrounds, challenges, and potentials.

Eva's story. When she first arrived from Egypt eight months ago, Eva entered the eighth grade at a suburban middle school. Although Eva did not speak a word of English, she quickly developed her social communication skills. Her clear pronunciation of English and her outgoing nature made it seem as if her English language skills were much more advanced.

In her native country, Eva excelled in mathematics and science. She loved working with technology, and at her home in the United States, she had all the latest gadgets and technical devices: a digital phone, an iPad, and a laptop with a wireless printer. Eva was capable of searching for information on the Internet with ease, and she assisted the other children in her ELD group with their individual and class projects.

As the school year progressed, Eva had an increasingly daunting task of keeping up in social studies class. Although Eva studied about some aspects of American life in her native country, she certainly did not study the subject to the extent that her American peers had. Additionally, her emerging academic language skills in English made reading her dense social studies textbook and responding to document-based questions about authentic resources a tremendous undertaking.

Consider This

All students who need to develop English language skills carry the same label, yet knowing a student's language proficiency level reveals little about what a student specifically knows or needs to thrive in a new school environment. Consider how you might be best able to determine the following to support Eva:

- How might you use Eva's technological expertise to support her language learning in English?
- How might certain religious and cultural influences affect her learning?
- What languages might Eva speak in addition to Arabic?

- How might you capitalize on her native language and literacy skills to support her learning American social studies content?
- What research-informed strategies might be implemented to improve Eva's comprehension of dense content-area texts?

Zhi's story. A bright and energetic boy, Zhi was eight years old when his family moved to the United States from Shanghai five years ago. They first lived in Los Angeles, where Zhi's father took a job in the restaurant industry, and Zhi attended his first U.S. school. Although he had no knowledge of English, Zhi entered second grade at an urban elementary school, where he made good progress developing his speaking, reading, and writing skills in English.

After two and a half years, Zhi's father had a better job opportunity, and his family moved once again to a small suburb just outside of New York City. By this time, Zhi was in the middle of fifth grade. His new class was engaged in studying the history of New York State, but Zhi had no background knowledge on the subject. Furthermore, his new school used a mathematics curriculum that was different from the way he was taught in Los Angeles. Zhi began to struggle a bit more academically, and he lost some of his confidence in his own ability as well.

When his father's brother arrived a year and a half later, Zhi was happy to be reunited with his cousins. However, both families decided to pool their resources, and Zhi's family moved once again, this time to Cary, North Carolina, where his father and uncle opened their own restaurant. Now, Zhi is attending a middle school where he must again adjust to a new school environment, with changes in school expectations and curricula. Frequent moves from place to place not only interrupted his schooling but also confounded his ability to meet with academic success.

Consider This

In spite of Zhi's many academic talents and the quality of teaching and learning available, family circumstances have placed Zhi and the teachers in charge of his instruction in a challenging situation. When trying to support the academic and language development of Zhi, consider the following:

- What are Zhi's strengths when it comes to learning?
- What are Zhi's talents and interests both inside and outside of class?
- How might you capitalize on Zhi's high levels of energy and steady progress in learning English?
- What social and emotional aspects of Zhi's learning might need to be addressed?
- What extracurricular programs might benefit Zhi to better adjust to his new school environment?

Now take another look at the profiles presented for Eva and Zhi and consider one more question: How might collaborative practices be used to find various possible answers to the two sets of questions posed for these ELs?

Eva and Zhi are two students among many ELs who are among the fastest growing subgroups of students in the United States. Most schools across this country have been welcoming an increasing number of culturally and linguistically diverse students for the past several decades. These students represent numerous subgroups and a complex array of within-group diversity. See Table 2.1 for a summary of diversity within the EL population.

Table 2.1	Diversity Among English Language Learners

Immigration status	• Recently arrived in the U.S. under typical circumstances • Recently arrived in the U.S. as a refugee • Recently arrived in the U.S. without legal documentation • Temporarily living in the U.S./visiting the U.S. • U.S.-born, U.S. citizen
Prior education	• Formal, grade-appropriate education in another country • Formal, grade-appropriate education in U.S. school system for a certain period of time • Limited formal, grade-appropriate education in another country • Interrupted formal, grade-appropriate education in another country • Interrupted formal, grade-appropriate education in U.S. school system
Linguistic development in language(s) other than English	• Monolingual in native language only • Bilingual in two languages other than English • Bidialectal, speaking both a standard language other than English and a dialect or Creole/Patois • Multilingual in three or more languages
Status of language proficiency and literacy in language(s) other than English	• Only receptive language skills • Productive oral language skills • Limited literacy skills • Grade-level literacy skills • Any or all of the above skills in more than one language other than English
Level of English language proficiency	• *Starting*: Being exposed to English with no or very limited language production • *Beginning*: Demonstrating receptive and emerging productive language skills • *Developing*: Employing basic oral and written language skills with predictable error patterns • *Expanding*: Employing more advanced oral and written language skills with fewer errors • *Bridging*: Approximating native language proficiency
Learning trajectory	• Demonstrating typical academic and linguistic developmental trajectories • Demonstrating academic and/or linguistic developmental challenges and difficulties that respond to interventions • Demonstrating academic and linguistic developmental challenges and difficulties that require special attention

By highlighting students' differences, our goal is to help better understand the *within-group* diversity that exists among ELs and to offer a framework to sensitize the entire school community to the varied experiences among ELs. We believe that as educators we need to resist a broad-brush approach to understanding and identifying ELs, and we must take the time to get to know them and understand the many dimensions of their identities and talents.

A powerful way to embrace such diversity is building on the concept of inclusive pedagogy—a student-centered approach that focuses on the needs of individual learners—to create a supportive environment that values multiculturalism, fosters social justice, and promotes the learning of all students. It has informed our work as a major framework and evidence-based practice. It is based on the premise that teachers recognize and respond to all students' needs and extend what is available to some students and make it accessible to all:

> Human diversity is seen within the model of inclusive pedagogy as a strength, rather than a problem, as children work together, sharing ideas and learning from their interactions with each other. The inclusive pedagogical approach fosters an open-ended view of each child's potential to learn. (Spratt & Florian, 2013, p. 135)

Although the notion of inclusive pedagogy is originally based on special-education instructional practices in the preK–12 context, it provides a useful framework for understanding and responding to diverse ELs' needs as well. At the core of successful inclusive pedagogy is teacher collaboration, often including or centering on helping students develop a true sense of belonging and become fully acclimated to the U.S. school context. Co-teaching practices—a unique way to create a shared learning environment—allow two or more educators to plan, deliver, and assess instruction for the sake of special populations while also setting challenging educational goals and delivering differentiated instruction for all students.

Keep in Mind: School Acculturation

Students who are not fluent in English very often are not familiar with American culture in general and, more specifically, the U.S. school system. They may not know what is expected of them and from time to time feel detached from and lost in their new surroundings. These students may become confused in unfamiliar situations or appear uncooperative in their new school environment; yet, their teachers may interpret their conduct differently. English learners may be misconstrued as inattentive, unfocused, or even defiant; however, they simply might not know what the common expectations are for their participation or, more seriously, be suffering from the effects of depression due to the trauma of leaving their native homes.

Teachers need to be aware of the common adverse reactions that students and their families face when entering a new country. There are a host of new situations new arrivals must negotiate, and dealing with an unfamiliar school system is just one of them. It is prudent to withhold judgments concerning these youngsters' ability to fully participate in the school community, or, as Lori Helman and her colleagues (2016) suggest, we could embrace a *benefit of the doubt pedagogy* that requires us to look through a compassionate lens each time we notice ELs facing challenges.

Why Collaboration Is Key to Knowing and Addressing the Needs of a Diverse EL Student Body

In their teacher preparation programs as well as through ongoing professional development, ELD/ELL specialists often receive extensive training in responding to the needs of culturally and linguistically diverse students. Whether or not they are bilingual or bicultural themselves, ELD/ELL teachers are frequently called on to serve as cultural interpreters, cultural mediators, or cultural brokers in their schools. They are asked to help immigrant families and the students in their schools to better understand American cultural expectations, most specifically, to help families navigate the cultural maze of the American school system. Oftentimes, when teachers collaborate, they better understand that ELs are not only challenged by difficult content and language barriers but also have to adjust to the cultural norms of a new teaching paradigm in the United States. From the frequent use of group work, differentiated instruction, project- or inquiry-based learning, to the types of questions teachers typically ask, ELs often experience a paradigm shift and have to redefine what a "good student" is, that is, what he or she must do to do well in school.

Principle 2: Create Conditions for Language Learning

Many of us who have studied a new language must recognize that we did so with varying degrees of success. Much of our personal achievement with learning another language may have to do with a range of factors, special circumstances, and carried contexts. Consider these questions as you reflect on your own experiences with language learning:

1. What were your reasons for learning a new language?

2. What did you think could be gained from knowing a new language?

3. Did you have a strong motivation to learn?

4. Did you believe that acquiring a new language could be accomplished?

5. Did you think it was worth the time and attention it required?

6. Did you have any fear and apprehension about learning a new language, and did you trust that you could overcome your fear?

Within the context of preK–12 education, these questions might play out quite directly. Our children do not have the choice to deliberate whether it is worth it or not and how long it is going to take to learn English. As teachers, our challenge is to create a learning environment that can assist rather than hinder students' progress toward acquiring a new language and develop academic knowledge and skills. In such an environment, students actively participate and develop agency in order to do the following:

- Take risks
- Develop confidence
- Remain positive
- Maintain focus
- Foster enthusiasm
- Find passion
- Build a strong sense of self-esteem
- Become self-directed, independent learners
- Take responsibility for their own learning
- Become life-long learners

*Why Collaboration Is Key to Addressing
an Effective Language-Learning Environment*

What is important to keep in mind is well captured by a recent National Education Association (2015) publication: "ELLs desperately need educators who believe in them, who recognize their assets, and who have the support and training they need to do their best by all of their students" (p. 19). Fred Genesee and Kathyrn Lindholm-Leary (2013) remind us that when content and language instruction are integrated, there is "authentic communication in the classroom about matters of academic importance that provides critical context for learning the communicative functions of the new language" (p. 6). On the other hand, if English learners do not have access to the core content and have limited opportunities to engage in authentic, meaningful communication with their peers, language acquisition as well as content attainment may suffer. Additionally, when teachers, administrators, and all members of a school community agree on the importance of developing the "whole" child, a commitment to address the academic and social environment becomes a shared concern.

Principle 3: Design High-Quality Lessons for Language Development

Consider the task of acquiring a new language while learning grade-appropriate content in all the core subject matters. Think about the complexities it would entail. You would need to understand what is being said or what you read even if you had no prior knowledge about the topic. You would need not only to know the proper words to use, but you also would have to have a sense of how the words could be strung together into complete sentences when you speak or write. Further, you would need to be able to read a range of different texts across genres and subject matters, engage in academic conversations about those topics, and write about them with a critical voice. That would be no small feat to accomplish!

For ELs to be successful, their teachers need to be highly skilled and intentional in their lesson planning and delivery. Therefore, teachers need to plan with specific outcomes in mind, and students need to be aware of these outcomes as well as how they may be achieved; additionally, teachers need to use appropriate strategies, conducive to language and content learning for ELs, as well as provide multiple, frequent opportunities for students to engage with others using the target language and content (TESOL International Association, 2018).

*Why Collaboration Is Key to Designing
High-Quality Lessons for Language Development*

ELD/ELL teachers use language-learning techniques to assist ELs in developing the necessary skills to become fluent in English. Ongoing collaborative practices between ELD/ELL and general-education teachers provide a clear path for sharing strategies to support new-language acquisition in the general-education classroom as well as how to best create opportunities for students to apply their language and content learning in authentic ways. Table 2.2 outlines some of the approaches ELD/ELL teachers apply when developing language competence with ELs.

Table 2.2   Instructional Strategies to Develop Language Competencies

What ELs Need for Language Competence	What Teachers Need to Do to Develop Language Competence
Vocabulary	<ul><li>Create multiple meaningful encounters with target vocabulary.</li><li>Preteach essential vocabulary.</li><li>Use explicit instruction.</li><li>Provide opportunities to use new words in speaking, reading, and writing.</li></ul>
Grammar	<ul><li>Teach grammar skills in context.</li><li>Use students' actual speaking and writing to provide mini-lessons.</li><li>Provide lessons that include both inductive and explicit grammar teaching.</li><li>Include one aspect of grammar as a part of students' writing assignments.</li></ul>
Literacy Skills	<ul><li>Read aloud to students.</li><li>Access prior knowledge.</li><li>Explicitly teach phonological awareness of problematic sounds.</li><li>Promote writing to increase reading skills.</li><li>Integrate vocabulary development.</li><li>Have ELs reread familiar texts to increase fluency.</li></ul>
Pragmatics	<ul><li>Explicitly teach cross-cultural differences in social settings.</li><li>Create role-playing activities for students to practice compliments, greetings, refusals, etc.</li><li>Share stories from home culture, and explore ways to develop bicultural and multilingual identities.</li></ul>

Research on the impact of teacher collaboration has consistently substantiated the practice. John Hattie's (2015) latest work has documented a groundbreaking discovery of the importance of collaborative expertise as well as recognizing the power of collective efficacy. He identified that the greatest barrier to students' academic achievement is within-school variability. For this reason, meaningful teacher collaboration—sharing successful instructional strategies, examining student data, reflecting on effective teaching practices, and so on—is key. When teachers collaborate and form high-functioning teams, the whole is greater than the sum of its parts, and their collective efficacy—their effectiveness—is increased (Eells, 2011; Krownapple, 2015). Teachers' collective efficacy indicates the shared belief—a new frame of reference—that together they can achieve success with ELs.

Principle 4: Adapt Lesson Delivery as Needed

When someone tells us a story, we tend to form pictures in our minds about what is happening in the story. As the storyteller reveals further details, we change our minds' visual patterns in an attempt to match what is being said. In essence, we use our own experiences regarding what we have already seen and heard to visualize and make sense of what we are being told. However, if the storyteller introduces something that is unfamiliar to us in the storyline, we may lose the solid point of reference we previously held and begin to place the story within a familiar frame of reference. If sufficient explanation and details are not provided, if the context is not available for making sense of new information, we may no longer comprehend what is being said.

Helping students to connect their own stories to what is being taught in class plays a significant role in how teachers adapt lessons and their instructional delivery for English learners. Tapping into students' prior knowledge, creating lessons that are relevant to students' lived experiences, and building the background knowledge of ELs are strategies that provide students with avenues to successful content and language acquisition. In addition, checking students' understanding in effective, meaningful ways is an important step in informing how to adjust lessons for their learning.

Knowing what students understand, the knowledge they are able to apply, and any misconceptions they may have are key to adapting lessons for English learners. Teachers need to develop the flexibility and expertise to make on-the-spot changes in the overall direction of their lessons to make learning more accessible for ELs. These changes may include the following:

- The manner in which new information is being provided
- The pace of the lesson
- The language being used
- The level of text complexity
- The types of scaffolding selected for support
- The way students are grouped for interaction
- The amount of time students require for learning

Why Collaboration Is Key to Adapting Lesson Delivery as Needed

When teachers collaborate, they exchange techniques and strategies to capitalize on students' prior learning, build their background knowledge, check for student understanding, and adjust lessons and instructional delivery to meet students' needs. It is certain that all students have unique sets of knowledge, abilities, and personal experiences they can tap into when learning new content and skills. Teachers must use their students' skills and strengths to help them make connections to new concepts presented in their classes. By collaborating, teachers can discover how to best support all students to build on their existing knowledge and to connect what they already know with what they are learning. Teachers need to incorporate specific strategies on an ongoing basis in order for academic growth to occur. Furthermore, building teacher capacity through collaboration and the development of professional learning communities is another essential ingredient for effective instruction.

Keep in Mind: Curricular Variations, Continuity, and Accessibility

Students come from various backgrounds that have provided them with excellent literacy and mathematics skills in their native language. They may also be well versed in the areas of music, art, global studies, and science. Yet, when they arrive in the United States, apart from having to learn a new language, these students may not be well prepared for the curriculum taught in American schools or for the assessments they have to take in order to meet state and local achievement standards.

No longer can ELD/ELL teachers deliver isolated skill lessons to their ELs in vocabulary, grammar, reading, and writing. Programs developed for English learners must be comprehensive and long-term to accomplish language and content-area objectives. Frequently, ELD/ELL teachers modify existing curriculum intermittently for students in their programs. This modified curriculum is rarely shared with classroom or other ELD/ELL teachers. If a comprehensive program that examines all levels of language proficiency and content instruction were carefully devised over time, it would have long-term benefits for the instruction of ELs as well as assist teachers in economizing their planning and preparing of revised materials and resources.

Curriculum mapping that identifies the goals and learning objectives in the core subject areas can help ensure curriculum continuity for ELs. It is a method for documenting the content material, related skills and strategies, and the assessment procedures for each core subject taught. A comprehensive grade-level curriculum map can be an important resource for ELD/ELL teachers to have in order to plan instruction for ELs that is congruent with their general-education curricula.

Materials for English learners often need to be adapted according to students' levels of proficiency to make content more accessible. For this to be accomplished, teachers need adequate professional development to understand how to accommodate the learning needs of ELs. Ongoing teacher collaboration between ELD/ELL and general-education teachers can help meet this demand.

Principle 5: Monitor and Assess Student Language Development

Observing, checking, and keeping track of the language development of English learners is an integral part of what ELD/ELL teachers do on a daily basis to advance the English proficiency of ELs. Yet, teachers who are not certified in English for speakers of other languages (ESOL) or endorsed frequently teach English learners in elementary grade-level classes, special subject areas (e.g., art, music, physical education), and secondary content classes. At best, in the course of an average student schedule, ELD or bilingual education services are furnished only one to two periods of study per day. For this reason, English learners typically spend the majority of the school day in general-education classes that offer little to no learning support other than what the general-education teacher can provide, along with whatever technology is available in the classroom. Formal training for regular classroom teachers to meet the needs of these diverse learners is crucial yet woefully inadequate. If we embrace the idea that all teachers are teachers of ELs, then all teachers need to be concerned about and develop their expertise in the language development of ELs in addition to content learning, monitor the progress of students as they develop English skills, and support ELs to become proficient in English through their daily instruction (Gottlieb, 2016).

Why Collaboration Is Key to Addressing Monitoring and Assessing Student Language Development

When teachers have sufficient time to collaborate, they can begin the process to change how progress monitoring and assessment is planned for ELs. They can share their personal knowledge that can facilitate learning for these youngsters, and they can devise alternative assessment procedures for ELs to accurately demonstrate what they have learned. Through collaborative practices, ELD/ELL teachers have the opportunity to share their extensive knowledge base with their general-education counterparts. Such a knowledge base includes

1. the distinction between academic and social language; more specifically understanding the differences among conversational fluency, discrete language skills, and academic-language proficiency (Cummins, 2001);

2. the impacts age, motivation, attitude, confidence, classroom climate, and learning style have on second language acquisition;

3. issues related to acquiring the new school culture, such as understanding academic expectations, discipline, formality, and social adjustment; and

4. national and state learning standards for ELs.

There is no formula for determining the special needs of English learners; each EL is unique in his or her own way. In addition, these students bring their own set of challenges to school with them when they enroll. That is why we are such strong advocates for teacher collaboration. So very often, ongoing professional conversations between teachers and other school personnel can help all educators to better understand the unique needs of ELs.

Principle 6: Engage and Collaborate Within a Community of Practice

The final principle directly suggests that teachers must create communities of practice and take on the challenge of responding to the complex needs of ELs in collaboration with each other. Yet, collaboration does not come automatically or easily to some teachers. For generations, teachers in the United States have worked in isolation, in some respects due to the very nature of traditional teaching—working alone with specific groups of students in separate rooms. In turn, school administrators often disregarded the abundant knowledge base held by teachers in their very own schools. However, teacher collaboration is being viewed increasingly as the most important practice implemented by educators. According to TESOL International Association (2018), collaboration provides opportunities for teachers to do the following:

- More fully meet the challenges of teaching
- Provide optimal instruction for students
- Engage in reflective practices
- Participate in ongoing learning and grow professionally
- Co-plan and co-teach
- Strengthen relationships with colleagues
- Develop as teacher leaders

This principle encourages administrators to develop a "community of practice by creating a climate of respect for all staff, especially valuing the role of the ESL/ELD and bilingual specialists in the school" (TESOL International Association, 2018, p. 88).

Not only are the six principles concrete and accessible guidance for identifying the core tenets of teaching English learners, but they also challenge all educators of ELs to develop their knowledge, instructional environments, lesson planning and delivery, assessments, and collaborative efforts to truly support the learning of English learners.

> ### Vignette Revisited
>
> Let's revisit Katie from the "Voices From the Field" section, earlier in this chapter. Katie shared with us how she and her team responded to the new administrative directives.
>
> *After processing what had been presented in the meeting and speaking with an ELD specialist whose school had been granted permission to co-teach in certain grade levels, my concerns started to dissipate. Given the district vision, my partner and I felt conflicted with the continuation of pull-out services, and rather than being upset or annoyed at the prospect of collaborating with classroom teachers, we were motivated to work closely with classroom teachers in order to support the vision of connectedness and congruity for ELs. We began to look into co-teaching as a possible alternative. We saw the potential for students to achieve greater success in both language development and depth of content knowledge if we could collaborate with classroom teachers to co-plan lessons in which we could share our respective expertise for effectively teaching both content and language. More importantly, we saw the value in co-delivering the lessons, so that ELD students would not have to receive language instruction in a separate setting. Our goal was to transform language instruction from an isolated session taking place outside the regular classroom to an integrated approach where students could engage in language-rich discussions about texts, information, and content concepts in their regular classrooms along with their peers.*

Vignette Reflection

Katie's unique approach to creating curricular continuity has grown out of her and her colleagues' interest and commitment to keep ELs included in their home rooms where instructional practices may be fully integrated. Katie and her collaborating teachers share the belief that language acquisition and literacy development may be well supported within the context of a co-taught classroom, where both ELD/ELL specialists and classroom teachers work together to ensure academic success for English learners.

CHALLENGES SCHOOL ADMINISTRATORS FACE

Program Compliance and Accountability

Collaboration and co-teaching initiatives are not created and implemented in isolation. Instead, they often are closely aligned to the federal guidelines outlined in the *English Learner Tool Kit* (U.S. Department of Education, 2017), an online document that offers guidance on every aspect of English learners' services to state education agencies (SEAs) and local education agencies (LEAs). Chapter 4 in the tool kit emphasizes the requirements related to English learners' access to equitable curricular and extracurricular opportunities.

Both SEAs and LEAs have the dual obligations to not only provide programs that enable EL students to attain English proficiency, but also to provide support in other curricular areas that will ensure ELs have equal opportunities to participate in the curriculum. LEAs may use a curriculum that temporarily emphasizes English language acquisition over other subjects, but any interim academic deficits in other subjects must be remedied within a reasonable length of time. LEAs may also offer EL programs that include grade-level content instruction in the student's primary language. (Chapter 4, p. 1)

The tool kit also identifies key curricular and extracurricular considerations for ELD and offers the following checklist as a self-assessment tool for LEAs to examine how collaborative and integrated their services are for ELs:

English Language Development

- Does ELD instruction prepare ELs to participate in the academic curriculum in English?
- Is the ELD instruction tailored to and does it build on students' levels of ELP [English language proficiency]?
- Is there ongoing, systematic assessment of ELs' progress toward English proficiency?

Curricular and Extracurricular Programs

- Do the EL programs provide access to the same standard grade-level curriculum—or to a comparable curriculum, equally rigorous—as is offered to never-ELs, while also providing appropriate language assistance strategies in core instruction?
- Are ELs integrated into the school's educational programs, extracurricular offerings, additional services, and student body?
- Do ELs have equal access to all of the school's facilities (e.g., computer labs, science labs, cafeteria, gym, and library)?
- Are ELs assessed in the core-content areas with appropriate and reliable evaluations and testing methods?
- Do content assessments indicate that ELs are making academic progress while in the EL program, and that former ELs are performing comparably to that of their never-EL peers? If not, are timely services provided to ELs to accelerate academic progress? Are those services offered within the school day? (Chapter 4, p. 2)

Chapter 5 cautions about reducing unnecessary segregation of ELs from their English-speaking peers: "As part of an inclusive school climate, LEAs should implement educationally sound and effective EL programs and limit the degree of segregation of ELs to what the program requires" (Chapter 5, p. 1). The tool kit also provides a checklist to reflect on the degree to which students are integrated by way of participating in inclusive schools that reduce the amount and type of segregation. Use the following select questions to examine the degree to which your school is inclusive and supportive of all ELs.

Student Integration

- What steps have been taken to develop positive and inclusive school climates for ELs?
- What are the stated educational goals of the EL program? Is the degree of segregation necessary to achieve those goals?
- Does the degree of segregation decrease commensurate with ELs' rising ELP levels as well as their time and progress in the EL program?
- Do EL students participate with their non-EL peers during
  - grade-level curriculum?
  - extracurricular activities?
  - after-school activities?
  - other subjects (e.g., physical education, art, music)?
- Is the EL program carried out in the least segregative manner, consistent with achieving the program's stated educational goals?
- How is EL student progress monitored and assessed throughout the school year to inform instruction and placement? (Chapter 5, p. 2)

Supervision, Evaluation, and Professional Development

Supervising and evaluating all teaching and nonteaching staff as well as providing opportunities for ongoing professional development for the faculty are demands school leaders need to balance with all other aspects of their jobs. In *Bringing Out the Best in Teachers: What Effective Principals Do*, Joseph Blase and Peggy Kirby (2009) summarize several critical actions and behaviors they observed among the most effective principals. We adapted their findings and created the following list of reflective questions for school leaders:

- How do I praise teachers for their professional accomplishments associated with school goals?
- How do I communicate and model high expectations for student achievement?
- How do I support teacher involvement in significant schoolwide decisions?
- How much professional autonomy do I grant teachers regarding curriculum and instruction when they exhibit professional readiness?
- How do I support teachers with material resources, protection of instructional time, professional development, and assistance with student discipline and parental concerns?
- How do I encourage individual growth through advice, feedback, and professional development?
- How do I exercise my authority?
- How do I consistently model effective practices congruent with principals' ethical code?

When school goals embrace diverse student needs and teachers' collaborative practices support all learners' social, emotional, academic, and linguistic development, all students are better able to achieve. School cultures should provide a secure, supportive environment for teachers as well as encourage risk taking and experimentation with innovative practices. If teachers are better able to hone their instructional skills, it will directly affect the achievement of ELs together with all learners.

Considering, Responding to, and Balancing the Needs of All Stakeholders

In an educational institution, well-known stakeholders who stand to gain from its success can be identified as students, faculty, and administrators as well as parents and community members (Godwin & Gross, 2005). The challenge all school leaders face, regardless of geographic location, is that they must understand, value, and respect all stakeholders' perspectives and needs as they make important decisions about local policy and practice. (See a detailed discussion of all stakeholders in a school community in Chapter 3.)

Building Partnerships

The practice of teachers working in collaborative teams is consequential to the development of school-learning communities, which can be effective catalysts for instructional change. These collaborative partnerships comprised of general-education teachers and subject-area specialists in conjunction with school administrators are a tremendous source of teacher empowerment. Sharing their expertise and providing feedback in collaborative settings are activities that enable teachers to be a part of the decision-making process in their school. It is particularly important for all teachers with special knowledge of English learners to have a venue to act as advocates for these diverse learners.

When teachers are able to consistently work together as teams, ELs' class participation and academic performance are often much improved. In spite of the many positive aspects and benefits of working as teams, some teachers are frustrated by collaborative-team efforts. They may not know what is expected of them or may harbor certain assumptions about the team's purpose that are not readily shared by others in the group. Some practitioners, by their participation in collaborative teams, believe they may be relinquishing control over what is being taught in their own classrooms. Others do not understand the collective purpose of team effort and think they would be much more productive on their own.

Thus, shared professional collaboration continues to be a challenge for some school districts. This is partially due to the lack of a proper collaborative framework, set expectations for its purpose, and sufficient time scheduled for meetings to regularly occur. As part of any overall collaborative plan, activities and associated expectations should be identified to make professional learning communities as productive as possible.

Creating a Positive School Culture

Based on the demands placed on students, teachers, and school administrators, we concur with Terrence Deal and Kent Peterson's (1999) seminal research regarding school climate. They found that schools with a strong, positive school culture were not only safe and secure places for all to learn but shared a common set of norms and values and demonstrated success in the following areas:

- Fostering effort and productivity
- Improving collegial and collaborative activities that, in turn, promote better communication and problem solving

- Supporting successful change and improvement efforts
- Building commitment and helping students and teachers identify with the school
- Amplifying energy and motivation of staff members and students
- Focusing attention and daily behavior on what is important and valued (Deal & Peterson, 1999, pp. 7–8)

Prominent among Deal and Peterson's (1999) findings are the benefits of collaborative practices, a shared commitment to school improvement efforts, and a special focus on the diverse school population. Similarly, based on an extensive meta-analysis of studies on successful school leadership, Robert Marzano, Timothy Waters, and Brian McNulty (2005) establish that a school leader has at least twenty-one responsibilities.

To create a purposeful community from which a strong leadership team can be created, Marzano et al. (2005) narrow the list to nine items as being the most essential. The short list includes being the optimizer, offering affirmation, sharing ideals and beliefs, demonstrating situational awareness, having visibility, building relationships, enhancing communication, building culture, and offering input. Aligned to Deal and Peterson's (1999) work, of these nine, we conclude that building a culture (i.e., meaningfully creating shared values, norms, and beliefs) that "positively influences teachers, who, in turn, positively influence students" (Marzano et al., p. 47) is most likely one of the most fundamental challenges and responsibilities school leaders face.

WHY COLLABORATION IS THE ANSWER TO THE CHALLENGES TEACHERS AND ADMINISTRATORS FACE

Since the first Little Red School House opened up, an age-old problem has perpetuated: Most teachers often work in isolation from each other. Close to two decades ago, Richard Elmore (2000) recognized the isolation of teaching as a vocation. He further observed that "individual teachers invent their own practice in isolated classrooms, small knots of like-minded practitioners operate in isolation from their colleagues within a given school, or schools operate as exclusive enclaves of practice in isolation from other schools" (p. 21). To some degree, teacher isolation continues to challenge our profession. On the other hand, collaboration allows teachers and administrators to build a learning community, as shown in the following examples:

- When teachers move from isolation to collaboration, collaboration breaks the isolation cycle and allows for "respecting, acknowledging, and capitalizing on differences in expertise" (Elmore, 2000, p. 25). Teachers with general-education, content-specific expertise offer their knowledge of the subject matter content, general-education curricula, and local, state, and national content-related standards and assessments to all other teachers on staff. At the same time, ELD/ELL specialists have the opportunity to share their expertise in second language acquisition, cross-cultural understanding, bilingualism and biculturalism, and literacy development. As a result, *students benefit*.

• When the school leadership is collaborative, both the responsibilities and the decision-making power are shared in a more democratic fashion. Such collaborative leadership is often referred to as distributed leadership (DeFlaminis, Abdul-Jabbar, & Yoak, 2016), which suggests mutual interdependence among multiple members of the school:

> The expectation that principals be content experts across all disciplines, not to mention the accompanying pedagogical approaches particular to each subject and field of study, is unreasonable. In reality, principals must know instruction, but they also must be able to tap into the knowledge and expertise of other educators. (p. xvi)

What collaborative leadership means for ELs is that multiple school community members' knowledge and expertise in curriculum, instruction, and leadership capacities are used to make the school a more effective and nurturing place to be. As a result, *students benefit*.

• When the entire school community shares a collaborative culture, members of that community work together effectively guided by shared norms, values, and principles. Diverse experiences, ideas, and points of view are respected rather than negated, marginalized, or trivialized. Thus, even if people disagree, their shared purpose helps them move forward. As Carl Glickman (1998) and many others after his seminal work *Renewing American Schools* report, in successful schools teachers are always questioning their current practices to be able to improve them. Teachers work collaboratively as they offer feedback to each other and plan instruction in coordination. Members of such successful schools "exercise collective autonomy … in making professional decisions about matters of schoolwide teaching and learning" (p. 28) and participate in collegial discussions about how to continuously improve instruction and enhance the learning environment for all students. Finally, the norm is both to be critical consumers of educational information as well as to produce data and information "by seriously studying their students and programs and by considering outside information before making schoolwide decisions" (p. 28). As a result, *students benefit*.

WHY CO-TEACHING IS A POSSIBLE ANSWER TO CHALLENGES TEACHERS AND ADMINISTRATORS FACE

Teacher collaboration and a team approach to the teaching profession may become all-important notions for a number of critical reasons. As early as 1992, Sandra Fradd discussed the promising positive outcomes of teacher collaboration implemented to serve all kids with special needs, including ELs. The most important question on teachers' and administrators' minds might be, "Does it yield increased student achievement?" An exciting line of research is documenting the impact of teacher collaboration and co-teaching on EL student learning. Priscilla Pardini (2006) was among the first to describe the results of an ongoing, multiyear initiative in the Saint Paul Public Schools in Minnesota, where traditional ELD programs are completely replaced by a collaborative program model. ELD/ELL and general-education teachers at all grade levels team teach. Pardini (2006) notes that between 2003 and 2005, the gap in reading achievement between the district's ELL and non-ELL students fell from 13 to 6 percentage points, as measured by the percent of students showing proficiency on the Minnesota Comprehensive Assessment. In math, the gap fell from 6.7 to 2.7 percentage points. The district's ELL students also did well when compared with their peers statewide, outscoring them in each of the last three years in reading and math as measured by the Test of Emerging Academic English. (p. 21)

In fact, ELs in Saint Paul Public Schools have made steady gains on all standardized tests administrated in the state in closing the achievement gap between EL and non-EL students. In the past decade, many more school districts reported outstanding student achievement gains due to co-teaching and teacher collaboration (Dove & Honigsfeld, 2018).

As a final note, in a most recent report, the National Commission on Teaching and America's Future (NCTAF) (2009) called attention to alarming demographic trends among teachers and administrators. Because more than half of the educators working in the K–12 setting are Baby Boomers, many of them may retire within the next five years. In the 2010–2011 school year alone, more than 100,000 experienced teachers were expected to leave full-time positions, whereas in the next decade more than 50 percent of currently practicing veteran teachers could retire.

A possible solution suggested by the NCTAF is forming teacher teams, which would allow veteran teachers to stay on in part-time or consulting/mentoring roles because they team taught with novice teachers. The consequences of such a shift may be far reaching: "This could be the decade in which we move beyond the notion that the stand alone teacher can do everything and instead reinvent American education to give us a global competitive edge for years to come" (NCTAF, 2009, p. 4).

Richard Ingersoll and Michael Strong (2011) argue that "teaching is complex work, that pre-employment teacher preparation is rarely sufficient to provide all of the knowledge and skill necessary to successful teaching, and that a significant portion can be acquired only while on the job" (pp. 202–203). Currently, the professional learning community movement is among the most widely recognized initiatives in the United States to support teacher collaboration. Collective teacher efficacy being cited as having the highest effect size on student achievement affirms the notion that administrators must harness teachers' collective expertise and offer ample opportunities for collaboration (Hattie, 2015, 2018).

ADMINISTRATORS' ROLE: CREATING A SCHOOL COMMUNITY TO SUPPORT EFFECTIVE INSTRUCTION FOR ELs

Based on the demands on students, teachers, and administrators outlined earlier in this chapter, and the research base that supports teacher collaboration, shared knowledge base, and collaborative inquiry, we suggest that school leaders do the following:

1. Create an inclusive, welcoming school learning community with a shared vision of respect and acceptance of everyone's cultural heritage and background.

2. Build a professional learning community that continually engages in collaborative inquiry on all students' needs, including ELs' linguistic, academic, and cultural challenges.

3. Establish "flexible teaming" that allows for both horizontal (on grade level) and vertical (across grade level) teacher teams, as well as cross-disciplinary teamwork to support ELs' curricular, instructional, and extracurricular needs.

Summary

The need for collaboration in pursuit of the academic success of English language learners has been identified through the challenges of students, teachers, and administrators. Each of these stakeholders has particular demands they must confront and an important investment in the success of collaborative practice.

Discussion Questions

VIDEO 2.1

Why Collaboration?

http://www.resources
.corwin.com/
CollaboratingforELs

1. In Video 2.1, what do Andrea and Maria mean when they suggest that an asset-based philosophy informs their work?

2. Reflect on your own teaching experiences and generate a list of challenges you face. Are they similar to or different from the demands on teachers discussed in this chapter? Compare your list with the one presented in this chapter and highlight the differences. Explore possible explanations for the differences.

3. In collaboration with your colleagues, develop a proposal for your school and district administrators to implement a collaborative ELD service delivery model or enhance an existing model, with the possibility of including co-teaching.

4. In 2015, National Policy Board for Educational Administration published the revised *Educational Leadership Policy Standards* under a new title, *Professional Standards for Educational Leaders*. Review the standards below and identify aspects of the standards that are intended to support a collaborative school culture, teacher collaboration, co-teaching, and building a professional learning community. Generate a list of recommendations for your leadership team to put these standards into operation and apply them to your own school context.

Standard 1. Mission, Vision, and Core Values

Effective educational leaders develop, advocate, and enact a shared mission, vision, and core values of high-quality education and academic success and well-being of each student.

Standard 2. Ethics and Professionalism

Effective educational leaders act ethically and according to professional norms to promote each student's academic success and well-being.

Standard 3. Equity and Cultural Responsiveness

Effective educational leaders strive for equity of educational opportunity and culturally responsive practices to promote each student's academic success and well-being.

Standard 4. Curriculum, Instruction and Assessment

Effective educational leaders develop and support intellectually rigorous and coherent systems of curriculum, instruction, and assessment to promote each student's academic success and well-being.

Standard 5. Community of Care and Support for Students

Effective educational leaders cultivate an inclusive, caring, and supportive school community that promotes the academic success and well-being of each student.

Standard 6. Professional Capacity for School Personnel

Effective educational leaders develop the professional capacity and practice of school personnel to promote each student's academic success and well-being.

Standard 7. Professional Community for the Teachers and Staff

Effective educational leaders foster a professional community of teachers and other professional staff to promote each student's academic success and well-being.

Standard 8. Meaningful Engagement of Families and Community

Effective educational leaders engage families and the community in meaningful, reciprocal, and mutually beneficial ways to promote each student's academic success and well-being.

Standard 9. Operations and Management

Effective educational leaders manage school operations and resources to promote each student's academic success and well-being.

Standard 10. School Improvement

Effective educational leaders act as agents of continuous improvement to promote each student's academic success and well-being.

Key Online Resources

Professional Organizations

American Association for Applied Linguistics (AAAL)
www.aaal.org

American Association of School Administrators (AASA)

www.aasa.org

American Educational Research Association (AERA)

www.aera.net

American Federation of Teachers (AFT)

www.aft.org

Association for Supervision and Curriculum Development (ASCD)

www.ascd.org

Council of Chief State School Officers

www.ccsso.org

International Literacy Association

https://www.literacyworldwide.org

National Association for Bilingual Education (NABE)

www.nabe.org

National Association for Multicultural Education (NAME)

www.nameorg.org

National Council of Teachers of English (NCTE)

www.ncte.org

National Education Association (NEA)

www.nea.org

Learning Forward

https://learningforward.org

Teachers of English to Speakers of Other Languages (TESOL)

www.tesol.org

Research Centers

Center for Applied Linguistics (CAL)

www.cal.org

Center for Research on Education, Diversity, and Excellence (CREDE)

www.cal.org/what-we-do/projects/crede

Collaborative for Academic, Social, and Emotional Learning (CASEL)

www.casel.org

Education Northwest
www.educationnorthwest.org

Mid-Continent Regional Educational Laboratory
www.mcrel.org

UCLA CRESST
http://cresst.org

WestEd: A Research, Development, and Service Agency
www.wested.org

Other Related Resources

The Co-Teaching Connection (Marilyn Friend's website)
http://www.marilynfriend.com

Education Week
www.edweek.org

Kansas University, Special Connections
http://www.specialconnections.ku.edu

National Clearinghouse for English Language Acquisition (NCELA)
www.ncela.ed.gov

Office of English Language Acquisition (OELA)
www.ed.gov/about/offices/list/oela/index.html

Teaching Diverse Learners, The Educational Alliance, Brown University
https://www.brown.edu/academics/education-alliance/teaching-diverse-learners

Who Does Teacher Collaboration and Co-Teaching for ELs Concern?

We are caught in an inescapable network of mutuality, tied in a single garment of destiny. Whatever affects one directly, affects all indirectly.

—Martin Luther King, Jr.

OVERVIEW

The goal of this chapter is to identify all stakeholders in a multilingual educational community and to describe their unique roles and responsibilities in developing and sustaining a collaborative school culture. We will present and analyze the unique experiences (both benefits and challenges) each constituent encounters while teachers engage in collaborative practices and co-teaching for the benefit of English learners (ELs). We will consider the roles played by those who initiate, design, implement, monitor, and evaluate collaborative practices.

Voices From the Field

Joyce Dallas, second/third-grade combo teacher at Garfield Elementary School in Boise, Idaho, reflects on her first experience collaborating with Molly Fuentealba, an EL specialist, for the sake of a student.

The first full month of school has begun. As a veteran teacher with a great track record for student success and growth, I am still concerned about Amani's progress. For the past year, I have taught a second-/third-grade combo class at Garfield Elementary in Boise, Idaho. I was Amani's teacher last year when I first voiced my concerns in our problem-solving intervention team (PSIT). I have already collected data and observations about Amani's progress this year suggesting that my previous concerns are still valid.

Amani has been in the country for two years, emigrating from Uganda as a refugee together with her family and many siblings. We have a highly successful EL teacher who offers Amani 45 minutes of English language development in a stand-alone setting every day. Last year, she also received an intervention in-class online language application, which did not necessarily fit her learning needs. This year, Amani has language development, language intervention, and Tier 2 reading interventions in addition to the small group and one-on-one support that I provide in my classroom. At times she is engaged and at other times she is reluctant to participate, which is why I brought this student up again during our PSIT meeting.

Today in the meeting, the district EL consultant, Molly Fuentealba, listed several suggestions. Frankly, I felt her suggestions were instructional techniques that were already components of my lessons. After a moment Molly asked, "Joyce, how would you feel if we worked together with your students in your very classroom? We could try out strategies together, explore, see what is working and if there might be any ideas we could come up with together." Neither one of us really knew the other but we both agreed and set the wheels in motion.

We decided to work together during math instruction because we have several ELs during that time, as well as students with an IEP [individualized education program] and 504 plans and a range of math abilities. This is how we began our collaborative journey: At first, Molly came in and we tried to wing it. We quickly recognized that we needed to plan so we started to exchange weekly e-mails. What typically took place was that I focused on the math concepts and skills, and Molly would offer language support: writing out key words, explaining symbols, and offering examples. How did Amani fare? Molly and I agreed that she seemed to have benefitted from the visual support and guidance presented on the whiteboard and the charts Molly prepared. But we knew we needed to do more.

Vignette Reflection

Joyce and Molly's story is one example of the many teacher voices we hear around the country. It expresses the challenges teachers encounter when they try to figure out and respond to the complex needs of ELs. It also reflects the desire teachers have to participate in ongoing, regularly scheduled discussions with their colleagues. When teacher isolation is replaced with opportunities for educators to learn from one another, they engage in joint problem solving, which in turn impacts the power of instruction for ELs.

ALL STAKEHOLDERS

Who walks through the front door of your school in the course of a day? In the course of a week? Or by the end of the year? Whose voice is heard? Who makes decisions? Who is involved in every aspect of the school life? Who is included in the school community and who is not? Who abides by those decisions and who hesitates? To establish a collaborative school community, we must identify the stakeholders first: What is unique about them? How do they benefit from collaborative school practices? Finally, what are their roles and responsibilities when teacher collaboration becomes enhanced and co-teaching is introduced for the sake of English learners?

Our Students

English-Speaking Students

Enter any classroom in the United States, or across the globe, for that matter, and you will find that students represent diversity not only in race, gender, ethnicity, languages, and socio-economic status; they also bring a variety of life experiences, display a range of learning needs, represent multiple intelligences, and show varied interests, talents, and readiness levels. With such apparent diversity, one teacher alone cannot respond to every student's needs, especially if working in isolation.

What are the benefits for English-speaking students when their teachers collaborate? They receive the following:

- More differentiated instruction due to collaborative teacher planning
- More varied instructional materials and resources
- More carefully crafted lessons
- More authentic and meaningful assessments that are adapted to the needs of students who are struggling or at risk
- More appropriate instructional adaptations for students who are struggling or at risk

Furthermore, if teachers engage in co-teaching and if students are taught by two rather than one teacher, students will experience the following:

- Fewer interruptions caused by pull-out programs at the elementary level
- More individualized or personalized attention as a result of reduced teacher–student ratio in all K–12 classes
- Enhanced social and emotional development due to deeper awareness of classmates' needs
- More chances to engage in collaboration with their classmates
- More opportunities to observe cooperation, interaction, and communication by their teachers collaborating in action

> *A few words of caution:* English-speaking students need to be prepared to welcome and accept all of their classmates, including ELs. It is the teachers' responsibility to foster development of heightened sensitivity to students' needs and an understanding of the basic premise that *fair does not mean equal.* When a co-taught class is set up, students need to be ready to adhere to the principles and dynamics of a collaborative classroom: Both teachers should be treated with the same respect. Each teacher will take on the role of leading a lesson or providing support to the other. Students will also need the opportunity to come to an understanding that each classmate may have different needs and that two teachers will respond to these needs through collaborative planning, co-teaching, and differentiated instruction.

English Learners

The LEP (limited English proficient) designation is the label of the past. Reflecting a deficit model, students' limitation in their language proficiency was emphasized by this classification. The richness of culture and language students bring to the classroom must be recognized, emphasized, and celebrated. According to a deficit perspective, some students would be considered to be at a disadvantage because of their cultural, social, and linguistic backgrounds, including their lack of ability to communicate in English. In contrast, an assets-based model of education considers and intentionally builds on the values, lived experiences, language patterns, and background knowledge as advantages that support learning. As Aida Walqui and Leo van Lier (2010) note, the assets-based approach "looks ahead to what students can become and that builds on the knowledge, beliefs, and values all students bring to school" (p. x).

Cultural and linguistic diversity are no longer unique to big cities or urban, inner-city schools. Many rural and suburban school districts face the same challenges of addressing the needs of a multilingual student body. The diversity of languages spoken in U.S. homes has also increased manifold. Based on 2011 Census Bureau data, Camille Ryan (2013) reports that the top ten languages spoken in U.S. households other than English are Spanish, Chinese, French, Tagalog, Vietnamese, Korean, German, Russian, Italian, and Portuguese. The top ten languages spoken by English language learners reveal a different picture. According to the Office of English Language Acquisition (2017), the top ten languages spoken by English learners across the United States are Spanish, Chinese, Arabic, Vietnamese, Haitian/Haitian Creole, Somali, Tagalog, Hmong, Portuguese, and Russian. The patterns of languages and ethnic groups will vary from state to state and region to region, but effective collaboration and co-teaching can equally benefit any multilingual community.

Language Proficiency Levels. There is considerable variation in how many language proficiency levels are differentiated to describe ELs. The number ranges from four language proficiency levels to six. In Texas there are four levels: Beginning, Intermediate, Advanced, and Advanced High. In California, there are three: Emerging, Expanding, and Bridging. New York State recognizes Entering, Emerging, Transitioning, Expanding, and Commanding. Similarly, states that use the English Language Proficiency Assessment (ELPA) use five proficiency levels, simply referred to as Level 1, Level 2, and so on (see www.elpa21.org). In states that are part of the WIDA consortium, six levels of proficiency are recognized: Entering, Emerging, Developing, Expanding, Bridging, and Reaching (indicating near-native proficiency). WIDA, established in 2002, has thirty-five member states and four additional educational agencies (such as the District of Columbia) at the time of this book's publication, so we recognize many of our readers will be familiar with their *2012 Amplification of the English Language Development Standards: Kindergarten–Grade 12*. We also note that the consortium is gearing up for a 2019 publication of the standards-based instructional framework.

EL Snapshots

ELs are a diverse group. Yet parts of their personal histories often have a lot in common. You have heard from Joyce about Amani in the chapter-opening vignette ("Voices From the Field"). Now meet José, Tianika, Andy, Gerry, and Kristina. You might recognize their stories, which belong to students in your school with different names. Or one day, children like them might be in your classes, each with their own story.

José was born in the United States. Raised by a hardworking extended family, he never left his community, except for short trips to the Dominican Republic. Now he is five and ready for kindergarten. José speaks fluent Spanish and has had a rich exposure to his family's cultural traditions, songs, and stories. He did not have the opportunity to make English-speaking friends or watch educational television shows such as *Sesame Street* or *Dora the Explorer* in English. Like his siblings and cousins, he is a child of first-generation immigrants who live in a relatively secluded metropolitan community where most people speak the same language. Store signs are in two languages, but most stores are frequented by shoppers who share the same native tongue as the store owners. Most day-to-day business can be conducted successfully in the native tongue. Now José is leaving his "linguistic island" and embarking on a new experience: learning English and, to compound matters, learning *in* English.

Tianika is fifteen. She used to go to private school in Nigeria, speaks two dialects of Hausa, and is literate in two languages other than English (being a child of diplomats who have lived in Russia and France). Her teachers seem to assume her silence comes from lack of ability, and they often group her with students who are struggling learners. In fact, she turns out to be a high-achieving, very focused student who seems frustrated by not being able to express herself well in English. She is self-conscious of her distinctive accent and seems rather shy and reluctant to make friends with her classmates.

Andy is a serious, rather reserved eleven-year-old. He barely speaks English with his classmates and hardly ever raises his hand in class. Andy is a completely different person after school: He studies diligently every day, he takes karate and music lessons, he goes to Chinese school on Saturdays and Bible school on Sundays. Much to his teachers' surprise, his writing is improving considerably faster than his speaking skills, and he is already outperforming his classmates on most of the math and science assessments.

Gerry is nine, but he spent less than three years in school in the Philippines. What he learned though, as he guided tourists up a nearby mountain to view Taal Volcano every day, was many life lessons. He learned to take care of his mule and how to be the fastest person

(Continued)

(Continued)

back to the base to be in line for the next tourist. He earned enough money to support himself and his sister. He even picked up some English: "Balance, ma'am, balance!" and "Thank you!" In his U.S. classroom, he is friendly and gets along with his classmates. Once recess is over, however, he seems lost in the classroom and does not seem to be able to relate to what is going on in the lesson.

Kristina was adopted from a Russian orphanage. At eight years of age, she owns her own winter coat, books, schoolbag, and toys for the first time. In the orphanage, she was used to sharing, and even fighting for, the warmer coat or stronger pair of boots. She reads and writes in Russian and has some basic English skills. She receives occupational therapy, and a private tutor works with her to improve her English. Despite all the effort, care, and nurturing they offer, Kristina's parents are seeing their daughter act aggressively and lethargically in turn. They fear Kristina is not adjusting well to life in the United States.

Each child entering school in the United States has a story—stories that we need to not only hear but actually listen to! Whether starting kindergarten or joining eleventh grade near the end of the school year, each child will bring unique experiences and challenges to the classroom. Despite the challenges the children and their teachers face, the National Education Association (2015) reminds us,

> There is nothing wrong with English Language Learners—no deficit to fix. They are whole students we must reach and teach in ways that open their minds to the amazing possibilities of their lives, and language must not be a barrier to that goal. (p. 19)

With such an asset-based approach to planning and delivering instruction for ELs, we invite you to reflect on some key questions: What should teachers and administrators know about ELs? How can all educators learn more about this population? Take a look at Figure 3.1 and consider the questions that will help you better understand each aspect of a student's background. Then review the textbox following the figure to see what additional information you might need.

What are the benefits for ELs when their teachers collaborate? ELs receive the following:

- Greater continuity of instruction: fewer interruptions in their school day
- More carefully aligned curriculum that yields adaptations
- More differentiated instruction due to collaborative teacher planning
- Effectively coordinated interventions for students at risk through response to intervention (RTI) programs
- More focus on their linguistic needs: instruction at their level of language proficiency
- More focus on their academic needs: preteaching necessary skills for understanding
- Greater understanding of their school behaviors and sociocultural needs
- More empathy from all teachers

Figure 3.1 Key Questions About ELs

What Information Is Helpful?

1. **Languages Spoken**
   - Language(s) or dialects spoken in the home
   - Dominant language in the home
   - Receptive skills in a language or dialect other than English
   - Level of native-language development
   - Family literacy

2. **Context of Immigration**
   - Country of origin or U.S. born
   - Date of arrival in United States
   - Unusual or traumatic experiences surrounding the arrival

3. **Educational Background**
   - Prior formal education: type of school, number of years
   - Additional educational opportunities provided by the family or community

4. **Cultural Background**
   - Dominant cultural background of the student and family
   - Basic beliefs concerning education (e.g., attendance, roles and responsibilities of teachers, students, parents)
   - Basic beliefs concerning family, friends, religion
   - Important days of celebration

5. **Family Situation**
   - Primary caregivers
   - Parents, siblings, extended family, and living situation
   - English-speaking relatives
   - Family status in the United States: permanent or temporary
   - Awareness of available community services and resources in their home language and culture

6. **Personal Interests, Abilities, Health**
   - Student's special interests, abilities, and talents
   - Extracurricular activities
   - Notable physical or health conditions that influence learning or instruction (i.e., vision, hearing, food allergies, childhood illnesses, etc.)

If two teachers work together to provide instruction in a co-taught setting, ELs will experience the following:

- Greater stability at the elementary level by receiving more instruction in their regular classrooms
- More individualized attention because of reduced teacher–student ratio in all K–12 settings
- Increased exposure to their English-speaking peers
- Enhanced social and emotional development as a result of diverse peer interaction
- More exposure to adult linguistic models, including an additional teaching professional
- More experience with grade-appropriate content
- Greater opportunities for acculturation by staying integrated in their regular classes
- Increased confidence in their ability to learn grade-level work

A few words of caution: ELs—especially beginners and students with interrupted or limited formal education (SIFE or SLIFE)—may have significant gaps in both their academic knowledge and their understanding of U.S. school norms. Because of their differing background experiences and the linguistic and academic challenges they face, they might feel more at ease during small group instruction or in a specially designed SLIFE or newcomer program that assists with their basic language development needs. Some adolescent ELs might find it challenging to learn new school procedures and adjust to school norms and routines.

Teachers

As of fall 2018, approximately 3.2 million full-time teachers have been employed in public schools in the United States with a student–teacher ratio of 16 to 1, a ratio that has been consistent since 2010 (Institute of Educational Sciences, National Center for Educational Statistics, 2018).

Gallup's recent research reveals a teacher shortage in almost all U.S. states in some of the major content areas (McFeely, 2018). It was also found that approximately half of teachers (48%) are either actively looking for a different job or waiting for opportunities to do so. According to Dennis Vilorio (2016) citing the U.S. Department of Labor, Bureau of Labor Statistics, between 2014 and 2024, there will be about 1.9 million job openings for preK–16 teachers.

Currently, high-stakes standardized tests and ongoing test preparation, increased accountability, mandated curricula, scripted literacy programs, and lack of planning time and resources are among the top challenges classroom teachers face across the country. At the same time, more and more educators are expected to work in an inclusive setting, sometimes without collaborative support, and still must meet the needs of students with a range of abilities learning in every classroom.

Elementary General-Education Teachers

Many elementary teachers comment that their students receive multiple support services during the day from Title I service providers, speech and language pathologists, social workers, occupational therapists, and psychologists. Academic intervention service (AIS) providers, reading teachers, and remedial math specialists also provide additional instruction to those who will benefit from it. Instrumental music, chorus, dramatic arts, and other special practice sessions and programs add to the time some children spend outside of the classroom. Pull-out programs abound in some schools; numerous other interruptions occur in many others.

In light of the often fragmented nature of a school day, there is a lot to gain for elementary classroom teachers and other general-education elementary instructional staff in collaborating with English language development/English language learner (ELD/ELL) specialists. Their roles and responsibilities change in the process in rather complex ways.

If general-education teachers collaborate with ELD/ELL specialists, they will do the following:

- Regularly exchange ideas with colleagues trained in a different discipline.
- Share their knowledge of the general-education curriculum.
- Align the content curriculum mandated by state and local standards to ELs' language proficiency levels.

- Learn to adapt their curriculum to bridge the gap ELs have in their prior knowledge.
- Help ELs socialize more successfully.
- Help ELs learn about the norms of American schools.
- Modify their lessons in varied ways that may benefit other students at risk in the class.
- Develop a better understanding of the unique linguistic, cultural, and academic needs of ELs.

If general-education teachers co-teach with ELD/ELL specialists, they will do the following:

- Share their classroom space, available class time and resources, and all instructional responsibilities with a colleague.
- Expose ELs to state-mandated general-education curricula along with best practices for second language learning.
- Better communicate goals and objectives for ELs.
- Enhance their academic communication skills, including interactions with ELs, by observing an ELD/ELL specialist interact with ELs.
- More effectively facilitate small-group instruction that actively involves ELs.
- Become reflective about their shared teaching experience.
- Adopt the use of strategies that are modeled by the ELD/ELL teacher.

Secondary (Middle and High) School Content-Area Teachers

If content-area teachers collaborate with ELD/ELL specialists in the middle school and high school context, they will do the following:

- Enrich the curricular content mandated by state and local standards to address ELs' unique experiences.
- Actively engage ELs in their content classes by considering their language proficiency levels.
- Adapt their curriculum and instruction to bridge the gap ELs have in their prior knowledge.
- Help ELs socialize more successfully.
- Help ELs learn about the norms of American schools.
- Modify their lessons in varied ways that may benefit other students at risk in the class.
- Develop a better understanding of how to address the unique linguistic, cultural, and academic needs of ELs by watching an ELD/ELL specialist interact with ELs.

If content-area teachers co-teach with ELD/ELL specialists, they will do the following:

- Help ELs be more engaged in each lesson that focuses on grade-appropriate content.
- Reduce ELs' tendency to become invisible or voiceless.
- Focus both on content and language goals.
- Better understand how able ELs are to learn new and difficult information.

Co-Teacher Snapshots

Tan Huynh, English language development teacher in the secondary school at Vientiane International School, Laos, shared some composite vignettes with us that represent different teaching styles and preferences and how co-teachers negotiated the instructional practices in the classroom to better support ELs. All names are fictitious.

The Person in Charge

Mr. Jameswright works in a secondary school as the workshop teacher. He is a master artisan in his own right and wants students to leave with the same passion he has for design. Because he is so driven to produce high-quality products, he insists that students follow his process exactly. To do this, he spends a significant portion of his class modeling several steps at a time, resulting in a course that feels like a lecture rather than a makerspace. Although modeling is an effective strategy for all learners, especially ELs, Mr. Jameswright dilutes its effectiveness by using technical language and talking for far too long. After the extensive modeling, the ELs often run to Ms. Rivers, the language specialist assigned to co-teach with Mr. Jameswright, to ask her to clarify the instructions.

Once Ms. Rivers sets the ELs to work, Mr. Jameswright pulls her over and says, "I don't understand why they are in my class if they can't follow the instructions! Can't you take them and work on their language skills first instead?" He seems to assume that any difficulties ELs face in his class stem from their language deficiencies rather than his teaching style.

Ms. Rivers smiles and gently replies, "I know ELs' developing English skills can make it difficult for teachers at times, and you're doing some great things already. In our next planning session, I can share some ideas that work with your teaching style."

A Co-Teacher's Response

As promised, Ms. Rivers and Mr. Jameswright meet to co-plan. Ms. Rivers goes into the co-planning with an asset-based mindset, which means offering strategies that align with Mr. Jameswright's teaching practices. She knows focusing their co-planning on what Mr. Jameswright brings to the class will grow their positive, collaborative relationship.

Ms. Rivers brings out her tablet computer and suggests that he prerecord his modeling. She explains that students can then pause the video, rewatch sections, and slow the speed so they can better understand his instructions. Mr. Jameswright likes the idea because it doesn't require him to abandon his approach; it simply changes the way students receive it. They proceed to spend the rest of the session recording Mr. Jameswright modeling his instructions.

After recording, Ms. Rivers asks if Mr. Jameswright would like her to present their new approach to the entire class. Mr. Jameswright agrees because he sees the value in letting Ms. Rivers share her own expertise. When language specialists focus on what the content teachers are bringing to the class, there's always a way to collaborate.

The Storyteller

Mr. Nam walks toward Ms. Hernandez's eighth-grade science class, not quite sure how he will be of service today. Ms. Hernandez is beloved for her ability to build relationships with students.

The students love asking content-related questions that always produce long-winded, elaborate, and eventually off-topic stories that consume most of the period. Ms. Hernandez feels like she is engaging students with these interactions, which is true because normally glazy-eyed teenagers lean forward in rapt attention to the campfire-like stories. No wonder she is well liked! She relies heavily on her strength of making content engaging. However, sometimes our strengths can be barriers to learning for ELs: They can't keep up with run-on tangents that have no connection to the lesson they're expecting.

Conscious of not wanting to hurt her feelings or to come off like he is judging her practice, Mr. Nam delicately brings up the topic with Ms. Hernandez during a weekly co-planning session. However, despite Ms. Hernandez's best intentions, the classes proceed just the same. Mr. Nam knows that his time is wasted by waiting on the sidelines during these impromptu stories, but what is he to do? What are the ELs to do besides feel frustrated at trying to catch words that buzz by?

A Co-Teacher's Response

Mr. Nam and Ms. Hernandez have a great relationship based on mutual respect. Mr. Nam is impressed by the way the students who fight and resist other teachers are subdued when listening to Ms. Hernandez. And Ms. Hernandez admires Mr. Nam's ability to get even beginning ELs to understand grade-level content.

Because of their respect for each other, Mr. Nam decides to adopt a "Yes, and" approach. He doesn't restrict Ms. Hernandez from her narrative teaching style. Instead, he simply asks, "Can I take the ELs into a small group and teach them the content that you're going to cover anyway?"

Being a reflective person, Ms. Hernandez says, "I guess you have a point. The ELs must be lost when I go into one of my stories. Yeah, why don't you go take them and work on something specific with them."

Though this is not the best approach in many situations because it reinforces a "your student, my student" mentality, it is the best we can do here to walk the delicate line between maintaining positive relationships with our co-teachers and serving ELs. Mr. Nam knows that collaborative relationships are earned, not assigned. The "Yes, and" approach helps us earn the respect of our colleagues while still improving the learning experience of our ELs.

The Well-Meaning Traditionalist

There are three or four hands raised waiting to be called on. Ella, the student who usually answers, is called on yet again. The other hands remained raised in anticipation while Ella offers an answer about feudalism in Japan. Most of the other students are zoning out, eyes straight ahead, not looking back at Ella or really anywhere else. Mr. Tsong, a secondary history teacher, nods to show that he is listening to Ella's response, which is actually thoughtful. Unfortunately, no one else is listening.

Why should they be? Everyone knows that it's Mr. Tsong's job to ask the questions, pick a student to answer, and evaluate the answer. Round and round this traditional, teacher-centered model of instruction goes. Ms. Washington, the language specialist who has a fantastic relationship with

(Continued)

(Continued)

Mr. Tsong, notices that Mr. Tsong adds to what Ella says and then asks another question to get students to think more deeply. "He does want deeper engagement," she thinks. "He just might not know how to get it."

Because Mr. Tsong respects Ms. Washington, she has a lot of space and freedom to spontaneously join in and guide the class as needed. However, how can she shift this repetitive question-and-answer structure on the spot while keeping their positive relationship intact?

A Co-Teacher's Response

Mr. Tsong is a student-centered teacher. He designs lessons that empower students to actively construct understanding rather than passively memorize content. Mr. Tsong is also collaborative and inviting of Ms. Washington as a co-teacher. He is often heard saying, "Ms. Washington and I created this scaffold to help you through the process," and "If you have questions, you have two teachers here for you." During a pause in the traditional question-response-evaluate activity, Ms. Washington walks over to Mr. Tsong and says, leaning in, "Some students are really engaged in this conversation. Seems like they are ready for a different structure to get even more students talking. What if we introduced the Harkness Discussion method now?"

Being a collaborative and student-centered teacher, Mr. Tsong says, "Yeah. Can you facilitate it?" Mr. Tsong steps back from the front of the class as Ms. Washington steps forward to have students form a circle and face each other. Then she has them pose questions to each other. They, not Mr. Tsong or Ms. Washington, are responsible for answering and evaluating each other's responses.

Language specialists are grateful when they have the opportunity to work with teachers like Mr. Tsong who recognize that each educator can contribute from their unique skill set. In these collaborative, mutually honoring relationships, language specialists are seen as teachers of all students, not just ELs, because everyone needs support to access content, engage in learning experiences, and use academic language.

A few words of caution. Teacher autonomy and collaboration are not mutually exclusive. Katrien Vangrieken, Ilke Grosemans, Filip Dochy, and Eva Kyndt (2017) studied teacher autonomy and collaboration and concluded that

> Autonomy does not exclude collaboration and vice versa. In this regard, it is important to create a collaborative school climate that does not exclude teacher autonomy. This can be realised by giving teachers voice in decisions about the collaborative structures in schools while also making room for bottom-up collaborative initiatives. (p. 313)

Both elementary and secondary general-education and content-area teachers need opportunities (a) to build a collegial relationship with ELD/ELL specialists and (b) to develop knowledge and skills related to working with ELs. It takes much needed time, administrative support and encouragement, and team-building strategies to make it successful.

ELD/ELL Specialists

In the wake of the Common Core State Standards and Next Generation Science Standards, it has been noted EL professionals increasingly take on new roles such as being experts, advocates, and consultants (Staehr Fenner, 2013; Valdés, Kibler, & Walqui, 2014). Traditionally, ELD/ELL teachers are at the forefront of addressing the needs of ELs. They are specially trained in second language acquisition, childhood bilingualism, culturally responsive teaching strategies, literacy development, and content-based ELD/ELL instruction. ELD/ELL teachers and the services they provide are sometimes misunderstood by the school community. One school district (Bellevue School District, Washington) that has embraced a collaborative approach to serving English learners posted the roles and responsibilities of an ELD/ELL facilitator as follows (https://bsd405.org/services/english-language-learners/):

- Provides support for Emerging and Progressing ELs by supporting the classroom teacher through:
  - Joint planning
  - Curriculum mapping and alignment
  - Co-developing instructional materials
  - Collaborative assessment of student work
  - Co-teaching
- Leads building-level professional development that is specific language development
- Develops appropriate EL instructional strategies to support K–5 students in successfully meeting academic standards
- Serves as a member of the core team of decision-making professionals in the elementary school environment in order to advocate and support ELs and their families
- Organizes and involves families in school events
- Serves as case manager for building ELs
- Instructional intervention in English development as needed

Although the role of the ELD/ELL teacher or specialist is critical, he or she cannot do the job alone. Serving ELs is much larger than a single job description. During professional-development sessions that we offer, we frequently pose the following questions: *What type of English language development support do ELs receive in your school or district? What is the role of the ELD/ELL program?* The responses vary greatly, but here is a representative sample:

- It is a necessary program.
- It is just like resource room.
- It is helping kids learn English as a second language, full of growing pains. It could be helpful, difficult, challenging, beneficial.
- It bridges the gap between bilingual classes and general-education instruction.
- It is extra help for English learners.
- It should be an opportunity to acquire the skills necessary to succeed in an English-speaking culture.

- It should be taught collaboratively with the classroom teacher and the ELD/ELL teacher.
- It should be taught using the same materials as in the regular classroom.

Recently, when we have posed the same questions, we have found that teachers frequently cite shortcomings of ELD/ELL programs with specific emphasis on the lack of collaboration and curriculum integration:

- ELD programs do not correlate with what is happening in the classroom or curriculum.
- There are not enough ELD services for our kids because there are not enough ELD/ELL teachers in our school.
- The ELD program needs to address all of the students' needs at their current level. It should provide support in all content areas.
- Our ELD program is not well constructed and does not respect the need for collaboration between classroom teachers who know the curriculum and the ELD/ELL teacher. We need time to develop a relationship and to plan together. It is all about the kids!
- The ELD programs are haphazard in my district. What is happening across our seven elementary schools is very different from each other.

The previous comments—collected anonymously—reveal a range of ideas, expectations, and misconceptions teachers might have about the ELD/ELL program in their respective schools. A common thread that emerges from these comments reinforces the need for enhanced communication and collaboration among all teachers who share the responsibility of teaching ELs. General-education teachers need to know that their ELD/ELL specialists have a lot to offer in terms of content integration with language and literacy development, differentiating instruction and assessment practices for all learners, and supporting all phases of planning, teaching and assessing English learners. Valentina Gonzalez (2017) summarized all the different roles and responsibilities she has taken on as an EL specialist, and it filled a two-page chart on her blog. Because of the complexities of the task, we strongly advocate for collaboration among school faculty. What are the benefits for ELD/ELL specialists when they collaborate with classroom teachers and content-area specialists? They will be able to do the following:

- Appreciate the challenges (a) general-education elementary teachers face being in charge of classes of 20 to 30 students of varied needs all day long, or (b) their secondary-content-area colleagues encounter as they teach up to 150 or more students per day.
- Understand national, state, and local content standards better.
- Enhance their knowledge of grade-appropriate content curriculum and related assessments.
- Have the opportunity to offer insight into making grade-appropriate content accessible to ELs.
- Experience increased camaraderie and a stronger sense of belonging within the school.

What are the benefits for ELD/ELL teachers when they co-teach? They will experience the following:

- Have the opportunity to work with an entire class of students rather than only with small groups.
- Take on the role of educating their colleagues about the needs of ELs.
- Help ensure that general-education content becomes accessible to ELs.
- Combine content and language development in a single lesson.
- Develop more complex classroom management skills.
- Understand the demands placed on classroom teachers and students regarding standardized test preparation.

A few words of caution. ELD/ELL specialists who enter into a partnership are able to establish their roles as equals in the classroom rather than being treated as assistants. Even though teacher assistants are also highly valuable members of such a collaborative team effort (see next section), ELD/ELL teachers should not accept the role of support personnel. The following textbox is a summary of assets teachers who collaborate can share.

What Do Collaborative Teachers Have to Offer Each Other?

1. **Pedagogical Knowledge**
   a. Understanding child development and the learning process
   b. Instructional strategies
   c. Classroom management skills
   d. Organization for differentiated instruction

2. **Content Expertise**
   a. Familiarity with the curriculum
   b. National and state content and ELD standards
   c. Strategies to best teach challenging, grade-appropriate content
   d. Anticipation of areas of difficulty for ELs

3. **Second Language Acquisition (SLA) Processes**
   a. Stages of SLA
   b. Reasonable but high expectations for ELs at each language proficiency level
   c. Culturally and linguistically responsive and sustaining pedagogy
   d. How to challenge and support English learners

4. **Cross-Cultural Understanding**
   a. Twenty-first-century immigrant experience
   b. Students born in the United States

(Continued)

(Continued)

    c. Culture of schooling

    d. Bias and prejudice against immigrants and language learners

    e. Acculturation versus assimilation processes

5. **Interpersonal Skills**

    a. Communication skills (*You can talk to me...*)

    b. Relationship building (*You can count on me...*)

    c. Encouragement (*I have an idea...*)

    d. Inspiration (*I can help...*)

Teacher Assistants

In many schools, teachers are assisted by paraprofessionals, paraeducators, teacher assistants (TAs), educational assistants (EAs), teacher aides, or instructional aides. According to the U.S. Department of Labor, Bureau of Labor Statistics (2016–2017), more than 1.3 million teacher assistants, whose educational qualifications range from a high school diploma to some college training, are employed in the United States. Their roles also range considerably, from offering noninstructional or clerical support—such as filing paperwork, duplicating instructional materials, taking attendance, or supervising recess activities—to participating in such instructional activities as checking homework. Teacher assistants participate in other instructional activities, including reinforcing what was already taught to the class, individually or in small-group settings, and helping students use print resources (dictionaries, encyclopedias, other reference books) and educational devices (laboratory equipment and computers).

What are the benefits for teacher assistants when they are involved in collaborating with both classroom teachers (content-area specialists) and ELD/ELL teachers? They will be able to do the following:

- Develop or enhance their skills working with diverse student bodies.
- Communicate about the needs of English language learners with more than one educator and share their insights.
- Coordinate their support activities with more than one teacher.
- Provide better-defined instructional support to ELs while observing how both general-education and ELD/ELL teachers interact with this population.

A few words of caution. Bilingual teacher assistants should not be required to merely offer simultaneous translations of a teacher's direct instruction even though we—along with researchers and practitioners alike—recognize the value of native- or home-language use and translanguaging (García, 2009; García & Li, 2014)—the use of different languages together. Teacher assistants need to be positioned to receive the same respect that teachers do. They should be invited to participate in all staff meetings and professional-development opportunities that teachers have and be included in collaborative planning work as well.

Other Teaching and Nonteaching School Staff

In addition to administrators, teachers, and teacher assistants, many other instructional and non-instructional school staff members interact with ELs and their families on a regular basis, including special-subject teachers (art, physical education, music, band), librarians, remedial math and reading teachers, guidance counselors, school psychologists, social workers, and nurses. How can they be included in a collaborative approach to ELD/ELL services? *Inform and be informed* is the motto of one principal we have worked with. When the entire school staff is informed about ELs' needs and appropriate strategies to be used with this population, everyone's professional practice is enhanced. When all staff and faculty members are informed and committed to serving and advocating for ELs, all students benefit.

Administrators

School administrators manage the day-to-day operation of a school and offer instructional leadership to their faculty. Principals' and assistant principals' responsibilities range from hiring faculty to creating a master schedule for all teachers, from managing student discipline to supervising and evaluating teachers and staff. We also recognize administrators as instructional leaders, who deeply care and are committed to the learning that takes place in the building. For the past ten years, we have been asking K–12 principals and assistant principals to share with us the biggest challenges they face as school leaders of culturally and linguistically diverse students. The responses included mostly questions, asking for guidance in the following areas:

- How do you develop shared ownership of English learners?
- How do we ensure we do not limit or decrease expectations for ELL students?
- What kind of professional development would all teachers benefit from in a school to support ELs?
- How do you support teachers to develop strong co-teaching partnerships?
- How do you offer family and community support in a linguistically diverse school?
- What is the best way to get your district/building to implement changes in the ELD program?
- How can we organizationally structure a large program when we cannot consistently hire qualified teachers?
- How do you differentiate curriculum for EL students?

Administrators, both new and experienced, grapple with similar challenges. Quick fixes are in demand but are in short supply. Raising faculty-wide awareness about ELs' needs, solving problems collaboratively, sharing in the decision-making process, and setting realistic common goals that are attainable for all parties are all steps in the right direction. Jamie Ponce (2017), a former co-teacher for ELs and current assistant principal in Elmwood Park, Illinois, puts it this way:

> Inspiring students to become voracious learners is my simplest goal each year; co-teaching allowed me to model my greatest hope for them every day because I was always learning and growing from my partnership and collaboration with my fellow teachers. (para. 18)

If teachers and administrators take joint ownership of creating a powerful learning experience for ELs and are engaged in dialogue to discuss instructional challenges and successes, students will benefit from their collaborative efforts. These viable leadership practices, which result in student achievement, generate support for the decisions that are reached and policies that are enacted. What are the actions of administrators when they work to establish a collaborative school culture? They accomplish the following:

- Set common goals for the school.
- Establish a common focus for the entire school regarding serving ELs.
- Build a common language about and for the sake of ELs.
- Support collaboration with effective resource management (human, time, budget, equipment, materials).
- Acknowledge and embrace teacher leadership for those who engage in regular collaborative practices.
- Provide effective and appropriate professional-development opportunities to faculty at various stages of their involvement in collaboration and co-teaching.
- Reach out to the community at large to expand the collaborative school culture beyond school walls.

A few words of caution. Teacher collaboration and co-teaching cannot be owned or successfully championed by an administrator alone. Being sensitive to other leaders in a building, such as department chairs and teachers who have earned the respect of others, may be critical to developing and fostering collaboration. Administrators may recognize that some teachers are more willing than others to collaborate. In this case, allow a small group of teachers to spearhead collaborative or co-teaching initiatives while offering incentives to those who volunteer to participate.

Parents and Community Members as Collaborative Partners

Parental Involvement

Parents and caregivers play an important part in their children's education and schooling experience. According to *Partners in Education: A Dual Capacity Building Framework for Family-School Partnerships* (Mapp & Kuttner, 2013), all families are recognized to take on seven essential roles:

- *Supporters* of their children's learning and development
- *Encouragers* of an achievement identity, a positive self-image, and a "can do" spirit in their children
- *Monitors* of their children's time, behavior, boundaries, and resources
- *Models* of lifelong learning and enthusiasm for education
- *Advocates/activists* for improved learning opportunities for their children and at their schools

- *Decision-makers/choosers* of educational options for their children, the school, and community
- *Collaborators* with school staff and members of the community on issues of school improvement and reform (p. 11)

Supporting parents in these roles is expected to result in home–school collaborations that support children's academic, social, and emotional development. If parents and teachers communicate high yet reasonable expectations for their children and provide opportunities for successful academic development, then the chances of success in school increase significantly.

What are the benefits for parents when their children receive instruction in a collaborative school culture that may also include co-teaching?

- There are opportunities to help teachers more fully understand students' backgrounds and cultures, thus developing a shared goal for the students. At the same time, they may receive support and assistance with understanding child and adolescent development and creating home conditions that support learning at each age, grade, and language proficiency level.
- More effective communication with all school professionals involved in their children's academic, cultural, and linguistic development is realized.
- Invitations are offered to assist as volunteers in class-based or schoolwide events and as audiences at a range of school activities.
- Involvement with their children increases in academic and language learning activities at home, including helping with homework and other curriculum-related activities.
- There is inclusion in school decisions, governance, and advocacy activities through school councils or improvement teams, committees, and parent organizations.
- Parents are made aware of and supported when seeking community-based resources.

A few words of caution. Parents of English language learners may appear to be among the hardest-to-reach members of a school community. Often both parents work (they may even hold multiple jobs); thus they might not be available during regular school, or even after-school, hours. Many might not be able to answer calls in English. Concerted efforts and creative ways of reaching all parents are needed and will vary from school to school. This may involve recruiting bilingual community members to act as liaisons between the school and students' homes or scheduling meetings when parents are most available, such as evenings and weekends.

Community Involvement

In 2014, ASCD expanded on the original framework for community engagement offered by the ASCD Commission on the Whole Child. The Whole School, Whole Community, Whole Child (WSCC) model responds to the call for greater alignment, integration, and collaboration between education and health to improve children's cognitive, physical, social, and emotional development. School districts and local communities vary tremendously in size, location, demographics, and resources. However, Hugh Price (2008) suggests that all schools mobilize the communities of which they are members by doing the following:

- Provide volunteers with clear objectives, strategies, tools, and resources to accomplish set goals.
- Brainstorm long-term activities that will foster children's linguistic and academic development.
- Employ media strategies to send the message of community involvement (cable newscasts, church bulletins, the Internet, shoppers' newspapers).
- Establish a steering committee to define tasks and divide the workload among participating groups.
- Remember to keep the focus on the children and not let adult needs and issues drive the community mobilization.
- Set up a clear and comprehensible vision that all collaborators share.
- Organize opportunities for consultation among partners to keep the interest alive and updates vocalized.

What are the benefits for all community members when students receive instruction in a collaborative school culture that may also foster co-teaching? They have the opportunity to do the following:

- Volunteer in the classroom and school.
- Contribute their time, talents, and resources.
- Include intermediaries such as local institutions of higher education or businesses in community activities.
- Witness the impact the entire community has on the school and its ELs.
- Make greater use of district resources.
- Increase their interaction with graduating students and job candidates.
- Experience an inclusive school culture reaching beyond the school grounds.

ADMINISTRATORS' ROLE: DEVELOPING AND SUSTAINING A COLLABORATIVE SCHOOL CULTURE

Who really decides what happens in the classroom, in a school, in a district? In a classic publication, Douglas Reeves (2006) notes that decision making may be best perceived on three levels within a school. Let's examine how such a model sheds light on supporting ELs through the development of a collaborative school culture.

On Level 1, teachers make decisions individually and behind closed classroom doors. As such, teacher autonomy is reinforced. It is teachers' own discretion whether or not they will engage in collaborative practices. Each teacher may decide what type of collaboration and co-teaching practices he or she favors. Even when a co-teaching framework is in place, there are numerous choices to explore (e.g., we offer seven possible co-teaching models in Chapter 4).

WHO DOES TEACHER COLLABORATION AND CO-TEACHING FOR ELs CONCERN? **63**

On Level 2, decisions are made collaboratively. Teachers and administrators identify and solve problems as a team. They agree on the type of collaborative model to employ (including the possibility of co-teaching) within the various ELD/ELL instructional delivery models used in the building.

On Level 3, school administrators make sovereign decisions about issues that do not require collaborative decision making and fall outside the realm of teacher collaboration and co-teaching. Decisions regarding school safety and security fall into this level.

On the basis of their case study of two successful, visionary leaders for ELs, George Theoharis and Joanne O'Toole (2011) describe the complexities of creating an inclusive school:

> With their social justice vision for educating ELLs, the leaders collaboratively planned and delivered inclusive ELL services. This meant the principal, general education teachers, ESL teachers, bilingual paraprofessionals, and other school personnel had to *learn new skills and new roles*. This required time for meetings and for collaborative planning of instruction as well as sustained professional development. (p. 679)

We added the italics in the previous quote to emphasize learning new skills and new roles. Similarly, in his work on the role of the building principal, Michael Fullan (2014) highlights key factors that increase a school leader's ability to amplify student learning. One aspect found to be most powerful in positively affecting student outcomes is the extent to which the school leader engages as a learner. In building a collaborative school culture, "The principal's role is to lead the school's teachers in a process of learning to improve their teaching, while learning alongside them about what works and what doesn't" (p. 55). As part of a framework to impact teacher learning, Fullan describes how school leaders must "invest in capacity building with a focus on student results" (p. 67).

So, what defines a collaborative school culture for ELs? We believe it is a culture in which a collective vision is developed, philosophical beliefs and values are shared, and a common purpose is articulated. In collaborative schools and districts, curricula are consistently aligned to national, state, and local content and ELD/ELL standards. Teachers implement research-based instructional practices consistently across content areas and grade levels by sharing in the three phases of instruction: planning, teaching, and assessing. Finally, effective frameworks are established and supported for ongoing professional development that promotes teacher interaction and student inclusion to result in positive student outcomes for all. For a summary of key features of a collaborative school culture and their implications for English language learners, see Table 3.1.

Table 3.1 Features of a Collaborative School Culture

Feature	What It Is	What It Means for ELs
Shared vision and mission	Clearly agreed-on desired outcomes, shared values, and goals that focus on all students characterize the vision.	A culturally responsive school in which ELs are not marginalized is the result.

(Continued)

Table 3.1 (Continued)

Feature	What It Is	What It Means for ELs
Curriculum alignment	Through curriculum mapping and coordinated curriculum development programs, coherence is established.	Curriculum changes and modifications consider ELs' linguistic and academic needs. ELs are meaningfully included in general-education curriculum learning.
Shared instructional practices	Planning, implementation, and assessment practices are coordinated among all faculty.	Differentiated instruction is designed and implemented with ELs in mind.
Ongoing shared professional development	Individual teacher learning is integrated into collaborative efforts to enhance all teachers' practice.	All faculty interacting with ELs understand and implement research-based methods for instructing and interacting with ELs.
Student-centered approach	Instructional focus is on the needs of the learner; students develop their own understanding through active learning techniques.	ELs are able to build their background knowledge and complete self-selected projects at their own level of linguistic ability.

Vignette Revisited

Let's revisit Joyce and Molly's teaching partnership as Joyce shares how they continued to develop their co-teaching through their yearlong journey of collaboration and where they are hoping to go next.

Our collaboration, both the planning and the delivery, has gone from "I" to "we"—on both sides. We find the time to talk about upcoming units of study ahead of time. We change roles and teaching models as they fit the lesson and unit. As a result, students see both of us as their teachers. Our instructional approach has evolved as well. We experiment a lot with the language of mathematics and try to make it visible and comprehensible for all. We have increased the use of academic language by students through partner-work, triads, chants, songs, class-made charts and Thinking Maps. We know we have each other's back, and we feel we can be vulnerable with each other. To further benefit my students, I am extending the language strategies we use in math to other areas of my teaching.

And how is Amani doing? Amani frequently shares her knowledge, teaches her classmates math terms in Swahili, and practices academic language with her partners. Transitioning from her ELD class to math is still a challenge at times but she is doing better. We found out that Amani has a new baby sister and is frequently tired in group. She has even fallen asleep at the table with her peers chattering around her. We have learned that she may be helping her mother with the baby during the night. After missing a few days, instead of taking her to the side of the room to catch up on missed math work and concepts, I suggested keeping her with the group for the new learning. Both Molly and I were surprised that Amani just jumped right in and stayed on par with her peers learning the new concepts. We both wonder what Amani would have missed if we had followed the old "let's catch them up first" model instead of working together to support her learning in class, alongside her peers. We are looking forward to long-term planning and protected weekly co-planning. We think we can really take all of our students, and especially our struggling students further along than we ever have by backward planning, looking not only at our math scope and sequence but thinking ahead to what language supports are needed to make learning visible and comprehensible.

Vignette Reflection

When we reflect on the initial question posed by this chapter—*Who does collaboration and co-teaching for ELs concern?*—we find the answer in part embedded in Joyce and Molly's story— each *individual* child. The teaching partnership that developed between these two teachers most certainly benefitted one student in particular. Yet, in examining all the instructional interventions put into place within this co-taught classroom, it is safe to assume that the various instructional approaches implemented by this dynamic teaching pair supported many other students as well.

Collaborative School Culture

Of all the stakeholders we discussed in this chapter, who will develop a collaborative school culture? Who will nurture it and help sustain it? A collaborative school culture is a result of shared responsibility and shared leadership, which are equally intertwined with having collaborative classrooms (the microcultures of schooling) and a culture of collaboration in the larger educational community (the macroculture of schooling). School culture as a separate entity is nestled between the unique culture of each classroom and the unique culture of each community (see Figure 3.2).

Creating an inclusive school culture is a complex undertaking. It requires both administrators and faculty to be a part of a community of learners who focus on improving the academic performance and social and emotional development of *all* students. Effective school cultures are collaborative in nature. They have common achievable and measurable goals that are

Figure 3.2   Collaborative Cultures

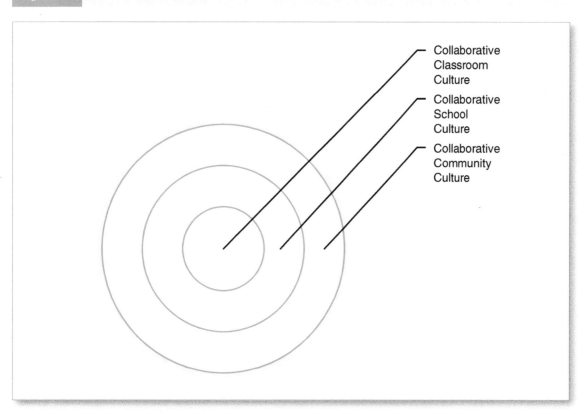

Collaborative Classroom Culture

Collaborative School Culture

Collaborative Community Culture

established through a collaborative process. Members of productive school cultures have protocols in place for clear communication and are able to maintain focus over an extended time period. It takes time, patience, and persistence to develop a school culture that supports learning for ELs.

Summary

All those involved in a child's education will be key stakeholders in a multilingual school community, each with a unique role in helping to shape best practices and educational opportunities for English language learners. A majority of students in the school community will benefit from teacher collaboration and ELD/ELL co-teaching, which facilitate instruction in the general-education class and use strategies that benefit all learners. All stakeholders are responsible for developing and sustaining a collaborative school culture in which co-planning and co-teaching can flourish. Frequently, it is the ELD/ELL teacher who initiates, designs, and implements co-teaching practices for the sake of ELs, but support from classroom teachers, administrators, paraprofessionals, as well as parents and community members, is vital.

Discussion Questions

VIDEO 3.1

Context for Collaboration

http://www.resources
.corwin.com/
CollaboratingforELs

1. Andrea and Maria discuss the larger context for collaboration and coteaching for ELs in Video 3.1. What is their argument for broadening this understanding and what are the components of a collaborative school culture?

2. Take an inventory of your entire school community. Who are all the stakeholders in your own community, and what is at stake for each constituency?

3. Engage ELD/ELL and general-education or content-area teachers in a collaborative inquiry project with a focus on ELs' in-school and out-of-school experiences. Discuss ways in which ELs' lived experiences are or are not connected to or represented in school activities. Explore possible avenues to introduce, enhance, and validate ELs' lived realities through either the taught or hidden curriculum or both.

4. Sketch out a case study vignette about one of your ELs. Briefly discuss his or her background, the home and school context, and the challenges the student faces. Add suggested strategies to help the child with cultural, academic, and linguistic development.

5. Consider the challenges ELs face as discussed in this chapter, and explore your students' specific needs. In collaboration with your colleagues, discuss possible steps you can take to meet those needs.

6. Generate a graphic overview or a summary chart of all existing practices that encourage parental participation and community involvement in your school. Brainstorm ways to involve parents of ELs more effectively.

Key Online Resources

Professional Organizations

Association for Supervision and Curriculum Development
www.ascd.org

National PTA
www.pta.org

Teachers of English to Speakers of Other Languages
www.tesol.org

Other Related Resources

National Clearinghouse for English Language Acquisition
https://ncela.ed.gov

4

What Are the Essential Components of an Integrated, Collaborative Service Delivery for ELs?

Collaboration allows teachers to capture each other's fund of collective intelligence.

—Mike Schmoker

OVERVIEW

The goal of this chapter is to explore the collaborative practices that teachers engage in. We will address the types of collaboration among English language development/English language learner (ELD/ELL) teachers and general-education teachers that yield effective instruction to meet the diverse academic and language development needs of English learners (ELs). Both formal and informal, as well as instructional and noninstructional, collaborative activities are presented.

We will examine seven co-teaching arrangements teachers use and will explore the advantages and challenges of each. Finally, we will identify the steps to creating a collaborative ELD/ELL program, including launching a co-teaching program.

Voices From the Field

Carlota Holder, EL Coordinator, Enlace Academy, Neighborhood Charter Network in Indianapolis, Indiana, shares her experience with promoting collaboration and co-teaching practices for the sake of ELs in her school.

I started at Enlace the fall of 2016 as an EL coordinator. I was intrigued to be working at a school where the EL population was 70 percent and in order to meet the needs of all learners, all classes were co-taught. Though intrigued, I immediately noticed some issues about our co-teaching model. My initial concern was that I was observing just one single teacher when visiting classrooms instead of their co-teaching partnerships. There were lots of opportunities where the co-teacher could have been more involved with the instruction, instead of sitting at their small group table doing what I would describe as "paperwork."

The most pressing issue was to enhance instructional strategies for ELs in the general-education classroom setting. This was a perfect setting to expose teachers to Sheltered Instruction Observation Protocol (SIOP) (Echevarria, Vogt, & Short, 2016), so that's where I started. When I was preparing for my second year, I decided to continue teaching SIOP in addition to actual co-teaching models and strategies to perfect what we're already trying to do. Everything seemed to have fallen into place.

At the end of my first school year at Enlace, the IDOE [Indiana Department of Education] announced that they would be providing a train-the-trainer collaboration and co-teaching workshop for EL educators across the state. I explained the opportunity to administrators, and we invested in six copies of Collaboration and Co-Teaching for English Learners *(Honigsfeld & Dove, 2010) for the instructional leadership team to read before the train-the-trainer workshop.*

Getting the instructional leadership team's buy-in was now "our" project and not my own. Our next step was to develop a summer professional-development session around collaboration and co-teaching, before the assistance of the train-the-trainer workshop. So, who did I go to for advice? None other than my amazing PLN [professional learning network] on Twitter. I explained what I was starting to do and the ideas just poured in.

We started by having teachers reflect on their current collaboration and co-teaching practices. Then we moved to the reason behind our collaboration and co-teaching efforts—our needs. We ran a two-teacher classroom to support English learners by providing them the language services that they needed within all content areas, so the better our collaboration and co-teaching practices, the more effective our instruction. Collaboratively we have one goal: to improve instruction and enhance the learning environment for all students. Each teacher contributed their unique kind of expertise to our school—content knowledge, cultural knowledge, social and emotional knowledge, curriculum, or language. The staff needed a reminder that we all have something to contribute, and we needed to capitalize on that through collaboration as Enlace is rooted in the belief, "Every child CAN and WILL learn."

After reflecting on the teachers' responses, we decided to engage in a shared exploration. I made posters of all seven co-teaching models. We orally reviewed them with the

English-as-a-second-language (ESL) teachers and then gave them time to do a gallery walk with their co-teachers. They used a reflection template to identify three co-teaching models that they would use in their classrooms and identified the different instructional blocks where they would attempt them. Teachers enjoyed the posters so much they requested that we put them in a shared physical space as a reference, in addition to a Google Drive. So we decided to hang them in our teacher workroom. Little did we know that they would be so valuable. Teachers would regularly get them and bring them to their team meetings to hold each other accountable for using different co-teaching models. Our collaboration and co-teaching initiative was off to an impactful start.

Between the time we provided professional development over the summer and attended the train-the-trainer workshop in October, the instructional coaches followed up with effective co-teaching models during classroom observations. We were slowly improving, but still had a long way to go. Halfway through the fall semester, we were given many new initiatives and collaboration and co-teaching were put on the back burner. When a member of the leadership team and I attended the train-the-trainer workshop, we learned about the collaborative instructional cycle of co-planning, co-teaching, co-assessing, and co-reflection. We immediately began to see its applicability to our new initiatives. Yet we knew we had to be mindful about not putting too much on our teachers' plates.

Vignette Reflection

As Carlota's vignette illustrates, she found herself in a context in which co-teaching had already been implemented, but systemic collaborative practices, such as honoring the collaborative instructional cycle consisting of co-planning, co-teaching, co-assessment, and co-reflection, had not yet been part of the school's culture. In addition, she noticed that most of the teams defined co-teaching as tag teaming, or taking turns teaching: One was in front of the students while the other teacher was attending to administrative duties. Carlota's initial experience confirmed what Deanna Kuhn (2015) also noted: "It is not enough simply to put individuals in a context that allows for collaboration and expect them to engage in it effectively. Intellectual collaboration is a skill, learned through engagement and practice and much trial and error" (p. 51). For Carlota's team, capacity building began through a range of informal and formal collaborative practices, which we explore next.

INFORMAL COLLABORATIVE PRACTICES

Engaging in informal professional conversations with colleagues who share common concerns and experiences is among the most rewarding experiences many teachers report. It is through conversations that teachers negotiate their own practice, through reflecting on what they are thinking and what they are doing in service of their students. Professional conversations may be successfully included in both formal and informal collaborative practices such as collegial circles, critical friend groups, mentoring and peer coaching, and so on. Charlotte Danielson (2016) emphasizes how critical the role of the *other* is in all types of professional conversations: "They supply the mirror, the sounding board, the sympathetic (and indeed sometimes challenging) voice" (p. 5).

At the same time, informal collaboration may also be accomplished through distributing or sharing information via teacher mailboxes or designated folders, school e-boards, e-mail correspondence, blogs, wikis, and Twitter. (See Chapter 5 for a more detailed discussion of electronic collaboration tools.) From our own experiences, informal collaborations may take place at the morning lineup, in the hallway, at recess, in the teachers' lounge, at lunchtime, and at dismissal. It often involves a quick chat to share anecdotal evidence about a student, an update, a question and answer, an opportunity for clarification. Informal occasions as well as formal practices are necessary components of ongoing teacher collaboration.

Isolation Replaced With Relationships

If teachers have more opportunity to interact socially, they build friendships.

If teachers have more opportunity to interact professionally, they build partnerships.

FORMAL COLLABORATIVE PRACTICES

Most teachers agree, however, that although informal interactions keep teachers connected, they do not support sustained, professional collaboration. In a recent RAND study (Johnston & Tsai, 2018), it was found that "schools and districts should consider providing protocols to guide collaboration and provide scaffolding for meaningful follow-through on an ongoing basis" (p. 13). For successful collaboration, formal structures and procedures must also be developed, implemented, and maintained. Such formal collaborative practices may have a more or less direct instructional or noninstructional focus. Instructional activities include (1) joint planning, (2) curriculum mapping and alignment, (3) parallel teaching, (4) co-developing instructional materials, (5) collaborative assessment of student work, and (6) co-teaching.

Noninstructional activities include (1) joint professional development, (2) teacher research, (3) preparing for and conducting joint parent–teacher conferences, and (4) planning, facilitating, or participating in other extracurricular activities.

The following subsections detail each of these collaborative instructional and noninstructional activities.

Instructional Activities

1. Joint Planning

When ELD/ELL teachers are invited in grade-level meetings (at the elementary school) or team or department meetings (at the secondary level), they are not only included in the planning process but also treated as essential and equal partners. Some teachers we know do not wait for formal invitations; they invite themselves, listen to the discussion, and proactively offer their input. In a different context, team-based, collaborative planning may periodically take place to prepare for special projects such as field trips, school plays, harvest festivals, Earth Day celebrations, field days, school–community events, and more.

The purpose of a more focused joint planning process—also referred to as cooperative or collaborative planning—is to allow ELD/ELL specialists and classroom teachers (at the elementary level) or content-area teachers (at the secondary level) to share their expertise as they (a) discuss students' needs and (b) plan lessons and units that they may deliver jointly or independent of each other. Sharing responsibility for ELs through collaborative planning ensures that a sustained professional dialogue takes place. As a result, instruction offered by the teachers involved is aligned rather than disjointed or fragmented. Joint planning helps ensure that the curriculum is made accessible to ELs through scaffolding, tiering, or other differentiated instructional techniques.

Effective Co-Planning Needs ESCROW

To maximize the effectiveness of collaborative planning, we suggest you build your **ESCROW:**

Establish and stick to set meeting times.

Start by discussing big ideas and setting essential learning goals.

Concentrate on areas of special difficulty for ELs; scaffold learning, adapt content, modify assignments, and differentiate tasks.

Review previous lessons based on student performance data.

Overcome the need to always be in control.

Work toward common understanding of ELs' needs.

A unique form of co-planning is when general-education and ELD/ELL teachers use the Sheltered Instruction Observation Protocol (SIOP) (Echevarria et al., 2016), the Expediting Comprehension for English Language Learners (ExC-ELL) protocol (Calderón & Slakk, 2018), or the Universal Design for Learning (UDL) (Novak, 2014). Content specialists or general-education teachers focus primarily on the content goals and objectives, and ELD/ELL teachers help generate appropriately aligned language goals. Similarly, content teachers or classroom teachers provide the required curriculum along with instructional resources commonly used to teach that curriculum, whereas ELD/ELL specialists provide supplementary materials and help adapt difficult texts, assignments, or assessment tools based on ELs' needs.

Co-planning basics. Regardless of grade level or instructional program model, key co-planning activities include the following:

- Identifying academic content standards and language proficiency standards for the lesson
- Aligning language objectives to content goals
- Adapting required reading, textbook passages, and assignments to reduce their linguistic complexity
- Selecting supplementary materials that help bridge new content to ELs' background knowledge

- Developing differentiated, tiered activities that match ELs' language proficiency levels
- Designing formative assessment tasks and matching assessment tools that will inform you about student progress and lesson effectiveness
- Identifying essential questions that scaffold meaning and clarify information
- Using individual student profiles to differentiate instruction

As suggested by TESOL (2018), ELD/ELL teachers are encouraged to not only collaborate and co-plan instruction or other activities with content-area teachers and classroom teachers but also form communities of practice. They may work with bilingual teachers (to tap into ELs' first language), literacy or math resource teachers (to share results of diagnostic and formative assessments), or special-education teachers (to review student data together, to attend prereferral and individualized education planning meetings, to inform parents about available services). In addition, it is beneficial to collaborate with school administrators (to design, implement, and coordinate the ELD/ELL program, to design professional development for the entire staff, to enforce local, state, and national regulations) as well as district-level administrators and curriculum directors or coordinators (to align the ELD/ELL program with other programs).

When planning time is scarce, teachers need to develop communication strategies that consistently keep all parties informed and allow for shared decision making. Resourcefulness regarding planning and implementing instruction is often supplemented with creative ways to communicate with each other about students, lesson ideas, teaching strategies, and instructional materials. A shared planbook or aligned curriculum maps can serve to frame the major concepts and skills that all students must learn for a particular unit of study and assist the ELD/ELL and the classroom teacher to organize lessons. (See Chapters 5 and 6 for more ideas.)

2. Curriculum Mapping and Alignment

Curriculum mapping. Many educators and researchers agree that curriculum mapping is an effective procedure for collecting data about the taught curriculum in a school or district using a yearly or monthly calendar as the framework (Jacobs, 2011; Jacobs & Johnson, 2009; Udelhofen, 2014). The key components of each map include the content we teach, the skills we develop, and the assessments we use to measure outcomes. Heidi Hayes Jacobs (2011) urges that "each element needs to be revised for timeliness and aligned for coherence" as teachers work together each year (p. 26). When ELD/ELL and general-education teachers collaborate to map the taught curriculum for ELs, they carefully document students' actual learning experiences in the various content areas. The goal is to engage in a dialogue to ensure alignment and explore possible misalignments of essential knowledge and skills needed for content attainment and language and literacy development. In her seminal work on curriculum mapping, Jacobs (1999) notes,

> The fundamental purpose of mapping is communication. The composite of each teacher's map in a building or district provides efficient access to K–12 curriculum perspective both vertically and horizontally. Mapping is not presented as what *ought* to happen but what *is* happening during the course of a school year. Data offer an overview perspective rather than a daily classroom perspective. (p. 61)

Curriculum planning, mapping, and alignment among ELD/ELL professionals are receiving increasing attention. In Table 4.1, we summarize what is targeted and what is to be accomplished when curriculum planning is the focus of collaborative efforts for the sake of ELs.

Most maps to support ELs reveal four types of information: the content (essential knowledge taught), the processes and skills used to teach the content, the assessment tools, and key resources used. The year-at-a-glance template we like to use allows intentional integration of content and language goals. Figure 4.1 shows critical components of teacher collaborative planning. Joint planning opportunities must be part of the regular school schedule; common preparation time is often the most frequently cited obstacle to successful teacher collaboration (see Chapter 6).

Curriculum mapping may be carried out both by looking back (backward mapping) and looking ahead (forward mapping). Table 4.2 offers a useful summary to reflect on the advantages and disadvantages of different types of curriculum mapping from the ELD/ELL perspective.

Curriculum alignment. What does the ELD/ELL curriculum look like in your district? When we pose this question, the answers vary greatly. We hear anything from "I don't have a set curriculum, I have kids from several grade levels all at the same time in my class, I have to focus on the four language skills," to "I follow the WIDA standards for ELD," to "I am a content-support EL teacher, and my job is to support what the students learn in their classes to be able to graduate from high school," to citing a published program as the mandated curriculum.

What are the curricular options?

1. A stand-alone ELD/ELL curriculum following a locally developed scope and sequence of language and literacy development

2. A stand-alone ELD/ELL curriculum following a statewide ELL/ELD curriculum framework

3. A stand-alone ELD/ELL curriculum based on a commercially available ELD/ELL program

4. A content-support ELD/ELL curriculum based on content standards

Table 4.1   What Is ELD/ELL Curriculum Planning?

What Is Targeted?	What Is to Be Accomplished?
Entire district	To establish common goals and a common curriculum framework from prekindergarten to high school graduation; the focus is on curriculum mandates, curriculum continuity, and meeting state regulations
Whole school	To plan instruction based on locally defined goals
Multiple grades	To plan a multigrade scope and sequence of the target content area to meet established district and school goals
A grade level	To plan learning experiences within the multigrade scope and sequence of the content
A class or group	To plan differentiated learning activities/resources/assessment tools
An individual	To plan individualized instruction for students by adapting curricula

Figure 4.1 Year-at-a-Glance ELD/ELL Curriculum Mapping Template

Month	Topic/Theme/Unit	Standards	Essential Questions	Content Skills	Language skills	Assessments	Resources

online resources Available for download at resources.corwin.com/CollaboratingforELs

Table 4.2 Backward (Journal) Mapping Versus Forward (Projection) Mapping

Initial Mapping Format	Advantages	Challenges
Backward mapping *(Sometimes referred to as journal or diary mapping)*	• This type of mapping is less time-intensive; it requires a small amount of time on a regular basis to record the ELD/ELL and general-education content, language skills, and assessments taught each month. • When various levels of language proficiency are considered, this type of mapping allows for a more accurate account of what was actually taught to various groups of ELs.	• It slows the completion of the initial mapping cycle, as teachers cannot proceed to the editing step until maps are completed. • The next steps probably would not occur until the beginning of the subsequent school year. • The curriculum mapping process can lose momentum. • Monthly check-ins must occur with each teacher to keep abreast of everyone's progress.
Forward mapping *(Sometimes referred to as projection mapping)*	• The initial curriculum maps are completed within a short time frame, enabling teachers to move to the next steps of mapping much faster. • If a district allocates the appropriate amount of time, the initial cycle of mapping can be completed in one academic year.	• It is more time-intensive. • Some teachers may have difficulty projecting future teaching. • It is troublesome for teachers who wish to document their differentiated maps for the three language proficiency levels.

Adapted from Udelhofen, S. (2005). *Keys to curriculum mapping: Strategies and tools to make it work* (p. 19). Thousand Oaks, CA: Corwin.

Carefully conducted curriculum alignment is expected to result in the following:

1. ELD/ELL curriculum aligned to grade-level literacy/English language arts program

2. ELD/ELL curriculum aligned to grade-level content courses

If the ELD/ELL program has a strong, purposeful connection to the grade-level content through curriculum alignment, instruction in the content classes becomes more meaningful for ELs. Without such curriculum alignment, the ELD/ELL services may become fragmented, the content delivered in each class may become disjointed, and the skills introduced and practiced may become confusing for ELs.

Curriculum development to integrate content and language. Among many others, Pauline Gibbons (2015) suggests that "in a well-planned integrated curriculum where there is a dual focus on both content and language, students have many opportunities to develop subject knowledge and relevant academic language simultaneously" (p. 93).

Curriculum development to build community. According to pivotal work by Thomas Sergiovanni (1994), curriculum development is a potential avenue to building a learning community. Although critical and helpful, no mention of English language learners is made in his work. Thus, we reviewed and adapted his eight platforms to indicate the key questions that need to be considered when curriculum development and community building in linguistically diverse schools are shared goals (see Table 4.3).

3. Parallel Teaching

ELD/ELL services may continue to be implemented in the form of a stand-alone, pull-out program. At the elementary level, ELD/ELL specialists often gather the children from one or more classrooms and take them to a designated ELD room. What happens while ELs are away from their regular classrooms? Their teachers are often puzzled by this challenge: what to teach and what not to teach while ELs are not in the room. One solution to this dilemma is for ELD/ELL specialists and general-education teachers to coordinate the objectives of their lessons by doing the following:

- Focusing on the same theme (In kindergarten, while learning about farm animals at the same time, ELs will match pictures to animal sounds and learn children's songs and nursery rhymes about farm animals.)
- Addressing the same essential questions (In second grade, while exploring why friendship is important, ELs will read *My First American Friend,* by Sarunna Jin.)

Table 4.3 Curriculum Platforms and Key Questions

Platforms	Key Questions to Consider When Servicing ELs
1. The aims of education	What is our goal, English acquisition or bilingual/multilingual development?
2. Major achievements of students this year	How are students doing? What have they learned? How do we know?
3. The social significance of the student's learning	In what ways do ELs improve their status in the school and community?
4. The image of the learner	How are ELs perceived by others?
5. The image of the curriculum	How does the ELD/ELL curriculum align to the general-education curriculum?
6. The image of the teacher	Who delivers instructions to ELs, the ELD/ELL specialist or all teachers?
7. The preferred pedagogy	What ELD/ELL methodologies are used?
8. The preferred school climate	Do we welcome students and parents from all cultural and linguistic backgrounds?

Based on Sergiovanni, T. J. (1994). *Building community in schools* (p. 79).San Francisco, CA: Jossey-Bass.

- Studying the same genre (In fourth grade, when reading autobiographies, ELs will create a timeline of their own lives and create a storyboard of their major life events.)
- Exploring the same topic by either building background knowledge or creating extensions of the shared objectives (In fifth grade, when studying about the Civil War, ELs create a summary chart of the two sides, while the general-education class analyzes letters written by soldiers from both sides.)
- Practicing the same or closely related literacy skills (In eighth grade, while enhancing note-taking skills, ELs receive various levels of modeling and scaffolding.)
- Preteaching or reteaching key concepts and skills (In ninth grade, while preparing to take standardized tests, ELs review the direction words and explore the language of test questions and prompts necessary to understand what is required of the students.)

At the secondary level, ELs are typically not pulled from content classes. Because the ELD/ELL courses are incorporated into students' schedules by design based on state and local regulations, the ELD/ELL program may parallel the general-education classes that help students master the content and skills necessary to earn a high school diploma. Alternately, some of these courses may focus on foundational skills needed by ELs.

4. Co-Developing Instructional Materials

When teachers collaborate with ELs' needs in mind, their attention may be focused on not only creating lesson or unit plans together but also developing instructional materials, resources, activity sheets, in-class and homework assignments, and assessment tools. There are many available classroom items that can be easily adapted for ELs. Sometimes, those involved in planning together for ELs can spend collaborative sessions conducting research on the Internet to gather appropriate information and materials for content, culture, grade level, and language proficiency for ELs. The following are examples of how ELs' lived experiences are reflected in the curriculum:

- In kindergarten, when the four seasons are introduced and reviewed, teachers consider each EL's country of origin and create illustrated diagrams that show how many seasons are in each of those locations.
- In second grade, when the three main types of communities (rural, urban, suburban) are explored, ELs' lived experiences prior to coming to the United States are recognized. Their countries of origin are featured in photographs, video clips, and other supplementary materials.
- In third grade, when the food pyramid is discussed, teachers locate ethnic food pyramids on the Internet that reflect ELs' home culture and dietary customs.
- In fourth-grade geography, when the continents and oceans are identified, ELs can share their experiences living in different parts of the world and discuss the continent they lived on and its adjacent oceans.

- In fifth grade, when the scientific method is introduced, ELs receive a native-language version of the five-step outline.
- In seventh-grade science, when the digestive system is presented, diagrams, summary charts, and three-dimensional models are made available for the students.
- In tenth-grade world history, when Peter the Great's accomplishments (and atrocities) are explored, authentic documents such as contemporary letters are adapted or excerpted to match ELs' language proficiency levels.
- In twelfth grade, in preparation for standardized tests necessary to earn a high school diploma, teachers collaboratively develop scaffolded essay templates and outlines that are appropriate for ELs' varied language proficiency levels.

The possibilities of material development are as diverse as lessons taught in the K–12 classroom!

5. Collaborative Assessment of Student Work

A powerful collaborative activity ELD/ELL and general-education teachers may engage in is sampling and carefully examining representative work by ELs. In one recently developed model, *Collaborative Analysis of Student Learning: Professional Learning that Promotes Success for All*, Amy Colton, Georgea Langer, and Loretta Gott (2016) suggest the use of rubrics within a framework of collaborative conversations and inquiry. Specifically, they propose that participating teachers focus on students' strengths and weaknesses and identify appropriate strategies to respond to patterns of learning problems. Using a protocol, members of teacher study groups analyze student work, offer plausible explanations for student performance levels, explore promising strategies to implement, and plan interventions. Once the teacher follows the collectively determined steps, new data are collected from the student, and the performance is assessed. This cycle is repeated, as teachers reflect on their students' learning and their own growth and needs.

Figuring out how to respond to English learners' language and literacy needs on the five proficiency levels, what the grade-level expectations are for each of those levels, and how to apply those expectations through scaffolding to individual contexts is no small feat! Tina Blythe, David Allen, and Barbara Schieffelin Powell (2015) summarize and compare two different protocols teachers typically follow when they examine student work. Each approach varies based on the answers to the following questions:

1. What is the purpose or goal?
2. What is the role of describing, interpreting, and evaluating student work?
3. What is the context in which student work is presented?

See Table 4.4 for possible answers to these questions in each of the two approaches.

In our work, we found it helpful to customize the protocol of examining student work by focusing on challenges shared by ELs and their teachers. We call our protocol Sampling Work by English Language Learners (SWELL). See textbox below for our recently revised protocol.

Table 4.4 Two Processes for Looking at Student Work

	Tuning Protocol	Collaborative Assessment Conferences
Purposes	To develop more effective assignments and assessment tasks To develop common standards for students' work To support teachers' instructional practice	To learn more about students' goals and interests To learn more about the strengths and needs of a particular student To reflect on and gather ideas for revising classroom practice
Role of description, interpretation, and/or evaluation	*Primarily evaluation:* The process asks participants to provide warm and cool feedback on student work samples and teachers' assignments, and so on.	*Primarily description, with some interpretation:* The process asks participants to describe the student work, to ask questions about it, and to speculate about the problems or issues in the work that the student was most focused on.
Presentation of the context for the student work	*Context presented initially:* At the beginning of the session, the presenting teacher typically provides descriptions of the assignment, scoring criteria, and so on.	*Context withheld until middle of process:* The presenter does not describe the context for the work until after participants have looked carefully at it and formulated questions about it.
Kinds and amount of student work typically shared	*Kinds of pieces:* A single assignment, task, or project. *Number of pieces:* Work from several students, often at different levels of accomplishment. May also be used with a single sample.	*Kinds of pieces:* Student work generated by an open-ended assignment (as opposed to worksheets). *Number of pieces:* One or two pieces of work from a single student. May also be used with multiple samples from a single student.

Adapted from Blythe, T., Allen, D., Schieffelin Powell, B. (2015). *Looking together at student work* (3rd ed. (p. 36)). New York, NY: Teachers College Press.

Sampling Work by English Language Learners (SWELL)

An Assessment Protocol

(Adapted from Gottlieb & Honigsfeld, 2017; Honigsfeld & Dove, 2010)

As you collaboratively examine student work samples produced by English language learners, use this checklist to document and address different aspects of learning.

Oral sample _____ Written sample _____ Language of the sample _____

Topic: _____ Date: _____

Student's Name: _____ Grade: _____

1. **Language Development**

   1a. _____ The work sample consistently uses some linguistic features. If so, which ones?

   1b. _____ The work sample shows specific linguistic challenges. If so, which ones?

   1c. _____ The work sample demonstrates that the student communicates meaningfully. If so, how?

2. **Conceptual Development**

   2a. _____ The work sample illustrates content-based knowledge and/or skills. If so, what?

   2b. _____ The work sample illustrates conceptual challenges. If so, which ones?

   2c. _____ The work sample shows that the EL has reached grade-level content attainment. If not, what do you suggest?

3. **Cultural Influences**

   3a. _____ The work sample reflects the student's cultural experiences. If so, which ones?

   3b. _____ The work sample reflects the student's experiential base. If so, how?

   3c. _____ The work sample exhibits cultural misunderstandings or misconceptions. If so, which ones?

4. **Social-Emotional Influences**

   4a. _____ The work sample shows evidence of motivated, self-directed learning. What is the evidence?

   4b. _____ The work sample shows student engagement in the task. How?

   4c. _____ The work sample shows evidence of task persistence. How?

6. Co-Teaching as a Framework for Sustained Teacher Collaboration

Co-teaching frameworks have been presented for special-education inclusion models by several authors. Most experts on co-teaching to support students with special needs talk about four to six possible co-teaching arrangements: In *A Guide to Co-Teaching: New Lessons and Strategies to Facilitate Student Learning*, Richard Villa, Jacqueline Thousand, and Ann Nevin (2013) identify four predominant approaches to co-teaching: supportive, parallel, complementary, and team teaching. They define supportive co-teaching as one in which one teacher takes the lead while the other teacher facilitates learning by rotating among them. In parallel co-teaching, two teachers work with approximately even sized groups in different parts of the classroom. When complementary co-teaching is used, one teacher works on enhancing the instruction previously provided by the other co-teacher. Lastly, team teaching involves both teachers sharing the instruction for the entire class as well as collaboratively planning, teaching, assessing all of the students in the classroom.

Wendy Murawski (2009) in *Collaborative Teaching in Secondary Schools: Making the Co-Teaching Marriage Work!* outlines five common approaches for co-instruction (one teach, one support; parallel teaching; station teaching; alternative teaching; and team teaching). Marilyn Friend and Lynn Cook (2016), Susan Fizell (2018), and most others discuss six co-teaching models in their work: one teach, one observe; one teach, one drift (or circulate); parallel teaching; station teaching; alternate teaching; and team teaching. When six models are considered, the supporting roles are more distinguished. This approach results in two different models, indicating whether one teacher takes on the support role of making observations or helping around the room as needed. Others further expand these commonly identified models to capture some nuances or variations; for example, Katherine Perez (2012) builds on Friend and Cook's basic set of six models by supplementing them with five additional variations, and Anne Beninghof (2016) identifies nine approaches to co-teaching. In recent publications, Elizabeth Stein (2017) and Wendy Murawski and Wendy Lochner (2017) caution to go beyond the basics and look beyond the models; Stein suggests examining the *why-to* not just the *how-to* of co-teaching; and Murawski and Lochner offer structures and protocols that sustain collaboration through leadership practices. In our own work, we have two additional publications in which we (a) explore the kind of leadership support needed to initiate, sustain and evaluate collaboration and co-teaching (Honigsfeld & Dove, 2015), and (b) unpack the collaborative instructional cycle that consists of co-planning, co-teaching, co-assessment, and co-reflection (Dove & Honigsfeld, 2018).

It has been well established that the goal of purposeful co-teaching is student achievement (Conderman, Bresnahan, & Pedersen, 2009). It must be well supported by several key factors or co-teaching components, such as interpersonal skills, content knowledge, teaching behaviors, philosophy of teaching, and co-teaching stage. Inspired by Greg Conderman and his colleagues' model, we have designed a visual representation of key factors that are necessary to address the unique academic, cultural, and linguistic characteristics and needs of ELs in an ELD/ELL co-teaching context (see Figure 4.2).

- *Shared Philosophy of Teaching*: Teachers must reflect on and share their fundamental beliefs about learning and teaching all children and, more specifically, about how ELs can acquire a new language and learn challenging academic content best.

- *Collaborative Practice*: Teachers must willingly and voluntarily engage in all four phases of collaborative practice: planning, implementing, assessing instruction, and reflecting on its impact on student learning.
- *Cross-Cultural and Interpersonal Skills*: To effectively co-teach, all involved must pay special attention to and further develop their cross-cultural understanding, communication, and interpersonal skills.
- *Bridging and Building Content Knowledge*: Teachers must recognize that ELs may bring both limited prior knowledge of the target content areas and a wealth of life experiences and other information to their classes. The challenge is to activate such prior knowledge, successfully connect it to new learning, or, when needed, effectively build background knowledge so students can understand the new content.
- *Consistent and Supportive Teacher Behaviors*: Teachers must recognize that they are role models to their students and are constantly being observed by them. So modeling consistent behavior sends a clear message to all students: Two teachers are in charge and are sharing equal responsibilities.

Figure 4.2 How to Create a Blossoming Co-Teaching Program

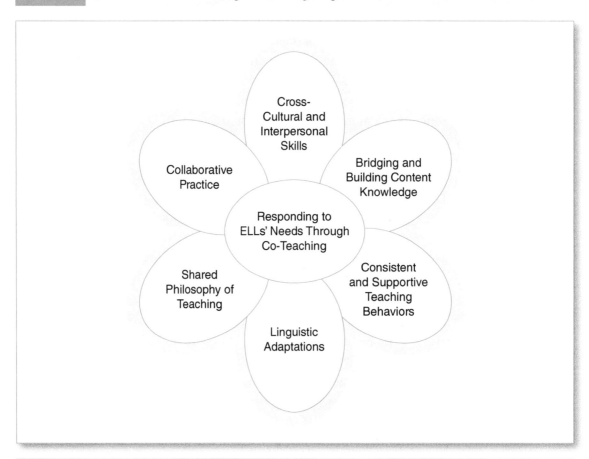

Adapted from Conderman, G., Bresnahan, V., & Pedersen, T. (2009). *Purposeful co-teaching: Real cases and effective strategies* (p. 16). Thousand Oaks, CA: Corwin.

- *Linguistic Adaptations*: The greatest challenge ELs face in any K–12 classroom is the linguistic complexity in spoken and written communication. Thus, collaborating teachers must purposefully work on adapting the difficulty level of tasks.

Co-Teaching Models

In our work with ELD/ELL teachers and their general-education colleagues, we observed the following seven co-teaching arrangements. In the first three cases, the teachers work with one large group of students. In the next three models, there are two groups of students split between the two cooperating teachers. In the final model, multiple groups of students are engaged in a learning activity that is facilitated and monitored by two teachers. Each of these configurations may have a place in any co-taught classroom, regardless of the grade level or the content area taught. We encourage our readers to consider both the advantages and disadvantages of each and pilot various models in their classes to see which ones allow them to respond best to the students' needs, the specific content being taught, the type of learning activities designed, and the participating teachers' teaching styles and own preferences.

1. One Group: One Leads, One "Teaches on Purpose"
2. One Group: Two Teach Same Content
3. One Group: One Teaches, One Assesses
4. Two Groups: Two Teach Same Content
5. Two Groups: One Preteaches, One Teaches Alternative Information
6. Two Groups: One Reteaches, One Teaches Alternative Information
7. Multiple Groups: Two Monitor/Teach

1. One Group: One Leads, One "Teaches on Purpose"

The general-education teacher does not always assume the lead role, nor does the ELD/ELL teacher solely serve in the role of "teaching on purpose," which refers to giving short, focused mini lessons to individual students, pairs of students, or a small group of students. Teaching on purpose might involve a follow-up to a previous lesson or a check and extension of what is presently being taught based on a teachable moment. Teachers who implement teaching on purpose may also keep a written log of information for each EL who needs follow-up.

Table 4.5   Model 1: One Group: One Leads, One "Teaches on Purpose"

Advantages	Challenges
The curriculum is accessible to everyone.	If not enough planning time is given, one teacher might take all the responsibility for teaching.
All students receive equal benchmark instruction.	
Formative data may be produced via logs (for follow-up).	The ELD/ELL teacher and teacher teaching on purpose feel like well-paid teacher aides.

(Continued)

Table 4.5   (Continued)

Advantages	Challenges
Constant monitoring of EL understanding is possible.	If the ELD/ELL teacher is the one taking responsibility, the general-education teacher might treat the co-taught time as a "break."
Personal, individualized attention may be given to students in need.	

Figure 4.3   What Does Model 1 Look Like?

Image Credit: New America

2. One Group: Two Teach Same Content

Two teachers are directing a whole class of students. Both teachers are working cooperatively and teaching the same lesson at the same time. For example, a general-education teacher presents a lesson, and the ELD/ELL teacher interjects with examples, explanations, and extensions of the key ideas. The ELD/ELL teacher can provide strategies to assist the students in better remembering and organizing the information that was presented.

Table 4.6   Model 2: One Group: Two Teach Same Content

Advantages	Challenges
There is more extensive modeling.	It needs a good amount of planning.
It allows collegial observation.	It requires time to get a smooth back-and-forth routine and time to gain comfort with material.
It provides immediate reinforcement/remediation.	It may be challenging for the ELD/ELL teacher to become thoroughly familiar with the general-education course content.
It allows the ability to take notes; offers authentic modeling.	
It adds clarity to the lesson.	
It is very effective when done well.	

Figure 4.4   What Does Model 2 Look Like?

Image credit: New America

3. One Group: One Teaches, One Assesses

Two teachers are engaged in conducting the same lesson; however, one teacher takes the lead, and the other teacher circulates the room and assesses targeted students through observations, checklists, and anecdotal records. The observing teacher may also take notes on which activities successfully engaged students, caused confusion, and so on.

Table 4.7   Model 3: One Group: One Teaches, One Assesses

Advantages	Challenges
There is opportunity to carefully observe students in action.	One teacher is responsible for the instruction of the entire class.
There is opportunity to collect a large amount of authentic data.	The observing teacher might not be perceived as equal by students.
The observing teacher can focus on specific subskills.	The observing teacher needs to be able to move into other models of co-teaching as needed.
The observing teacher may offer peer feedback on what worked and what did not for individual students to the colleague who teaches.	It is not an effective model if used too frequently.

Figure 4.5   What Does Model 3 Look Like?

Image credit: New America

4. Two Groups: Two Teach Same Content

The students in the class form two heterogeneous groups, and each teacher works with one of the groups. The purpose of using two smaller groups is to provide additional opportunities for the students in each group to interact, provide answers, and have their responses monitored by the teacher.

Table 4.8 Model 4: Two Groups: Two Teach Same Content

Advantages	Challenges
It decreases class size (small groups). It individualizes instruction. It provides safe environment for students to take risks.	Teachers will need a lot of time to plan.
Teachers can swap groups to allow for a fresh perspective. It provides students with an alternative way to learn the same content. Automatic differentiation	A lack of willingness to share the teaching/planning process and resources might sabotage this model.
There is more interaction due to a lower student–teacher ratio.	It could result in *two* separate classes pulled aside.
There is consistency with particular groups.	It might not work for all teachers; selected content might be more challenging for some ELD/ELL teachers to present.
Two brains are better than one!	The noise level might be distracting.

Figure 4.6 What Does Model 4 Look Like?

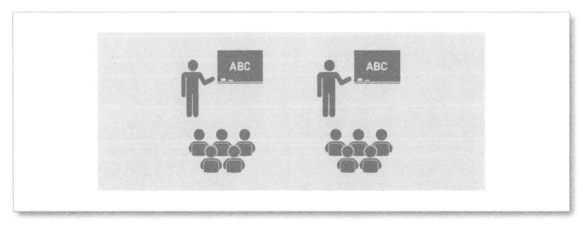

Image credit: New America

5. Two Groups: One Preteaches, One Teaches Alternative Information

Teachers assign students to one of two groups, based on their readiness levels related to a designated topic or skill. Students who have limited prior knowledge of the target content or skill will be grouped together to receive instruction. The teacher working with that group will have the opportunity to prepare students to bridge the gap in their background knowledge.

Table 4.9   Model 5: Two Groups: One Preteaches, One Teaches Alternative Information

Advantages	Challenges
Focused attention may be given to subgroups' unique needs.	It may appear as if two separate classes are being run in the same room.
It is ideal for tiered lessons and tasks or other forms of differentiated instruction.	The noise level might interfere with information processing.
It allows for building vocabulary for one group of students and expanding the vocabulary of another.	There are concerns that the time allowed for preteaching information might cause some students to have a less rigorous curriculum.
It allows for building background knowledge.	

Figure 4.7   What Does Model 5 Look Like?

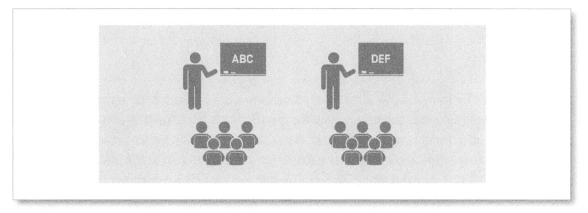

Image credit: New America

6. Two Groups: One Reteaches, One Teaches Alternative Information

Teachers assign students to one of two groups, based on their levels of knowledge and skills regarding the designated topic. One teacher will focus on previously presented material and offer the group an opportunity for reinforcement. In this flexible grouping arrangement, the group to which students are assigned is temporary and relates solely to their knowledge and skills regarding the designated topic. As the topic and skills that are addressed change, so does the group composition.

Table 4.10   Model 6: Two Groups: One Reteaches, One Teaches Alternative Information

Advantages	Challenges
It is ideal for differentiating.	You may need more than two groups.
It is flexible—only students who need reteaching or reinforcement will get it.	It is challenging to stagger the reteaching with the enrichment to stay at the same pace.
It provides enrichment for a higher level.	Students may quickly differentiate between "smart students" and "others."

Figure 4.8   What Does Model 6 Look Like?

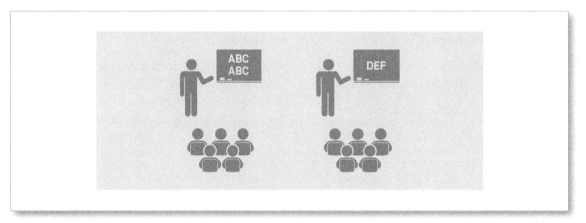

Image credit: New America

7. Multiple Groups: Two Monitor/Teach

This multiple-group format allows all or most students to work in either heterogeneous or homogenous groups, with selected students grouped for specific, skills-based instruction. This model can be particularly effective in language arts at the elementary level, when students with specific reading difficulties require specific and intensive small-group instruction or at the middle school level when students participate in literature circles or inquiry circles. Science or computer labs may also easily lend themselves to such instruction. It is also conducive to learning centers or learning stations, where students rotate from center to center (in the elementary classroom) or from station to station (in the secondary classroom) while two teachers monitor the learning.

Table 4.11   Model 7: Multiple Groups: Two Monitor/Teach

Advantages	Challenges
There is total engagement due to movement.	Students may be distracted or confused.
More individualized attention is offered.	Students can get off task.

Advantages	Challenges
There is increased student participation and engagement.	Grouping can result in a division within the class. Segregation
Co-teachers can cover more of the curriculum if the jigsaw technique is used.	Labeling
It lends itself to multicultural interaction.	
There is extensive opportunity for peer learning.	It demands a lot of preplanning and organization.

Figure 4.9   What Does Model 7 Look Like?

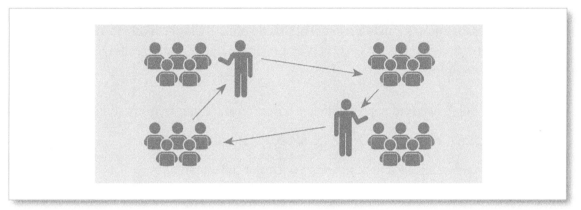

Image credit: New America

What Is Unique About Co-Teaching for ELs?

During any of the preceding co-teaching configurations, the partnering teachers will share the responsibility for planning instruction, implementing the lessons, and assessing student performance and outcome. In a co-taught classroom, ELs learn general-education content along with their monolingual peers. When learning groups remain heterogeneous, ELs have the opportunity to work with students who have various academic capabilities and English language fluency. This is in contrast to remedial or ELD/ELL pull-out programs, in which ELs are either grouped with youngsters who are below grade-level readers and writers or have limited English language proficiency.

ELs have unique needs. An ELD/ELL program should enhance students' understanding of English while they are learning classroom content as well as offer English-proficient peers to serve as language models. In our view, these are some of the basic ingredients of a successful co-teaching model. Within a general-education classroom, an ELD/ELL teacher can demonstrate strategies during a co-taught lesson, and the classroom teacher can continue to use the same strategies with ELs when the specialist is no longer present. Very often, the exchange of ideas between both teachers allows for more risk taking and the use of innovative strategies on the part of each teacher to benefit all students in the classroom.

Noninstructional Activities

1. Joint Professional Development

ELD/ELL specialists and classroom teachers or content-area teachers may benefit from participating in joint professional-development activities either at their school, within their district, or outside their own professional environment. If they attend external, off-site training programs together, they have an open forum to share their experiences, voice their concerns, and get feedback and responses both from colleagues from other school districts and from the course leader or workshop facilitator. On returning to their schools, teachers have the opportunity to share the information they gained both formally and informally with their colleagues. When they transfer the new information to their own practice and implement the new strategies in their own teaching, not only are they obtaining new skills, but they can also share these skills collaboratively with others who may not have attended the same training. When teachers participate in sustained professional learning experiences together, the benefit is even greater since they are able to support each other in their endeavors.

The collaborative professional-development practices that yield the most effective partnership and team building between ELD/ELL teachers and their general-education colleagues have the following common elements:

1. Regular, job-embedded opportunities to reflect on and improve instruction

2. Shared purpose and clearly defined professional learning goals

3. Team membership and commitment to norms of collaboration

4. Focus on teachers' instructional practices and how they impact students' learning

Our vision is aligned to the Every Student Succeeds Act (ESSA) definition of professional development, which is described as

> an integral part of school and local education agency strategies for providing educators (including teachers, principals, other school leaders, specialized instructional support personnel, paraprofessionals, and, as applicable, early childhood educators) with the knowledge and skills necessary to enable students to succeed in the core academic subjects and to meet challenging State academic standards; and [. . .] sustained (not stand-alone, 1-day, and short-term workshops), intensive, collaborative, job-embedded, data-driven, classroom-focused. (ESSA Definition of Professional Development, 2015)

We are in agreement with Stephanie Hirsch (2015), who notes that professional development should be a professional learning journey rather than isolated activities, and that it will vary based on the local context. She also cautions that "the definition doesn't equate to implementation. The hard work of planning, facilitating, implementing, sustaining, and evaluating professional learning happens every day in states, districts, and schools" (para. 14).

Collegial circles. Collegial circles are small groups of teachers who meet on a regular basis to discuss common questions, share concerns, offer solutions to common problems, and discuss appropriate instructional techniques. In a classic educational resource, *Looking in Classrooms*, Thomas Good and Jere Brophy (2008) suggest moving through three stages when designing a group discussion. To transfer this model to the current ELD/ELL context, we renamed the stages, adjusted the goals, and gave ELD/ELL-specific examples for each stage, as seen in Table 4.12.

Peer observations. One powerful school-based professional-learning opportunity for ELD/ELL and general-education teachers is created by visiting each other's classes. When observing the teaching–learning process and monitoring student outcomes in a classroom where ELs are placed, teachers may focus their observation on the following:

Kid watching: What are some of the observable challenges ELs face as the lesson unfolds? How do they respond to the tasks and activities presented by the teacher? How do they interact with their classmates? What opportunities do they have to meaningfully use and, thus, develop their English language skills? What do ELs do differently in the observed class?

Teacher watching: Are both content and language objectives implemented? If so, what are the language and content goals for the lesson? How clearly are they communicated? How does each teacher approach the varied needs of ELs? What types of adaptations are used? In what ways are the assigned texts, tasks, homework assignments, and assessment practices modified (if at all)?

Tonya Ward Singer (2015) promotes a systemic framework for what she refers to as observing together. She suggests that "to get specific about goals, student language use, and effective pedagogy for building academic language in tandem with content, educators must step into classrooms

Table 4.12 Phases of Group Discussions

Phases	Types of Knowledge	Goals	Examples Related to Collaboration and Co-Teaching
Phase 1	External Knowledge: ↓ Review and Discover	• Explore existing, research-based information. • Find out what experts say about the topic.	• Find recently published articles on a shared topic of interest, such as co-teaching.
Phase 2	Personal Knowledge: ↓ Reflect and Relate	• Engage in active listening. • Share personal experiences related to the topic or problem. • Connect and compare external knowledge to group members' own experiences.	• Discuss the pros and cons of each co-teaching model. • Invite everyone to share his or her personal experiences. • Compare own challenges and successes to those documented in the literature.
Phase 3	Future Actions: ↓ Revise and Devise	• Internalize new knowledge about the topic. • Review and revise prior understanding of the problem. • Develop a plan of action.	• Decide on the feasibility of the various models for one's own context. • Develop a plan to experiment with and implement new models.

together and learn from the specifics of dynamic classroom interactions" (p. 15). As teachers observe each other and students in action, they can collaboratively answer some essential questions we adapted from Singer (2015):

1. What is the goal for student learning?

2. What can students understand and do in relation to the goal?

3. What scaffolds and supports are in place to help them achieve the goal?

4. What evidence do we have to prove they achieved the goal?

Singer (2015) also suggests a collaborative inquiry cycle connected to peer observations that begins with a well-defined problem and authentic questions generated by the teachers. We adapted her model to emphasize the collaborative dimension of this endeavor (see Figure 4.10), in which participants (a) collaboratively plan, (b) may co-teach and be observed, or teach and observe each other; (c) collaboratively assess student progress or outcomes and analyze data together; and (d) collaboratively reflect on how to improve teaching. Because the cycle starts over, this protocol ensures continuous inquiry and improvement.

Dwight Allen and Alyce LeBlanc (2005) promote a simple yet effective collaborative peer coaching system they call the *2 + 2 performance appraisal model*. The name suggests that teachers who engage in this form of peer support offer each other two compliments and two suggestions following a lesson observation. We suggest several general and ELD/ELL-specific key areas to consider when offering each other feedback (see Table 4.13).

Collaborative coaching/mentoring. When teachers participate in a mentor/coaching program either as a mentor/coach or as a mentee, opportunities to improve or learn new techniques for ELs abound. Collaborative coaching and peer mentoring imply that teachers support each other's practice beyond conducting peer observations. Through a framework of collaborative coaching, teachers learn from each other, model effective instruction for each other, and provide sustained, job-embedded, and student-centered classroom assistance to each other. Jim Knight (2017) reminds us that "a dialogue is thinking with someone" (para. 19). Thus, collaborative coaching requires a more equal relationship between the two partners, such as the relationship between co-teachers or those who collaborate formally in other ways to provide instruction to ELs. It is effective (a) when both participants possess knowledge about the topic or issue, or (b) when the coach understands one part of a problem (content requirements of the curriculum) and the partner understands another part (ELs' linguistic development) (Villani & Dunne, 2012). Thus, collaborative coaching becomes a vehicle for professional growth for both the novice and the experienced teacher.

2. Teacher Research

When teachers engage in classroom-based practitioner research, they may do so individually or collaboratively using a number of different formats. Working in research and development (R&D) teams, participating in collaborative inquiry groups, and engaging in collaborative action research or lesson studies are briefly described next.

Figure 4.10 The Collaborative Instructional Cycle

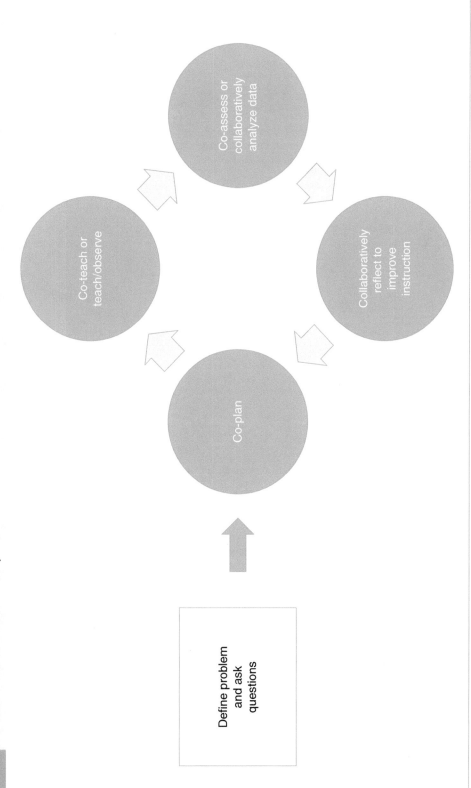

Table 4.13   Target Areas of Feedback in the 2 + 2 Model

General Feedback	Feedback Specific to Working With ELs	Comments
Clarity of lesson objectives	Language and content objectives	
Motivation	Connection to ELs' prior knowledge and experiences or building background knowledge	
Lesson sequence	Lesson accessibility	
Differentiated activities	Scaffolded and tiered activities	
Student engagement	EL participation	
Questioning techniques	Questions matched to ELs' language proficiency levels	
Grouping techniques	Using heterogeneous and homogenous groupings with the purpose of bilingual peer bridging	
Assessment techniques	Differentiation of assessment for ELs	

Adapted from Allen, D. W., & LeBlanc, A. C. (2005). *Collaborative peer coaching that improves instruction: The 2 + 2 performance appraisal model.* Thousand Oaks, CA: Corwin.

   Available for download at resources.corwin.com/CollaboratingforELs

Research and development teams. Research and development (R&D) teams are formed by small groups of teachers who more formally decide on a particular instructional approach that they study collaboratively. In some districts, R&D projects and accompanying teacher portfolios that document teachers' success with the target strategy may be used in lieu of more traditional teacher evaluations (which are often based on observations by an administrator and may only yield limited data on the teacher's performance).

After collaborating teachers review research related to the selected instructional approach, they collaboratively plan and implement lessons based on the approach, assess their own (and each other's) growth, and evaluate the student outcomes. In New York State and some school districts around the country, a similar activity is called the annual professional performance review (APPR). Tenured (or even untenured) teachers may choose to participate in it. The ultimate goal is to improve the quality of instruction and learning in the classroom while also documenting and assessing teacher learning.

Collaborative inquiry groups. When teacher discussion groups or collegial circles elect to engage in more in-depth explorations, they may decide to form collaborative inquiry groups. They may decide to investigate an overarching concept (such as the teaching–learning process or second language acquisition patterns) or choose more specific topics that deal with ELs' instructional needs (such as using effective note-taking strategies). Although teacher learning is certainly important, the shift to embrace is to more specifically measure the impact of teacher decisions and actions on student growth. We look to Jenni Donohoo (2013), who outlines four stages of participating in a collaborative inquiry process. We adapted her protocol to be specifically focused on the needs of ELs:

- **Stage 1: Framing the Problem.** Collaborative teams determine a meaningful focus related to the needs of ELs, develop a question about a particular link between professional practices and student progress or outcomes, and formulate a theory of action.
- **Stage 2: Collecting Evidence.** Collaborative teams develop a shared understanding and build additional knowledge and competencies about the unique academic, linguistic, cultural, and social-emotional needs of ELs. Teams determine what type of evidence will be collected as well as when, where, and how it will be collected.
- **Stage 3: Analyzing Evidence.** When teams have gathered enough information to address the question posed, they take a five-step cyclical approach to analyzing evidence. After they organize the data, they read, describe, classify, and interpret the data as a continuous cycle. Teams learn how to make meaning of data by identifying patterns and themes and formulating conclusions. As teams refine their understanding, they revisit their theory of action accordingly.
- **Stage 4: Documenting, Sharing, and Celebrating.** During this final stage, teams come together to document, share, and celebrate their new understandings. Teams consider next steps by identifying additional student learning needs and reflecting on what they learned through their inquiries. Finally, teams debrief the process by considering how their work was reflective of the characteristics of collaborative inquiry.

Adapted from Donohoo. J. (2013). *Collaborative inquiry for educators: A facilitator's guide to school improvement* (p. 5). Thousand Oaks, CA: Corwin.

In addition, we have also seen teachers adapting the traditional action research to take on the form of collaborative inquiry. We build on Geoffrey Mills's (2017) definition of *action research* as "any systematic inquiry conducted by teacher researchers, principals, school counsellors, or other stakeholders in the teaching/learning environment to gather information about how their particular schools operate, how they teach, and how well their students learn," the ultimate goal of which is "effecting positive changes in the school environment (and educational practices in general), and improving student outcomes and the lives of those involved" (p. 10). Jennifer Garvey Berger, Katherine C. Boles, and Vivian Troen (2005) identify the following six paradoxes that are inherently present in teacher research or practitioner research:

1. It must be mandated; it can't be mandated.

2. It must be championed by a strong principal; it can't be owned by the principal.

3. There must be an outside actor; the outside actor's role is questionable.

4. Teachers must learn research skills; teachers must trust their own knowledge so as not to be overwhelmed by the things they need to learn.

5. Teachers' teaching changes profoundly; teachers say their research confirms things they already knew.

6. For it to work as a whole-school reform, teacher research must be woven into the fabric of the school culture; teacher research is contrary to the culture of schools. (p. 103)

Despite the obvious challenges noted by Berger et al., when collaborative action research is woven into the school culture and supported strongly by both the administration and the faculty, it allows teachers to examine their practice systematically and participate in the highest level of professional learning by conducting authentic, classroom-based research. See the collaboration action research planning template we use with teachers in the following textbox.

Collaborative Action Research Planning Template

Action Research Outline

Background

Give a brief description of the educational issue.

Research Questions

Collectively generate questions that are researchable, answerable, and relevant to the students' needs.

Participants

Describe the community, school, and classroom in which the study will take place.

Describe the students (ability levels, language backgrounds).

Data Sources

Identify the purpose of each data source (instrument) and how it will help answer one or more of the research questions.

Data Collection Procedures

Describe week-by-week (if applicable, day-by-day) sequential steps for both instructional and research (data collection) activities.

Data Analysis

Plan how you will analyze and interpret the data in order to answer each research question.

Anticipated Outcomes

Identify some desired or anticipated outcomes.

Action Plan

Outline a possible collaborative action plan following the study.

Lesson study teams. The lesson study concept originated in Japan as a professional-development movement for experienced inservice teachers who wanted to regularly engage in examining their teaching practices to improve their effectiveness (Lewis, 2002). In the classic format, participating teachers jointly plan a lesson in response to a preestablished study question or goal. One teacher teaches the lesson while others observe. Next, teachers discuss the lesson, revise it, and another team member teaches the lesson in a new class. This process of observation and discussion is repeated and ends with a written report (Fernandez & Chokshi, 2002). Among many others, Jacqueline Hurd and Catherine Lewis (2011) reported on how to transfer the Japanese lesson study to the U.S. context and note that it is a seemingly simple idea that requires complex processes: "What could be more obvious than collaborating with fellow teachers to plan instruction and examine its impact on students?" (p. 3). The emphasis is on the latter—through a carefully designed lesson study, teachers are most interested in what students are thinking and doing as a result of the lesson and how to engage in a deep exploration what may be improved. Teachers we worked with used the SIOP model and the lesson study approach in a modified framework (Cohan & Honigsfeld, 2006; Honigsfeld & Cohan, 2007). We found that sustained lesson study projects need considerable outside support. These activities are not supported by most schools' current professional-development structures. Time, resources, incentives, and opportunities to share the group's findings are all necessary components.

3. Preparing for and Conducting Joint Parent–Teacher Conferences

When ELD/ELL teachers and their general-education colleagues compare ELs' linguistic behavior, attitudes, and overall academic performance in their respective classes, they may observe that the same child acts quite differently in two different settings. Use the blank note-taking template in Table 4.14 to generate a list of observable linguistic and academic behaviors in various instructional settings.

Table 4.14 Compare ELs' Observable Behavior

Observation Notes (Setting 1 _____)	Observation Notes (Setting 2 _____)

When ELD/ELL specialists and general-education teachers write progress reports and quarterly, semiannual, or annual report cards based on collaboratively reviewed student work samples, portfolios, and test scores, multiple perspectives are included. Such collaborative effort is beneficial in assessing students' linguistic and academic progress because it leads to providing a clearer picture of areas of strengths and needs for both teachers and families.

4. Planning, Facilitating, or Participating in Other Extracurricular Activities

Jointly preparing and facilitating parent outreach and family involvement programs, as well as other community-based activities, also enhances collaboration. What are some common and uncommon collaborative practices?

1. Parent Teacher Association (PTA) meetings

2. Parent Information or New Family Orientation Night

3. Parent Workshops

4. Family Game Night

5. Cultural Events

6. Collaborative Class, Grade, or School Newsletters

7. Family Field Day

8. Class and School Plays, Concerts, Talent Shows

Vignette Revisited

Let's revisit Carlota's school from earlier in this chapter. Carlota also shared with us what actions were taken to improve collaboration and co-teaching in her school.

We knew we had to start at the different planning stages—pre-planning, co-planning, and post-planning—so teachers would feel like they're working smarter, not harder. We started on restructuring grade level team meetings with communication, reflection, and reporting. Once reestablishing team norms, we laid out what the planning stages would look like in our building. We gave them time to work on their pre-planning responsibilities and asked them to execute the new planning stages in their next team meeting. To follow up with teachers and hold each other responsible, we sent teachers a Google form to fill out so we could use their feedback for next steps.

Not all teachers were following through the pre-planning stage and teachers needed more time to collaborate, so clear next steps included meeting with teachers once a month, during their prep time to assist in the planning process as a team. We were able to build this into our weekly PD schedule as we wanted teachers to understand that the collaborative process will help them work smarter, not harder.

Once the planning process is mastered, the goal is to perfect the rest of the instructional cycle: co-planning, co-teaching, co-assessing, and co-reflecting. Co-reflection has also been built into our

(Continued)

(Continued)

PD schedule with weekly data meetings. Teachers will have the opportunity to reflect on their data as a grade-level team and then begin the reteaching process by collaboratively planning for it.

Our success so far has been a result of hard work, expert advice, guidance from my twitter PLN (professional learning network), and some key co-teaching resources. We're hoping to create not only an exemplar school with collaboration and co-teaching practices, but also an exemplar school for EL students.

Vignette Reflection

Carlota's school is one example where coaches, school leaders, and teachers work together to establish norms and routines for co-planning. Having a framework or routine for co-planning truly helps to facilitate the practice. Co-planning routines create structure—they generally define what must be completed, the time frame needed to achieve it, and how to be most effective. They help teachers to focus on planning tasks whether teachers are preplanning or postplanning on their own, or co-planning together; they are a predictable system for being productive. Sometimes, co-teaching teams decide on their own co-planning routines, creating difficulty for the co-teacher who may have several teaching partners. As a result, these teachers might need to use different routines for accomplishing co-planning with each teacher. Having a system that all teachers agree on and adhere to can be one way to develop co-planning as part of the school culture. It sets expectations for all teachers to follow, and it allows for co-planning to be carried through year after year the same way even though co-planning partners may change.

ADMINISTRATORS' ROLE: CREATING COLLABORATIVE OPPORTUNITIES AND SUPPORTING COLLABORATIVE EFFORTS

Administrators play a critical role in providing the human and material resources necessary for teacher collaboration and co-teaching practices to develop and thrive. We propose that administrators consider the key components of an integrated, collaborative model for ELD/ELL service delivery as outlined in the following textbox.

An Integrated, Collaborative Model for ELD/ELL Services

What are the components of an integrated, collaborative model to serve ELs?

1. Interdisciplinary, cross-department (cross-specialization) conversations

    a. To discuss students and their ongoing linguistic and academic development

    b. To consider ELs' changing curricular needs and appropriate adaptations

    c. To explore extracurricular opportunities for ELs and to enhance parental involvement

2. Common planning opportunities

   a. To align curriculum

   b. To adapt curriculum

   c. To modify instructional materials

   d. To vary instructional strategies

3. Shared classroom experiences

   a. Classroom visits to observe each other's best practices

   b. Classroom visits to observe ELs' participation in various instructional settings

   c. Classroom visits to peer coach (2 + 2 model)

   d. Co-teaching to deliver instruction collaboratively

4. Individual and shared reflection and inquiry

   a. Based on teachers' experiences with students

   b. Based on teachers' best practices

   c. Based on a shared professional reading of emerging literature on collaboration and ELD/ELL strategies

5. Administrative support and feedback

   a. Establishing logistical support for all levels of collaboration

   b. Offering instructional leadership (being knowledgeable about both ELD/ELL and collaborative practices)

   c. Creating a professional learning community through the integrated, collaborative model to serve ELs and improve instruction for all students

WHAT ADMINISTRATORS NEED TO CONSIDER

In his inspirational work, Richard DuFour (2005) claims that "the powerful collaboration . . . is a systematic process in which teachers work together to analyze and improve their classroom practice. Teachers work in teams, engaging in an ongoing cycle of questions that promote deep team learning. This process, in turn, leads to higher levels of student achievement" (p. 36). In his essay "Masters of Motivation," Jon Saphier (2005) offers a simple yet profound formula to help administrators establish a shared understanding of a critical belief.

If you believe that teacher collaboration is critical to your school's success, then undertake the following actions:

- Say it.
  - Talk about it with conviction and passion but without stifling critical questions.
- Model it.
  - Show its importance by practicing collaboration.

- Organize it.
  - Create opportunities that value, encourage, and reward collaboration.
- Protect it.
  - Stand behind teachers who exemplify collaboration despite difficulties by allocating resources.
- Reward it.
  - Recognize and reward teachers who practice collaboration on a daily basis both privately and publicly.

Summary

We are confident that once they have tried it, many teachers will welcome the opportunity to regularly collaborate or co-teach and to be able to borrow from each other. When teachers collaborate, they share their wisdom about teaching, experience complex situations together, and reveal insights about instructional planning. When teachers successfully share their skills of delivering a lesson, or meet the challenges and enjoy the rewards of helping a new generation of ELs, their students become integrated into the fabric of the classroom, the school community, and, ultimately, into the larger society of the United States.

Discussion Questions

VIDEO 4.1

Formal and Informal Collaboration

http://www.resources
.corwin.com/
CollaboratingforELs

1. What types of formal and informal collaborative practices do Andrea and Maria highlight in Video 4.1? What is their favorite reflection strategy and how are they going to practice it after the video recording is done?

2. In his classic publication *Building Community in Schools*, Sergiovanni (1994) said, "If we are interested in community building, then we, along with other members of the proposed community, are going to have to invent our own practice of community" (p. 5). With your colleagues, validate or refute this statement by exploring the extent to which your school is engaged in inventing its own practice of community for the sake of ELs.

3. Bradley A. Ermeling and Genevieve Graff-Ermeling (2016) suggest establishing certain conditions to support collaborative improvement in a school context. Review the four conditions below and reflect on how and why they could support a collaborative integrated service delivery model for ELs.

   a. Stable settings

   b. Facilitated inquiries

   c. Recursive processes focused on improving instruction

   d. Peer observations and reflections on lessons

4. List all the formal and informal, as well as instructional, noninstructional, and collaborative, activities that you engage in during any given day. Consider the effectiveness and importance of each of these activities as they relate to the impact on student learning.

5. Review the seven co-teaching arrangements outlined in this chapter, and discuss appropriate teaching scenarios that may be aligned to each model.

6. Donohoo (2013) suggests the following rubric template to be used to gauge the level of implementation of some target instructional practices. Use this template and jointly develop rubrics for select collaborative and co-teaching practices introduced in this chapter.

Levels of Implementation Template (Classroom)

What does deep implementation of _____ look like in the classroom?

Beginning Level	Developing Level	Applying Level	Innovating Level

Reprinted with permission from Donohoo. J. (2013). *Collaborative inquiry for educators: A facilitator's guide to school improvement* (p. 63). Thousand Oaks, CA: Corwin.

Key Online Resources

Action Research, by Eileen Ferrance

https://www.brown.edu/academics/education-alliance/publications/action-research

Interdisciplinary Learning in Your Classroom

www.thirteen.org/edonline/concept2class/interdisciplinary/index.html

Internet Projects Registry (for Global Collaborative Projects)

www.globalschoolnet.org/gsh/pr

5

How Do Teachers Plan, Instruct, Assess, and Reflect Collaboratively?

Without leaps of imagination, or dreaming, we lose the excitement of possibilities. Dreaming, after all, is a form of planning.

—Gloria Steinem

OVERVIEW

Carefully coordinated planning, instruction, and assessment are integral parts of a successful collaborative program to teach English learners (ELs). This chapter will outline the necessary organizational techniques for English language development/English language learner (ELD/ELL) specialists, general-education teachers, and school administrators to implement collaborative practices and, more specifically, co-planning, co-teaching, and co-assessment strategies effectively. We will offer several frameworks for (a) creating collaborative teams, (b) engaging in collaborative planning, and (c) initiating, maintaining, and refining co-teaching practices. We offer suggestions on how to assess ELs cooperatively and also discuss the role technology tools play in teacher collaboration.

Voices From the Field

Jennifer Visalli, an English for speakers of other languages (ESOL) teacher from Garrison-Jones Elementary School, Pinellas County Schools, Dunedin, Florida, shares her experiences with collaborative teams.

Although collaboration and collegiality among the general-education teachers and the English for speakers of other languages (ESOL) teachers have always been positive at Garrison-Jones Elementary, our principal, Karen Buckles, had the vision of making the collaborative process more purposeful. Our district ESOL specialist, Dr. Natasa Karac, who supports our teachers, provided Ms. Buckles and me with a copy of a book about co-teaching for English learners. My principal and I participated in a book study together over the summer and exchanged ideas on how to create a framework for ongoing communication for teacher collaboration. Using the framework, I wrote a detailed plan on how to implement an integrated, collaborative model for ESOL services at our school. I am very delighted to share what is taking place during our first year of enhanced collaboration.

My schedule consists of teaching kindergarten through third grade ELs. I collaborate with all of their general-education teachers, but I am focusing my direct collaborative efforts with one of our second-grade teachers, Pam Hardy. Mrs. Hardy has seven ELs in her classroom. In addition to participating in a weekly professional learning community (PLC) meeting, I modified my schedule so that I can meet with Mrs. Hardy and the second-grade team each week during their collaborative planning period. During this co-planning time, we discuss best practices, curriculum, instructional strategies, interventions, and ways that the curriculum can be adapted to make it more comprehensible for our ELs. We talk about the academic, emotional, linguistic, and social needs of the students. We spend time reviewing and analyzing the students' assessment data. I also bring instructional resources from my ESOL lending library to share with Mrs. Hardy and the other second-grade teachers.

Besides meeting with Mrs. Hardy face-to-face, we send e-mails to each other as needed. She shares the second-grade curriculum maps with me electronically so that we can coordinate our lesson objectives. We also conduct joint parent–teacher conferences to keep the families of our ELs informed. We feel that our shared commitment to plan, instruct, and assess our ELs has made the implementation of our integrated, collaborative model for ESOL services a success. Together, we are looking forward to continue working collaboratively for the benefit of our English language learners.

Vignette Reflection

This chapter's vignette illustrates how leadership support is often a key factor in facilitating meaningful collaboration among educators even when there is a positive school climate for teaching teams to work together. Having school leaders who not only provide appropriate resources to teachers but also learn alongside them creates collaborative pathways between teachers and administrators that can make a genuine impact on the school experiences of English learners. There are certain aspects of an integrated collaborative service delivery for these students that cannot be developed or enhanced by co-teaching teams alone. For this reason, school leaders need to be aware of and create the infrastructure that is necessary to support co-teaching efforts to make these types of programs for English learners thrive.

MAKING A CASE FOR COLLABORATIVE EFFORTS

A common challenge among ELD/ELL teachers is the lack of time to collaborate with others in their schools. Very often, teachers substitute genuine collaboration with brief hallway conversations, two-minute exchanges before and after class, or last-minute text messages in an attempt to negotiate content and language goals that may be covered in class during a particular lesson. Although short-lived discussions provide some congruence between general-education and ELD/ELL curricula, they do not address the many issues that underlie best practices to help ELs achieve academic success.

Setting the Collaboration Stage

Ask any teacher if he or she collaborates with colleagues, and invariably you would receive a resounding "yes." Although teachers often say they collaborate with one another, the term means different ideas to different educators. Teachers sometimes use the term to refer to the informal discussions they have with friends and colleagues regarding routine school issues. Serving on school or district committees and grade-level and subject-area meetings are other situations that are a part of faculty members' collaborative activities. It appears that any situation in which teachers are not working in isolation and working in tandem with others might be deemed collaboration. Yet, the quality of such collaboration at times may come into question. Do these meetings include targeted discussions concerning student progress? Do they focus on analysis of data, standards reviews, or curriculum alignment? Are ELD/ELL teachers and other specialists attending them regularly and offering their input?

Effective collaboration among educators is a goal-centered enterprise that focuses on student achievement as its main objective. It encompasses targeted discussions, analysis of data, standards reviews, co-construction of essential curricula, lesson planning, development of assessment tools and techniques, and thoughtful examination and reexamination of instructional delivery. It is sustained via the support of committed teachers, empowering school administrators, as well as the development of a general school culture that reinforces the practice. It requires building relationships through the use of effective communication skills, purposeful participation, and respect for others.

Collaboration for the instruction of ELs in its many forms engages teaching teams to share their expertise, equipment, materials, skills, strategies, time, and physical classroom space to enhance student learning. Each teacher brings to the table a wealth of knowledge about appropriate resources to meet individual student needs. Whether ELD/ELL lessons are being co-taught in a single classroom or conducted in separate settings, teacher collaboration is essential to meet the unique needs of diverse groups of English learners (Nagle, 2013).

Building Collaborative Teams

To structure your school to initiate teacher collaboration for the sake of English learners, the members of teams first must be identified. Will your teams consist solely of an ELD/ELL teacher and a general-education teacher, or will they involve administrators, other faculty specialists, and paraprofessionals? We recommend that you consider how the organization of each team might strengthen plans and actions for the students you wish to support.

A common practice is to develop a core team, which generally involves a classroom teacher and an ELD/ELL teacher. However, we have also observed core teams that consist of teaching trios or quads in which three or four teachers occupy one classroom for instruction. With these teaching configurations, we have found two ELD/ELL teachers working alongside a classroom or content teacher, or a literacy specialist working in conjunction with ELD/ELL and general-education teachers, or even a team of teachers consisting of a literacy specialist, an ELD/ELL teacher, a grade-level teacher, and a special-education teacher aide. These types of partnerships can provide the backbone for larger collaborative teams that include additional members.

To form a core team partnership, we recommend the following strategies:

- At the onset, share with one another your expectations for collaborating for the sake of English learners.
- Outline for each team member your personal goals for the partnership, your philosophy about educating English learners, your expectations for ELs' performance and success, as well as your particular strengths in working with this population of students.
- Establish regular avenues of communication from the onset in order for the core team to practice ongoing collaborative activities—co-planning, co-instruction, co-assessment, and co-reflection.
- Identify the roles and individual responsibilities of each member.
- Outline decision-making strategies, such as which decisions can be made individually and which should be made in consultation with one another.
- Review available co-planning schemes, co-teaching models, and collaborative tools and techniques, and select those that are mutually agreed on.
- Make determinations as to when lessons will be conducted in the same classroom with both teachers or in separate classroom settings.
- Consider using protocols to structure face-to-face conversations to support better collaborative practices within limited amounts of time (McDonald, Mohr, Dichter, & McDonald, 2007).

In the building of collaborative efforts, it is most important to reflect on the general goals of a proposed team and decide if it should include interdisciplinary members, focus on subject-specific partnerships, have only grade-level members, or be self-selected groups of faculty. Support teachers such as literacy or special-education specialists can provide additional support to enhance the collaboration of the core planning team depending on each EL's individual learning needs. Literacy specialists may be able to offer insight into appropriate reading programs or present ongoing assessment information for individual students. Special-education consultants may also provide guidance for instruction regarding learning issues that go beyond second language learning.

Paraprofessionals such as teacher assistants and classroom aides can be an important part of a collaboration team. These team members often have a working knowledge of individual students' abilities and skills and can provide important insight during the planning and assessment process.

Figure 5.1   Flexible Collaboration Team Configuration

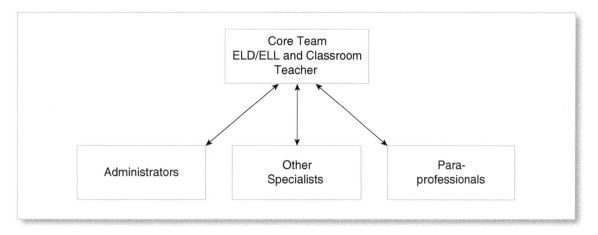

In addition, bilingual paraprofessionals can be invaluable to the success of some ELs who need native-language support.

Administrators need to be kept informed and may choose to participate in regular team meetings depending on their individual leadership styles. Some administrators prefer to be involved in day-to-day teacher collaboration by offering feedback on weekly written lesson and assessment plans. Others would rather be an integral part of the overall team process (see Figure 5.1).

LAUNCHING THE COLLABORATION TEAM: TOP DOWN OR BOTTOM UP?

An important matter to consider is who is initiating collaboration among teachers. If it is a top-down decision set into motion through an administrative directive, to what extent will administration play a part? In general, administrators may require teachers to collaborate but may themselves have limited experience with using strategies, techniques, or protocols for collaboration. Teachers in turn may be asked to work under the mandates established by the top-down approach without adequate support on how collaborative planning, co-teaching, joint assessment of student work, team decision making, and co-reflection of such practices will be accomplished. It is important to consider what strategies are necessary for a collaborative team's success, and administrators must be a powerful resource to provide appropriate support to institute collaborative teams.

An alternative to a top-down directive is a bottom-up approach, which may be prompted by an individual teacher who establishes a cooperative plan with one or more colleagues. ELD/ELL teachers, to support their ELs in learning grade-level curriculum, may make the first move toward developing a collaborative plan for instruction and assessment. We have observed other teachers as well who have taken the initiative to lead grassroots efforts to collaborate with colleagues for the sake of ELs. Yet, these teachers often face many challenges, so they should have a detailed plan for successful implementation.

A Grassroots Approach to Teacher Collaboration

Consistent collaborative activities among teachers can enhance the skills and strategies teachers use for instructing ELs in the general-education classroom. Collaborative planning helps general-education and ELD/ELL teachers establish content and language learning objectives, adapt instruction, identify opportunities to build background knowledge, prepare scaffolded materials, create alternative assessments, and so on. It can be a means for developing necessary supplementary materials that differentiate instruction for ELs and increase the odds of learning success. Co-planning also supports teachers' sharing information about students' cultural backgrounds as well as their individual physical and psychological needs. So how might teachers initiate the collaborative planning process to accomplish these ends?

As teachers start rethinking collaboration, we often recommend the following easy-to-follow start-up steps:

- Start small while considering the *BIG* picture. Avoid becoming overwhelmed by the various issues that often need to be discussed and addressed or the number of teachers to team with and engage in these discussions. Instead, narrow the focus of collaborative talks to one or two important issues and find ways to reach colleagues through communication strategies other than face-to-face meetings.
- Begin with simple conversations among teachers. Consider at first how collaboration might begin in informal ways. Take every opportunity to initiate conversations or ask colleagues for their opinions and advice. Building rapport with your fellow teachers is a natural way of gathering collaborative capital.
- Choose one or two teachers with whom to collaborate. Reducing the scope of your collaborative efforts will not only increase your chances for success but also help to hone your communication skills and strategies to use later with other teachers.
- Think creatively! Remove set notions about working with colleagues and lift any constraints or preconceived ideas you may have. Explore ideas about how to get things done with your teammates and allow ideas to flow. This step requires the building of trust among partners.

Figure 5.2 offers a summary and expansion of the previously listed ideas.

COLLABORATIVE TEAMS IN ACTION

Collaborative teams are created and sustained for numerous purposes—instructional improvement for students, learning opportunities for teachers, co-constructing curriculum for programs or initiatives, building teacher leadership, and so on. The following are just some of the many functions of collaborative teaching teams for the sake of English learners.

Understanding the Collaborative Instructional Cycle

For teaching pairs, trios, or quads who are either co-teaching or parallel teaching (see Chapter 4), and collaborative teams who directly devise integrated instruction for English learners, we

Figure 5.2 Teacher Collaboration: What to Do and How to Do It

What to Do	How to Do It
Start small while considering the *BIG* picture.	• Identify one or two major goals to attain. • Have realistic expectations for yourself and your colleagues. • Share a favorite lesson plan, a sure-fire activity, or effective resource with colleagues. • Offer to co-teach part of a lesson with a colleague.
Begin with simple conversations among teachers.	• Take an informal step toward discussing ELs' needs. • Follow up with some great resources. • Invite colleagues to see ELs in your classroom.
Choose one or two teachers with whom you could collaborate.	• Create positive relationships with colleagues. • Engage in professional conversations. • Get to know colleagues who seem to have teaching philosophies both similar and dissimilar to yours.
Think creatively.	• Look for "found time" for planning. • Explore electronic means of communication. • Listen closely to what colleagues have to say. • Co-construct solutions to challenges.

recommend that all members develop a clear understanding of the collaborative instructional cycle—co-planning, co-teaching, co-assessment, and co-reflection.

Co-planning is an essential activity; it provides teachers the opportunity to set general learning goals for students based on educational standards, to maintain continuity of instruction, to integrate curricula that include language and content objectives, to dialogue and discuss effective ways to differentiate instruction and assessment for English learners, and to co-create materials that give all students access to content while developing both their basic and disciplinary literacy. Without co-planning, there is no co-teaching, the second element in the integrated instructional cycle.

Co-teaching requires coordinated purpose, equal teaching partnerships, and shared responsibilities for a class community of learners who are not separated for instruction by their labels. It involves the thoughtful grouping of students for learning, a clear understanding of one's roles and responsibilities during the co-taught lesson, and the coordination of teaching efforts. It challenges teachers to remain flexible, be open to new ideas, and trust one another.

Co-assessment provides teaching partners with opportunities to consider ELs' individual strengths and needs by reviewing available student assessment data to establish instructional goals and objectives. This practice allows teachers to decide the need to further build students' background knowledge or the requisite for reteaching and review. Although the analysis of standardized assessment scores provides some information, in order for teaching teams to establish pertinent learning objectives, the examination of additional data (e.g., local school assessments, unit tests, writing samples, learning summaries, journal writing, student observations, and other formal and informal evaluations) may best determine individual student needs and be used more effectively for planning follow-up and continued instruction.

Co-reflection on educational practices has many aspects, and it frequently sets the parameters for the next collaborative instructional cycle. Co-reflection provides insight into whether or not strategies and resources used during lessons are affecting student learning and can be particularly useful when teaching teams want to hone their co-teaching skills. Successful teaching partners often reflect on both their challenges and their successes to refine instruction. To this end, some co-teaching teams digitally record their teaching and analyze the videos to gain insight. Other teaching partners document their reflective discussions and identify next steps to meet the identified challenges. In addition to examining their teaching practices, collaborative teams also reflect on their collaborative practices as well.

Developing Integrated Curricula

Integrated instruction for English learners demands integrated curricula—programs that develop both content knowledge and language acquisition skills in English for ELs to achieve mastery. These programs are crucial for the overall achievement and success of English learners. According to Linda Darling-Hammond (2010), "As the fate of individuals and nations is increasingly interdependent, the quest for access to an equitable, empowering education for all people has become a critical issue for the American nation as a whole" (p. 9). For this reason, educators must devise programs for ELs that truly incorporate high-quality, general-education curricula in conjunction with language development to provide equitable and powerful learning for these students.

The task of creating curricula for integrated instruction is not an easy one. It begins with anywhere from district- or school-wide initiatives to individual teaching teams involved in the following:

1. A thorough examination of state standards for content and language learning

2. A review of each grade-level/content curriculum already in place

3. The careful adaptation of grade-level content for ELs, distinguishing salient facts and material the students are expected to learn

4. The development and delivery of high-quality English-language instruction alongside content instruction to support the learning of language and literacy skills

Among the four tasks listed above, the final one—high-quality English instruction—is most critical. All too often, when integrated programs are initiated, co-teaching teams default to the general-education curriculum as the essential program for co-taught classes. English learners are offered a variety of supports to acquire the class content curriculum, but little is done to address the language learning needs of English learners in any systematic or consistent manner. In other words, lessons may contain objectives for both language and content learning, but the content learning takes precedence, and it is the part of the lesson that is most often assessed. Without the careful, regular planning of language instruction and its assessment, the language development of English learners will only be partially addressed.

Consider how collaborative teaching teams might identify broader content concepts to be addressed and also focus on the specific language concepts and skills to meet students' needs. For example, a math word problem focusing on converting improper fractions to mixed numbers may pose challenges for ELs on multiple levels. In addition to the math concepts needed for the lesson, ELs will have to understand the math-specific vocabulary use (*improper* and *mixed*), as these terms differ in meaning from their everyday usage. Yet, through attention to language—at the word level (vocabulary), at the sentence level (how words are combined to make meaning), and at the text level (focusing on overall comprehension)—teaching teams can provide a balance of language and content instruction. Figure 5.3 illustrates how content and language objects can be designated using each teacher's expertise.

By sharing information about ELs' academic and language needs, teaching partners can guide one another to devise appropriate lessons and in-class activities for all students. ELD/ELL teachers need to set specific language learning goals for ELs and encourage general-education teachers to incorporate language learning into their daily lessons for these students even when they are not co-delivering instruction. However, when co-teaching takes place, language learning goals may be accomplished during small-group instruction, in which each teacher works with students on sets of specific skills—either language or content—in order to (a) preteach select vocabulary, (b) develop basic comprehension of concepts, (c) build background for on-grade-level understanding, and (d) provide above-grade-level enrichment activities. Figure 5.4 is one example of a template to support weekly co-planning for teaching teams. It focuses on the co-development of language and content objectives for all students.

Sharing Students' Cultural Background

ELD/ELL teachers furnish information regarding ELs' cultural and family backgrounds, which can provide insight into the strengths students may have or challenges they may face in general-education classrooms. Students from other countries or whose family heritage differs from the majority of the school population may have different expectations and concerns about the school environment, issues of safety, or how teachers and students should interact with one another. They may still be in the process of trying to understand the different cultural norms of their new school and occasionally make missteps in their own behaviors or abilities to adjust. In addition, these youngsters may be reluctant or unable to obtain the much needed answers to their questions about their new school.

Family constellations, religious identities, socioeconomic status, and race or ethnicity can play major roles in how students are accepted and treated by others in school. Certain cultural groups might be devalued or accorded a lower status in the greater community (Goodman, 2015). ELD/ELL teachers can provide insight to both teachers and students to understand the unique features of different cultural backgrounds and how to best work with these youngsters and their families.

Understanding Students' Social and Emotional Well-Being

In addition to teaching teams exchanging ideas and resources on academic and language content for ELs, sharing information regarding English learners' social and emotional needs is vital to

Figure 5.3   Sample Matched Content and Language Objectives

	Content Objectives	**Language Objectives**
English Language Arts	Students will define and explain the concept of cultural diversity through a read-aloud of the book *People* by Peter Spier and a class comparison activity of similarities and differences.	Students will read for detail, take notes, and create a graphic organizer by discussing personal similarities and differences in groups of four. Each group will then share what they have found to create a class comparison chart depicting the diversity within the class.
Social Studies	Students will explore how the world is made up of major geographical and cultural differences, with a focus on the geography, climate, and culture of each student's native country or region through the creation of posters and culture boxes.	Students will write about their native country's geography, climate, and culture on a poster board. Students will also create a culture box, which contains five items paired with a tiered activity. Depending on proficiency level, the student should (a) only label the items, (b) write one descriptive sentence for each item, or (c) write a descriptive paragraph for each item. Students will present their board and box to small groups. Students will complete outcome sentences as a culminating activity.
Mathematics	Students will estimate, measure, and record specific body parts in nonstandard units of measure, such as the length of their foot using paper clips.	Students will discuss and create written notations for their estimates of nonstandard units of measurement on a worksheet and whiteboard to later compare and contrast the lengths of their own body parts and other common objects.
Science	After observing and participating in a hands-on sensory activity, the students will identify and differentiate the five senses.	Students will discuss in groups the experience of the workstations while completing a worksheet consisting of observations and recordings. Students will also complete a KWL chart that records what the students *know*, what they *want* to know, and what they *learned*.
ELA/Technology	Students will master the proper format of letter writing and apply it to the task of writing friendly letters to e-pals who are pen pals via the Internet. Students will also use the computers to type, spell check, and prepare their letters in proper form.	Students will label the parts of a letter with the correct terminology. Students will write their first letter to their e-pal and then maintain open communication via the Internet throughout the school year.

Collaboratively developed by Lucia Posillico and Andrea Honigsfeld.

Figure 5.4   Co-Planning Form for Classroom and ELD/ELL Instruction

ELD/ELL Teacher: _____ Classroom Teacher: _____ Grade _____

For the Week of: _____

Weekly Overview
What is the focus for the week? What standards are we going to address?

	Content-Area Objectives *Language Objectives* **What are we going to teach?**	*Teacher/Student Activities* **What will each teacher do? What will students do? How are we going to teach?**	*Resources/Materials* **What resources do we need?** **What materials do we need to develop?**
Monday			
Tuesday			
Wednesday			
Thursday			
Friday			
Daily and/or Weekly Assessments			

online resources   Available for download at resources.corwin.com/CollaboratingforELs

students' overall well-being and success. Many newcomers experience culture shock—feelings of disorientation and distress due to unfamiliar surroundings—and need time to adjust to the new culture, the norms and expectations of the society, and, more specifically, the norms and expectations of the school (Zacarian & Haynes, 2012). Many youngsters are separated from their parents and siblings in the United States. They may suffer from a number of maladies and negative repercussions, including post-traumatic stress syndrome, separation anxiety, and physical illness. Although creating a sensitive, nurturing, and culturally responsive learning environment is the responsibility of all teachers, ELD/ELL professionals may be more extensively prepared in cross-cultural awareness and more knowledgeable about the twenty-first-century immigrant experience. With these considerations in mind, ELD/ELL teachers can guide general-education teachers on what expectations they should hold for their newcomer students with respect to their class participation, homework completion, attendance, behavior, and attitudes.

In consideration of what collaborative teams need to share before and during the onset of teaching English learners, Table 5.1 offers some key tips as you embark on collaborative endeavors.

A FRAMEWORK FOR EFFECTIVE COLLABORATIVE INSTRUCTION

Setting a framework to organize what, how, and when content and language skills will be taught is a tremendous asset for collaborative teams to have as an overall resource. This type of organization can assist teaching teams in ensuring lessons are congruent with grade-appropriate instruction and can relieve teaching partners of the anxiety that often emerges as a result of the limited time to plan. In co-teaching arrangements, ELD/ELL and general-education teachers share common guides to content-area curricula, scope and sequences, state standards for content, language, and

Table 5.1 What to Do and What Not to Do When You Collaborate

DO	DON'T
Focus on all aspects of ELs' development: academic, linguistic, social, cultural, and emotional.	Blame or scapegoat anyone, especially the parents.
Document both the process and the outcome of collaborative activities.	Think you need to do it all on your own.
Request administrative support; find and create time to collaborate.	Be dissuaded by lack of time.
Share information, resources, and ideas.	Withhold information or resources.
Ask questions, listen carefully, and offer your input.	Put yourself or anyone down—ever!—or say "It's a stupid question . . ."
Expect conflicts and resolve them professionally.	Allow collaborative practices to dissolve due to different points of view.

literacy development, core texts, teacher-made materials, online programs, and any other resources that are essential to the planning of collaborative instruction. Subsequently, routines for lesson co-planning, co-instruction, co-assessment, and co-reflection can be established.

Before the School Year Begins

We often recommend that school administrators arrange to have collaborative teams meet over the summer months or right before school begins to allow for joint planning for the coming academic year. Although teachers may not be obligated to attend such meetings during the summer months, the benefits of collaborating before the academic year commences will increase tenfold once the first semester is under way. Grade-level/content teams can take the opportunity to reflect on and review the previous year as well as formally plan for the coming school year. One activity—building and revising curriculum maps—can be of great value for teaching teams to negotiate at this time. Curriculum maps may be arranged monthly, yearly, or by marking period and contain both broad-based topics and specific details of the curriculum, including activities, texts, literature, websites, grouping strategies, and so on. Establishing content and language learning goals, standards-based skills and concepts, formative and summative assessments, and major and supplementary resources for instruction will give teaching partners a strong anchor for planning throughout the school year. Additionally, meetings might even include a simple invitation to visit each other's classrooms to browse available resources. The hidden treasures you will find down the hall in your colleague's classroom just may surprise you!

In preparation for the new school year, establish some schoolwide, team, or partnership agreements; set the time for your first team meeting; and develop an introductory welcome letter to be sent home to parents.

During the School Year

Establishing routines and responsibilities for co-planning, co-assessment, and joint reflective practices within your co-teaching team is most effective when they are initiated early in the school year. Consider the amount of time you will be able to spend as a team to collaborate and create a protocol that will accomplish as much as possible within the time frame you have. For example, consider the flow of the following lesson planning protocol:

1. Identify the learning objectives—long-term and short-term goals—at the onset; consider how to differentiate learning expectations and assessment. (10 minutes)

2. Allow time for brainstorming ideas for the different aspects of lesson delivery as well as further discussion and negotiation of strategies and techniques to be used during the lesson. (20 minutes)

3. Come to consensus and summarize your plans of action. (10 minutes)

Creating a lesson planning template such as the one in Figure 5.4 can aid in the ongoing collaborative process. When face-to-face communication seems to be an insurmountable challenge, experiment with electronic methods of communication to inform each other about lesson ideas and student needs. Once your co-teaching team has an established routine, try to regularly collaborate with grade-level/content-area teacher teams to tap into the available expertise in your school.

At the End of the School Year

Celebrate your collaborative efforts by reflecting on the successes and challenges that you have met. Set aside time to evaluate all your collaborative efforts. Consider keeping and sharing reflective journals that each team member has personally updated throughout the school year. These journals can be part of the actual data used to improve practice and to obtain additional time and resources needed for collaboration to take place among team members. Alternately, you can keep a learning log on a shared Google Drive that documents the key takeaways from your collaborative experiences. In addition, plan on showcasing your success stories to your administrators, fellow faculty, parents, and school board members. Don't forget to find the time to spend with your collaborative partners to reflect on the challenges of the coming school year.

TECHNOLOGY AND COLLABORATION

Technology can play an important role in establishing ongoing collaboration among educators who, for whatever reason, are unable or for whom it is difficult to meet face-to-face. Telecommunication can alter the way in which teachers participate in shared decision making with their colleagues regarding lesson planning, curriculum selection, instructional strategies, reviewing student work, and reflecting on previous practices. Technology can provide an avenue for educators to correspond with others in the same school and even explore how teachers provide instruction in other areas of the world. Weblogs, wikis, tweet chats, online communities, and professional learning networks have redefined communication and interaction in the twenty-first century (Langer de Ramirez, 2009). The Internet is one of the most important innovations of our time, bringing substantial benefits to economies and societies, but also driving change in the way we live and work, and, ultimately, collaborate. What are the choices teachers have to communicate with each other more effectively?

E-Mail

E-mail is a very common, simple form of Internet use. Since most teachers have made the leap to planning their weekly lessons electronically, they may simply share lesson plans via e-mail or propose activities and ideas to each other—even from their portable or hand-held devices. If necessary, teachers may identify and set parameters for certain times during the week in which e-mail can be sent, received, responded to, and so on. Conversely, they can use this form of communication in the most informal, ongoing fashion.

Blogs

Blogs, short for *weblogs*, can take many forms, including personal online journals as well as platforms for the greater world community to post opinions and share commentary via the Web.

Teachers use blogs to exchange ideas on a variety of educational matters, share their personal knowledge, assist in instructional problem solving, and network with educators regardless of geographic location. Blogging is particularly useful for those ELD/ELL teachers who feel isolated in their school or district and would benefit from the support of other teachers. We follow a lot of enthusiastic co-teachers' and collaborative ELD/ELL educators' blogs who might devote their entire blog to collaboration and co-teaching or might address it periodically (see textbox).

https://elementaryenglishlanguagelearners.weebly.com

http://ellchatbkclub.blogspot.com

www.empoweringells.com

https://justingarciaell.com

www.readysetcoteach.com

Wikis

A *wiki* as an accumulation of information on the Web designed to allow anyone to contribute or modify its content. Invented by Ward Cunningham in 1995, a wiki is a collection of webpages in which its members often are encouraged to add or modify information. Wikis may be used to construct collaborative websites and frequently are implemented in businesses that use similar features on their networks for company employees to communicate and collaborate. In education, teachers can use wikis to collaboratively work on curriculum content or lesson planning instead of e-mailing and attaching documents back and forth. A wiki can serve as a collective of grade-level or subject-level materials and provide necessary curriculum maps and information for all teachers to use in their planning for ELs. There are ready-to-use, easy-to-implement wikis available for teachers who might hesitate to use new technology.

Text Messaging

Although it may not be suitable for complex planning, assessment, and reflection practices between teachers, text messaging has been incorporated successfully by teaching teams in a number of ways for collaboration purposes. It can be used to clarify information, verify lesson goals and objectives, suggest spur-of-the-moment ideas, identify new resources, and so on. This type of communication should be used only if it has been agreed on between co-teaching members.

Dropbox

Dropbox is a file-hosting service that offers file storage and sharing on a cloud platform. Users can create files on their personal computers that are synchronized to Dropbox and invite others to share the posted files that have been created. The service is free up to a certain amount of storage. Dropbox is an effective application for sharing files with one or more teachers. It can support online lesson planning, co-assessment of student work, and ongoing reflection of instructional practices. The only downside to using Dropbox is that only one person at a time can work on a document. If more than one person edits a document at the same time, Dropbox will create a duplicate and conflicting file.

Google Drive

Google Drive is Google's online document filing and sharing system that allows users to share files with one or more people. Unlike Dropbox, documents can more easily be worked on by more than one person at the same time. This feature allows teachers to collaborate with one another in real time. Teachers often use this application when they are working side-by-side with one another as well as when they are not meeting together. All team members can view how others on the team have edited a particular document in real time. Using Google apps is a popular choice for teachers who collaborate with one another.

Vignette Revisited

When we look back at the many strategies used for collaboration at Garrison-Jones Elementary School, we can better understand how incorporating these strategies helps teachers succeed. Teachers established frameworks or protocols for communication having a set organization for how collaboration takes place. They had face-to-face time to meet and plan together regularly for their students. They also used electronic means to communicate with one another outside the regular school day. This use of multiple collaborative strategies incorporating organization, routine, and documentation of planning, assessment, and reflection has been found to be most effective in accomplishing successful collaboration among many co-teaching teams.

CO-TEACHING FOR POWERFUL INSTRUCTION

Co-teaching is a dynamic component of teacher collaboration that employs its own special set of teaching competencies. Its major goal is to merge ELD and content instruction to increase the time ELs are exposed to general-education curriculum and thereby strengthen their overall academic achievement. Co-teaching often requires a restructuring of the school environment—a shift in ways to not only collaborate with other teachers but also to emphasize learning for all students; establish high standards for ELs; share responsibility for planning, instruction, and assessment; and take on new roles within the classroom.

Roles and Responsibilities

In practice, some co-teaching partners may appreciate the naming of individual tasks and the delineation of responsibilities each teacher will have to create successful classroom experiences for all students involved. Teaching roles should be flexible and interchangeable to ensure parity and coordinated support for ELs. Some of these teacher roles and responsibilities can be identified and described as follows:

- The *leader* keeps the lesson's pace, allows enough time for task transitions, and makes suggestions about how to reorganize lessons when there are time constraints.
- The *supporter* considers directions from the leader, follows the leader's cues, and supports spontaneous lesson changes.
- The *techie* takes charge of technology and prepares and sets up presentations from online, video, DVD, or teacher-made resources.
- The *scribe* writes spoken information, provides bulleted lists on chart paper, and copies directions on the board.
- The *illustrator* identifies information for students through simple board sketches, graphic organizers, or downloaded photographs off the Internet.
- The *devil's advocate* asks questions to the teacher leading instruction to provoke thought, clarify information, or to have information repeated with additional examples, illustrations, or language use.
- The *evaluator* uses a co-teaching journal to jot down a lesson's strengths and challenges for future discussion in collaborative team sessions.

Some of these identified roles are decided according to the co-teaching team's chosen model of instruction (see Chapter 4) for particular lessons. By determining each team member's responsibilities for each lesson, teachers can prepare instruction more effectively and be better able to obtain the materials necessary to meet their students' needs. When lessons are carefully orchestrated and teaching roles clearly established, what would otherwise be awkward or confusing instruction can be executed seamlessly. In this way, classroom activities are more likely to be of maximum benefit to ELs.

Co-Teaching Competencies

Each person on the co-teaching team must have a thorough understanding of the selected co-teaching model. As previously discussed in Chapter 4, some teaching teams prefer to use two or more models consistently, whereas others enjoy the flexibility of using different co-teaching models at different times or on different days. In addition, not all collaborative planning results in the use of co-teaching. Regular co-planning sessions establish important curriculum continuity even when teachers deliver instruction in separate class settings.

Although there may be little time for teachers to meet face-to-face, the need to collaborate is too important an issue to be hindered by inadequately scheduled planning time. Innovative planning methods need to be devised to ensure collaborative objectives are met.

Co-Teaching 101: A Quick-Start Guide

From our discussions with teachers, we often are asked how to get started with co-teaching. We offer the following guidelines to jump-start your program.

First Steps

1. Start by doing what you know best!! Think of your favorite, most successful lessons, activities, and tasks that have always worked in a one-teacher classroom. Be ready to try those out in a co-taught setting.

2. Make sure that common grade-appropriate, content-based objectives are identified for each lesson. Your ELs will learn the same content material in an adapted format.

3. Start the lesson together standing in front of the class. In this way, you establish parity; that is, you will have equal roles in the eyes of all students.

The following are lesson starters that can be used based on your lesson objectives:

   a. Use a graphic organizer, advance organizer, or some visual aid to offer an overview or introduce a concept.

   b. Role-play for your students (frequently taking advantage of the fact that two adult English language models are available).

   c. Read aloud (Teacher 1) and think aloud (Teacher 2), commenting on what Teacher 1 just read.

   d. One teacher introduces information; the other teacher clarifies, illustrates, writes key words on the board, shows related pictures or *realia* (real-life objects), and/or asks questions of key points.

   e. Teach a rhyme, use poetry or finger plays, sing a song or play music, or involve everyone in a game.

   f. Take turns talking. (Learn to take signals from each other.)

4. Consider student-grouping configurations for the next section of your lesson.

   a. Split the class into two, approximately even heterogeneous groups.

      i. Group A: learners who need extra support, scaffolding, preteaching, or reteaching in the selected content

      ii. Group B: more proficient learners in the selected content

         • Each teacher stays with his or her group for a set period of time working in a parallel teaching mode using differentiated instructional techniques.

         • Each group focuses on language and content that is needed to reach general-education goals.

   b. Split the class into three, approximately even homogenous groups.

      i. Group A: ELs who are entering or beginning students

      ii. Group B: learners who need extra support

      iii. Group C: highest-performing group working on advanced tasks independently

         • Teacher 1 takes Group A, Teacher 2 takes Group B, and Group C works independently for a set period of time. Each teacher stays with his or her group for a set period of time working in a parallel teaching mode using differentiated instructional techniques.

   c. Feel free to experiment with other models of instruction, such as setting up and monitoring four or five learning centers.

5. In the last section of the lesson, bring the entire class together for debriefing.

   a. Groups take turns sharing ideas and products, outcomes of learning, answers to worksheets, results of problems solved, etc.

   b. Teachers take turns asking review questions.

   c. Teachers play a closure game (e.g., Wonder Ball, where you toss a koosh ball to students and have them finish sentence starters such as *I wonder, Today I learned, I liked*, etc.).

   d. Teachers use some type of exit activity together. (Students respond to one of several possible summary questions on "exit cards," or "tickets to leave," slips of paper, or index cards. The ELD/ELL teacher or general-education teacher collects the "tickets" and uses them for assessment purposes.)

6. Remember to reflect daily (jointly or individually) on the co-teaching experience. Keep a simple "2+2" log: Jot down two things that worked and two things that could be done differently next time.

Date	Two Things That Worked	Two Things to Work On

Other Tips

1. Look for opportunities to create your unique set of co-teaching routines or rituals early on. Your students will notice and be able to anticipate the sequence of activities.

2. Bring your own talent forward. If you are a singer, introduce the topic through songs (www.songsforteaching.com). If you are artistic, illustrate key concepts for your students as the other teacher explains them.

3. Don't be afraid to think creatively and try new ideas.

4. Visit inclusive classrooms where colleagues have been co-teaching for many years.

   a. Ask them for their favorite techniques to collaborate.

   b. Visit them to watch a lesson they co-teach.

5. Be spontaneous; co-teaching does not have to be scripted.

6. Respect each other's comfort zones, but encourage each other to be adventurous.

7. Show your enthusiasm for being with the whole class together and for working with each other. (Students always pick up on nonverbal signals.)

8. Enjoy the experience.

How to Manage a Co-Teaching Situation

Managing a co-taught classroom—creating routines to determine who does what, when, and where—is a crucial aspect to powerful instructional delivery as well as making the most of co-teaching time. Many special-education experts (e.g., Conderman, Bresnahan, & Pedersen, 2009; Fattig & Taylor, 2007; Murawski & Dieker, 2013; Stein, 2017; Villa, Thousand, & Nevin, 2013) offer effective strategies for purposeful co-teaching in the inclusive classroom setting. As previously stated, ELs have rather different needs than students with disabilities. Expanding on Conderman et al.'s (2009) approach, we created a summary chart to represent the ELD perspective (see Table 5.2). What could each teacher do as he or she engages in the various stages of a co-taught lesson?

Table 5.2   Teacher Activities During the Co-Teaching Process

When One Teacher Is Doing This . . .	The Other Teacher Is Doing This . . .	Benefits of Collaboration
Taking attendance	Collecting or reviewing homework or introducing or reviewing a social or study skill	Instruction time is increased. Skills-based instruction is integrated into lessons.
Distributing papers or other resources	Reviewing directions or rules or modeling the first problem in the assignment	Instruction time is increased. Examples promote student understanding.
Presenting information through lecture or media (PowerPoint, video, or audio clip)	Modeling note taking on the board or overhead or filling in a graphic organizer	Content is accessible for all students. Strong connections are made between new and previously learned content. Student understanding is facilitated.
Giving instructions orally	Writing down instructions on the board or overhead or repeating or clarifying any difficult concept	Content is accessible for all students.
Checking for understanding with large, heterogeneous groups of students	Checking for understanding with small, homogeneous groups	Reteaching can occur without delay.
Circulating; providing one-on-one support as needed	Providing direct instruction to ELs one to one or in small groups	Learning is not merely incidental.
Prepping half the class for one side of a debate	Prepping ELs for the opposing side of the debate	Instruction time and student engagement are increased.

When One Teacher Is Doing This . . .	The Other Teacher Is Doing This . . .	Benefits of Collaboration
Facilitating independent, silent work	Circulating and checking for comprehension	Reteaching can occur without delay.
Providing large-group instruction	Circulating, clarifying key concepts or cultural information	Culturally challenging information is made understandable.
Monitoring the large group as students work on practice material	Preteaching or reteaching challenging concepts to a small group of ELs	Student language learning is enhanced.
Facilitating sustained silent reading	Reading aloud quietly with a small group or previewing upcoming information	Students are exposed to or internalize language structures they will need to apply to independent reading.
Creating basic lesson plans for standards, objectives, and content curriculum	Providing suggestions for language objectives, scaffolding activities, adapting instructional materials	Student needs are met through differentiated instruction. Lessons are created to meet the needs of student subgroups.
Facilitating stations or groups	Facilitating other stations or groups	Instructional materials can be tailored to the needs of ELs.
Explaining a new concept	Conducting a role play, modeling a concept, or asking clarifying questions	Students' interest and motivation are increased. ELs are engaged in varied activities.
Considering enrichment opportunities	Considering reinforcement opportunities	Everyone works toward essential understanding and skills. More options are available to meet student needs.

Adapted from Conderman, G., Bresnahan, V., & Pedersen, T. (2009). *Purposeful co-teaching: Real cases and effective strategies* (p. 31). Thousand Oaks, CA: Corwin.

How to Achieve Co-Teaching Success

Co-teaching can be accomplished through a variety of approaches and contexts. ELs can be well served when co-teachers acquire effective skills and generate lessons through collaboration. Here are some strategies for initiating your co-teaching programs.

1. Initiate a pilot program; secure administrative and peer support for piloting co-teaching in a limited number of classes.

2. Engage in informal and formal explorations of co-teaching with colleagues who might be potential co-teachers.

3. Request formal training in co-teaching practices from your administrators.

4. Following initial training, secure ongoing support in the form of mentoring, coaching, or establishing a collegial circle.

5. With your co-teaching partner, agree on two or three models and experiment with their practicability. For example, beginning the lesson together, moving to a certain grouping configuration, and then ending the lesson together is a well-established routine among successful co-teachers (Dove & Honigsfeld, 2018).

   a. When you establish a predictable routine or structure during a co-taught lesson, it requires less planning time and coordination between the teachers involved.

   b. As trust and mutual respect for each teacher's ability builds, additional models can be executed simply with rewarding results for both students and teachers. It is most successful when both the ELD/ELL teacher and the classroom teacher share the responsibility of taking the lead role. In this way, both teachers' individual talents can be used to benefit the students.

6. Establish daily or weekly routines and clearly defined expectations for each other and your students. Always talk about differences in teaching philosophies or preferred approaches, work to prevent potential problems before they arise, and resolve conflicts professionally and in a timely fashion.

7. Once you have established a co-teaching relationship, experiment with additional models of instruction (e.g., see Dove & Honigsfeld, 2018, where variations of the original seven models exceed thirty configurations). This works best when the ELD/ELL and general-education teachers have a good rapport with one another and their teaching styles can accommodate much flexibility.

   a. Teachers who have similar instructional and disciplinary styles are likely to select certain co-teaching arrangements.

   b. On the other hand, teachers who have differing styles—perhaps complementary styles—will use co-teaching arrangements that allow for each teacher's individual strengths to receive a more pronounced focus.

8. Document and share your successes.

COLLABORATIVE STUDENT ASSESSMENT

In their seminal work, Rick Stiggins and Rick DuFour (2009) suggest engaging in collaborative assessment practices to maximize the power of formative assessments:

In professional learning communities, collaborative teams of teachers create common assessments for three formative purposes. First, team-developed common assessments help identify curricular areas that need attention because many students are struggling. Second, they help each team member clarify strengths and weaknesses in his or her teaching and create a forum for teachers to learn from one another. Third, interim common assessments identify students who aren't mastering the intended standards and need timely and systematic interventions. (p. 641)

Collaborative assessment for ELs' linguistic, academic, and social development incorporates the use of a variety of data to determine student progress. Collaborative partners and co-teachers use ongoing, informal classroom assessment techniques, adapted formal assessment tools, and teacher-created, differentiated standardized-test preparation materials. Consider the following recommendations for student assessment:

- Use multiple, varied assessment measures to show student competence of a skill or content knowledge or language and literacy development.
- Develop a portfolio assessment system that allows including student work samples from a variety of content areas.
- Scaffold assessment tasks by incorporating visuals, graphic organizers, reduced linguistic content, and simplified directions.
- Permit students to use dictionaries, glossaries, and, if feasible, teacher and student notes and other resources.
- Schedule extra time for students to complete assessment tasks.
- Plan opportunities for individual student conferences and small-group assessment techniques.
- Keep teacher observation notes and periodically compare them with your colleagues.
- Offer students opportunities to reflect on and evaluate their own content-based and linguistic performance and progress.
- Develop tools such as checklists, rubrics, and rating scales for teachers to gather ongoing student assessment data and for students to self-assess.

ADMINISTRATORS' ROLE: EFFECTIVE MANAGEMENT OF RESOURCES

Although program administrators in charge of services for English language learners often understand the benefits of teacher collaboration and advocate its use, they are often unable to schedule adequate time for teachers to meet and plan activities on a regular basis. However, for successful implementation of educators' collaborative efforts, the following recommendations should be considered:

- Establish common planning time.
- Use staff development days to evaluate progress and establish long-term goals.
- Hire substitute teachers to provide release time for teachers to collaborate during the school day.
- Allow teachers time to collaborate during faculty meetings.
- Schedule meetings for collaborative partners during special student programming (e.g., assemblies).

Summary

A combined team effort is necessary for effective co-planning of instruction for English language learners. A core pair or trio of educators act as a base for the co-planning team, which also may include administrators, paraprofessionals, and other teacher specialists. A commitment to using a variety of planning, instruction, and assessment strategies will yield the most effective instruction to meet the academic needs of ELs. Teachers have no choice but to explore new options in order to find the time to plan cooperatively if they are to co-teach or co-plan with colleagues successfully. Administrators can support co-teaching and collaborative teams by providing the time, money, and staff development activities that ensure program success.

Discussion Questions

VIDEO 5.1

Getting
Started With
Collaboration
and
Co-Teaching

http://www.resources
.corwin.com/
CollaboratingforELs

1. In consideration of how co-teachers might get started with co-teaching, which teaching strategies that you already use might fit well into an initial co-teaching routine, according to Video 5.1?

2. In your current teaching situation, what personal and institutional roadblocks prevent teacher collaboration, co-planning, or co-teaching from taking place (effectively)? What recommendation do you have for removing those roadblocks?

3. How does a school commitment to equitable education for English language learners affect teacher collaboration, co-planning, or co-teaching efforts?

4. How do standards and standardized assessments affect the type of collaboration that teachers engage in?

5. How does teacher collaboration or co-teaching benefit general-education students and ELs in terms of (a) linguistic and literacy skills, (b) interpersonal and cross-cultural development, and (c) overall academic achievement?

Key Online Resources

Creating a Wiki
www.wikia.com/Special:CreateNewWiki

Education Alliance at Brown University
www.alliance.brown.edu

Learning the Language
http://blogs.edweek.org/edweek/learning-the-language

PBWorks: Online Team Collaboration
http://pbworks.com

Science for English Language Learners
www.larryferlazzo.com/eslscience.html

SIOP Model
www.siopinstitute.net

TeachAde: Online Community for Teachers
www.teachade.com

Teacher Tube (Teacher Community for Sharing Instructional Videos)
www.teachertube.com

6

When Do Teachers Collaborate and Co-Teach?

They always say time changes things, but you actually have to change them yourself.

—Andy Warhol

OVERVIEW

The benefits of ongoing teacher collaboration have been well established, yet challenges to consistent and meaningful professional conversations and other collaborative work efforts regarding instruction for English learners (ELs) persist. Lack of time is often cited as a major factor preventing some teachers from exchanging ideas, jointly planning lessons, evaluating individual student progress on a regular basis, and discussing appropriate interventions. This chapter will identify time frames in which collaboration among teachers can take place successfully. We will examine favorable occasions already built into current schedules as well as offer sample templates to consider and schedules for a range of collaborative practices, including co-teaching. We will conclude with suggestions on how to ensure adequate time for collaboration and co-teaching.

Voices From the Field

Melissa Eddington and Jennifer Wolf from Dublin, Ohio, describe their middle-school co-taught class and their commitment to their collaborative partnership.

(Continued)

(Continued)

The bell rings for first period classes to begin at Karrer Middle School. As the eighth-grade students enter our shared language arts class in Room 258, they have the understanding that they will not be sitting at individual desks. These students are free to choose where they sit each day, in small clusters around the classroom, and we expect them to work with a variety of other students because we use flexible groupings for teaming them up for different tasks.

As our students settle into their daily independent reading routine, they anticipate that we will be engaging them individually in brief reading conferences. In this classroom, the conferring teacher could be either one of the two of us, as we co-teach this language arts class. One of us (Melissa) is an English learner (EL) teacher with licensure in language arts, while the other (Jennifer) is a reading and language arts teacher with an endorsement to teach ELs. We feel fortunate that our classroom experience, knowledge, and licensure dovetail in this way, and we believe that co-teaching is a perfect fit for us. Furthermore, we are firmly committed to teaching and learning with each other and with a diverse group of students in our shared language arts classroom.

We both value collaboration and co-teaching. In addition, we are interested in innovative education and committed to improving our practice through evidence, feedback, and reflection. Most important, we are open to learning from colleagues and respect the knowledge and expertise of other professionals. With these values, we had discovered during the previous school year that we seemed to be well matched for a co-teaching classroom and pitched the idea to our building administrators. Our request for co-teaching in the following school year was granted, and our administrators ensured that our daily schedules were aligned to allow us to share a planning period and lunch.

During this time, we meet every day to discuss our students, our goals, our planning, and our reflections. As school days go, however, it seems there is never enough time. Outside of the school day, we often continue our collaborative efforts with the help of technology such as Google Drive and the app Voxer. Using such technology allows for ongoing collaboration with the added benefits of keeping a record, providing processing and response time, and offering us the flexibility to contribute at our convenience.

Vignette Reflection

As this vignette illustrates, Melissa and Jennifer have a strong commitment to collaboration and co-teaching, which is especially important as classrooms in their school district have become exponentially more diverse. For example, in Dublin City Schools where they teach, there are currently more than 1,750 ELs who speak over 61 different native languages and represent more than 50 countries. These two teachers firmly believe that diversity, such as in their own district, serves to strengthen schools and communities when it is recognized, valued, and celebrated.

Teachers and students benefit from instruction that is based on collaboration and strong co-teaching partnerships. Actualizing a shared vision of high-quality teaching and learning for all is possible only when classroom teachers and English language development/ English language learner (ELD/ELL) teachers commit to creating and maintaining powerful co-teaching teams.

TIME AND STRUCTURE FOR TEAMWORK

The setting of interdisciplinary teams for the purpose of collaboration is a worthwhile goal for schools and districts to pursue. These cross-subject collaborators generally consist of teams who teach the major content areas of the school curriculum or are a combination of grade-level teachers and subject specialists (mathematics, literacy, science, etc.). Teachers working in these groups share essential information about their teaching craft along with skill and content objectives that can be carried across the curriculum to enhance the continuity of instruction. In this way, ELs can be exposed to a wide range of educational experiences all anchored in similar goals and objectives based on the standards and benchmarks from core content curricula.

Members of any collaborative team need to develop cooperation and a shared interest in the group's collective purpose. Participants, whether they are core-subject or special-subject teachers, should be on an equal footing when it comes to agenda setting and group discussions. When given the opportunity to meet, administrators and collaborative teams must pay careful attention to how meetings are structured to make the best use of allotted time and to ensure that all members have equal time to contribute to team efforts by sharing their ideas, resources, concerns, and personal beliefs.

One way to focus an agenda or get to the heart of a matter is to invite meeting participants to anonymously respond to a simple question via an online tool such as www.answergarden.ch, which gathers responses and turns them into a word image—the larger and bolder responses are those that were offered by individual participants more frequently. By gathering this simple form of data, meetings can be structured to focus immediately on a pressing matter instead of spending meeting time figuring out the concern. An example is displayed in Figure 6.1, in which a group of educators at one of our workshops responded to a question about the most important ingredient needed to have successful collaboration and co-teaching.

Creating Teams for Collaboration

It is vital for all teachers to have a voice and carry equal weight in any interdisciplinary team. This idea may be challenging when teams already have well-established core members, either from the

Figure 6.1   Word Image

Image credit: www.answergarden.ch

same grade level or the same discipline, who are considered permanent members of teams, whereas other specialists—ELD/ELL, special education, literacy, speech/language, and so on—are members who rotate among these respective teacher groups. It is a common occurrence for specialists not to be included as permanent members of interdisciplinary teams; they are generally fewer in number and service students in multiple grade levels and across various disciplines.

Administrators often view the practice of rotating these teacher specialists as advantageous; it allows various teams the time and opportunity to have the counsel of different specialists throughout the school year. Considering the number of specialists per school is generally small, it creates challenges for administrators when assigning them to permanent interdisciplinary teams. With this in mind, a critical recommendation we have is to make sure ELD/ELL specialists are accepted and valued as contributing members of all school-based teams and professional groups and, as such, are fully included in collaboration at an established time and place.

Several issues arise from the practice of assigning nonpermanent members to teams. First and foremost, it does not allow teacher specialists to bond with other members of the team. According to Daniel Levi (2016), participants in any team effort need to develop some level of personal relationship with each other in order for good communication and trust to occur. When social relationships are lacking between group members, communication can break down. Rotating between teams does not allow specialists to form strong relationships or afford the opportunity to develop trust. In turn, communication is negatively impacted and specialists' ideas and concerns are minimized.

When special-subject teachers float between teams, they are perceived as guest participants and not as full members of the team. Teacher specialists may be marginalized in these type of meetings. The regular or core members may regard teacher specialists as resources for information when they need clarification about a discussion issue rather than fully participating members of the group.

Another problem that arises from this scheme is that rotating team members may be underused. The valuable expertise of ELD/ELL teachers and other specialists regarding youngsters with exceptional needs may not be given a voice during team meetings, which leaves classroom teachers, already challenged with the education of these pupils, without needed support. Additionally, when the knowledge of specialists is not shared, teachers restrict the scope of their collaborative meetings and reap fewer benefits from their teams. It is important to establish equal status among all participants and to give their ideas and opinions equal weight.

SETTING A PURPOSE FOR COLLABORATION

Before administrators can plan sufficient time for teachers to meet, the purpose of collaboration must be identified and carefully discussed. Most often, teachers cite the need to exchange their views on the *nuts and bolts* of lesson planning and student instruction with each other, as well as day-to-day organization and classroom management they commonly share. However, collaborative topics are much broader than classroom practices. They encompass a whole host of educational objectives that can be used as building blocks to transform a school culture. Before setting time frames for collaborative work, the rationale for collaboration must be identified. Once the purpose is set, a time frame for collaborative activities can be established.

Collaboration for Specific Purposes

In 2015, the administrator in charge of curriculum and development in a small suburban school district on the East Coast challenged her school principals to align their English language arts (ELA) curriculum with the new state standards. Each of the principals set about to gather his or her own team for the task; subsequently, select members of those teams met on a district level to finalize the alignment. In reviewing the new ELA curriculum, both teachers and administrators became keenly aware that the newly developed curriculum did not meet the needs of their large and growing population of English learners. As a second phase of the ELA curriculum revision, school teams, with the guidance of an outside consultant, created further revisions and additions to the curriculum to meet the unique needs of ELs. These curriculum teams are just one example of how teacher teams are created to collaborate for a specific purpose.

Certain collaborative activities easily lend themselves to having a set beginning and end. These types of collaborative practices may be for the purpose of establishing a basis for an overall shared mission or vision for ELs, to develop a common understanding of general information about English learners, or to decide the future goals for particular content curricula, grade levels, program models, or school resources. These collaborative activities may involve the whole faculty as well as the support staff so that there is a clarity of purpose regarding the education of ELs.

Collaboration for specific purposes may include broad topics such as the following:

- Brainstorming ideas to facilitate teacher collaboration
- Curriculum mapping to align ELD/ELL and content-area instruction
- Defining the collective purpose for specific programs and policies for the teaching of ELs
- Designing a plan for ongoing faculty and staff learning
- Examining beliefs and assumptions about the abilities of ELs
- Identifying state and local standards for ELD/ELL instruction
- Providing professional-development activities that promote a better understanding of a specific subpopulation of ELs

Additional activities may include:

- Classroom seating to assist English learners' comprehension
- Customs and observances of different cultures to be included in the curriculum or to bring relevance to classroom instruction
- Identification of students' language proficiency levels and how to accommodate instruction accordingly
- Interpretation of student assessment data
- Reviewing, locating, or developing online resources for ELs to learn specific information, strategies, and skills
- Developing or enhancing instructional strategies for teaching beginning-level ELs

Small-scale information usually is shared during teacher preparation periods, lunchtime meetings, or brief hallway conferences. In contrast, broad-based finite collaboration often is accomplished during general faculty meetings or days specifically scheduled for staff development. An outside expert may even be invited to conduct a single workshop or a series of workshops for a select group of faculty. Targeted professional development for specific purposes can be the stimulus for meaningful change in teaching and learning if the right approach is taken.

An Example of Collaboration for a Specific Purpose

Collaborative Task: ELD/ELL Program Revision in a K–12 District

Who is involved?

An eclectic team consisting of building and central-office administrators, elementary classroom and special-subject (art, music, etc.) teachers, ELD/ELL specialists, middle and high school content-area teachers, special-education professionals, social workers, and outside consultants will participate and contribute ideas regarding programs for ELs.

What are the team's short-term goals?

The team will strive to understand the challenges of ELs in all classes, identify the district's current programs for ELs, review assessment and other pertinent data to outline the strengths and limitations of the district's programs, and identify new programs and broad-based strategies to help meet the needs of the EL population. The following are the team's guiding questions:

- What beliefs govern the way programs are devised for ELs?
- What factors affect the academic progress of ELs?
- How can the district improve its policies and programs for ELs?

What are the desired outcomes?

Through collaborative efforts, the team will decide on three long-term goals for the coming school year, determine how each goal will be evaluated, and identify any necessary professional development or resources to accomplish established goals.

When and where do meetings take place?

Meetings are scheduled when school is not in session. Approximately 20 hours of commitment is necessary to accomplish the task. Participants are remunerated for their time.

Long-Term, Ongoing Collaboration

The characteristics of ongoing collaboration require continuous and planned opportunities for teachers and administrators to engage in meaningful dialogue about appropriate assessment practices, student data, research-informed instruction, and student progress. The need for consistent collaboration is embedded in the nature of the perceived or desired outcomes. Whether teachers are engaged in co-teaching for ELs, in-class coaching, mentoring new teachers, reciprocal classroom observations, or specific teacher study groups to increase understanding of ELs, continuous collaborative effort is necessary to implement these productive practices successfully.

The main challenge of ongoing collaboration is that a great deal of time is needed to plan, implement, revise, and reflect on selected practices with colleagues, much more so than with collaboration set for finite and specific purposes. Some schools have built time for collaboration into daily class schedules. Teachers are grouped into teams, often in one of the following configurations:

- *Grade-level planning teams*: Classroom teachers and ELD/ELL teachers are the core members who may be joined by literacy specialists, speech pathologists, special-education teachers, and other faculty or support staff. These teams may meet daily or weekly to discuss core curriculum, planning, and student assessment data and work to facilitate the implementation of the collaborative instructional cycle—co-planning, co-instruction, co-assessment, and co-reflection— for the sake of ELs.
- *Content-area planning teams*: ELD/ELL teachers meet on a weekly or monthly basis with specialists segregated by subject (English language arts, mathematics, science, social studies) to align curriculum and standards for ELs, identify ways to accommodate or modify the curriculum, and share instructional strategies in their areas of expertise for all students to meet grade-level content and language learning standards.
- *Cross-grade planning teams*: The main focus of multigrade team meetings is for all teachers to be aware of grade-level expectations both above and below their curriculum level and to better understand the demands of upcoming standards and assessments for ELs. Cross-grade planning may occur once per month or at specific intervals throughout the school year.
- *ELD/ELL planning teams*: ELD/ELL specialists meet weekly or biweekly to discuss their successes and challenges with co-planning, co-teaching, meeting curricular demands, specific issues regarding student learning difficulties, and the use of innovations and techniques with English learners.

Adapted from Roberts, S. M., & Pruitt, E. Z. (2009). *Schools as Professional Learning Communities* (2nd ed. (p. 16)). Thousand Oaks, CA: Corwin.

The following are various types of information teams may share in collaborative groups for the sake of English learners:

- Adaptation of materials
- Alternative instructional resources
- Assessment data
- Cultural norms
- Curricular concerns
- ELs with limited/interrupted education
- Facilitating use of home language

- Family history and issues
- Language proficiency levels
- Native-language literacy skills
- Referrals for special-education services
- Reporting progress
- Student motivation
- Student work

Contractual issues prevent some school districts from altering teachers' schedules in order to produce effective, ongoing collaboration. Other districts do not want to change the amount of teacher contact time with students in order to schedule collaborative team meetings; administrators often are concerned with not having community support for this practice. Yet, schools that value collaborative practices find creative ways to schedule meetings in already overburdened schedules. Whatever the case, a specific framework for structured and reoccurring meetings allows teachers to engage in dialogue in the most meaningful ways for their students. Table 6.1 illustrates the key components of an ongoing collaboration framework.

Time for Reflection

Ongoing collaboration should encourage teachers to reflect on their current practices. The process of reflection allows teachers to revisit what they have learned, share their experiences with their colleagues, and obtain insight into their own teaching (practices) by continually evaluating the impact of their efforts to assist English learners.

Teams involved in collaborative practice should include periodic reflection. This type of evaluative process can be accomplished through developing, discussing, and answering key questions regarding classroom instruction for ELs. Some questions that may be helpful for reflection are as follows:

- How have we provided a low-anxiety, stress-reduced learning environment for our ELs?
- How have we successfully differentiated instruction to meet the needs of English learners?

Table 6.1 Framework for Ongoing Collaboration

Identify the participants	• Grade-level teams • Content-area teams • Interdisciplinary teams
Set the purpose	• Data review • Lesson planning • Material adaptation • Reflection • Student learning • Study of specific content • Sharing strategies and best practices
Establish required time frame and scheduling logistics	• Before or after school • Scheduled congruence period • Lunchtime • Online
Determine needed resources	• Shared values • Supportive leadership • Protocols for conversation

- What are the overall successes ELs have had in learning academic content and meeting grade-level benchmarks?
- What issues need to be addressed to improve instruction for our English learners?
- How have we provided instruction to develop ELs' language and literacy in all classes?
- How can we improve our collaborative efforts to make instruction more meaningful for our English learners?

Because reflection is an essential component of both self-assessment practices and formative assessments, we will more fully explore the topic in Chapter 8.

An Example of Ongoing Collaboration

Collaborative Task: Planning Interdisciplinary Instruction for ELs in Grade 6

Who is involved?

An interdisciplinary team consisting of core content-area teachers (English language arts, math, social studies, and science) and an ELD/ELL specialist plan thematic units to benefit ELs.

What are the team's prevailing goals?

The team's purpose is to plan interdisciplinary instruction on an ongoing basis. Necessary goals will focus on the following:

- Identifying curricula elements that are conducive to thematic instruction
- Outlining components of each identified theme
- Selecting content standards that will be addressed
- Determining language and literacy goals
- Devising a differentiated assessment plan for both language and content learning
- Sharing ideas and strategies for individual lesson plans
- Determining evaluation of interdisciplinary thematic units

What are the desired outcomes?

Considering thematic instruction is an important key to English learners' academic success (Freeman & Freeman, 2016). An increase in English learners achieving English proficiency is desired. Additionally, the ability to identify successful units and retain them for future use is a suitable aim.

When do meetings take place?

Meetings are scheduled during a weekly congruent planning period. School schedules should be devised so that all ELs in Grade 6 are able to work with the interdisciplinary team creating thematic units.

TWO OBSERVATIONS OF ONGOING COLLABORATION

Effective Ongoing Collaboration: Teachers Plan Instruction for ELs

We have observed numerous groups of teachers working collaboratively to plan lessons for ELs. One group of third-grade teachers in cooperation with their shared ELD/ELL teacher had a unique way of developing instruction for their students. They formed a team that met during a specially scheduled time for one period each week with the expressed purpose of planning differentiated learning for all their students.

This team of teachers arranged themselves in front of a bank of computers. A five-minute brainstorming session elicited numerous topics, and a theme was chosen by consensus. At that point, the members of this group assumed different roles. The classroom teachers took on the positions of leader, reporter, and clarifier of content-area instruction. The ELD/ELL teacher acted as the in-house expert on materials and strategies for ELs.

The lead teacher used a checklist of the different elements necessary for the selected theme, the reporter keyed the information on the computer, and the clarifier identified standards, literature, and other materials as possible resources. The ELD/ELL teacher took notes, suggested ways to organize the theme components, determined activities that were appropriate for the different language proficiencies of the group of third-grade ELs, suggested language-learning activities that could be incorporated into each theme, and explained that she would need more time to devise some activities according to specific content.

These collaborative partners seemed to take their job seriously. They remained focused on their lesson-writing task and used a common lesson plan format that was situated in Google Docs and therefore made available to all team members. This team complained little, refrained from personal discussion, remained focused, and incorporated humor to keep up everyone's spirits. Each team member carefully debated how to present the theme's topics using appropriate strategies and resources for ELs. These teachers engaged in conversations about their students' abilities, tried to match activities that were appropriate to each level of instruction, and remained on task until the lesson plans they set out to devise at the onset were completed.

Collaboration Pitfalls: When Time to Collaborate Fails to Yield Desired Results

We observed a second group of teachers faced with a similar task—to develop lessons that incorporated differentiated instruction for their students. This group of teachers included three kindergarten teachers, an ELD/ELL teacher, and a student teacher. These teachers began by sitting at a bank of computers while the student teacher who was prepping materials (cutting out shapes) sat apart from them. The classroom teachers both individually and collectively looked through various file folders, and they expressed their concerns about duplicating copies of student handouts for future class activities while everyone engaged in various discussions that had nothing to do with differentiated lesson planning.

The teachers' topics of conversation ranged from housekeeping issues such as "Healthy Snacks Week" to curriculum activities such as events for Dr. Seuss's birthday. They rapidly moved from topic to topic, and their conversations thoroughly engaged everyone in the group. During a brief pause, one teacher turned to us and said, "Now this is collaborating." After approximately fifteen minutes had passed, the teachers focused on creating the differentiated lessons they were charged to do.

The group tried to search for previously written lessons, but after another fifteen minutes had gone by, they could not find them and decided to proceed without them. One teacher commented, "Lessons in math are already differentiated in the math text." The teachers moved forward in the planning process by individually searching through the math text for possible lessons to adapt.

The teachers engaged in personal discussions and gossiped about other faculty members. They used an established format for writing collaborative plan summaries on the computer to copy a lesson from the math book. With ten minutes left in the session, the teachers shared with each other ways to differentiate the established math lesson. As the session ended, the teachers' discussions again steered away from lesson planning. A variety of topics captured their individual attentions and amused them: from the way one eats a Reese's Peanut Butter Cup to what is entailed in incubating eggs in the classroom.

Time to Meet: Not the Only Issue

In both the kindergarten and third-grade groups, the teachers had established strong relationships among their peers. Each teacher seemed to accept the other for her contributions and role in the process. These teachers had the ability to console and amuse one another, and each exhibited trust in her colleagues. Yet, one set of teachers was better able to focus on its intended planning task while the other eventually accomplished its prescribed goal but in a more superficial way.

Although it appears that collaborative conversations may be effective in some situations, one cannot suppose that just providing the necessary time for professional discourse leads to desired outcomes. The problem some teachers face with the collaborative process may stem from the manner in which collaboration itself has been implemented. Change is a complicated issue, and although the purpose for collaboration may be set, the means for accomplishing its intended outcomes often are not. According to Michael Fullan (2015), teachers not only should understand the need for improved practices, they must also have a clear understanding of the beliefs and practices they are asked to implement. Participation in the collaboration process is no different. Without a clear understanding and a strong buy-in to its purpose and beliefs, teachers will focus on superficial goals to satisfy an administrative directive instead of engaging in activities that are meaningful to the group as a whole.

Braden Welborn (2012) identifies six keys to successful collaboration as (a) clarity of purpose, (b) individual commitment, (c) time, (d) understanding how to collaborate and communicate, (e) supportive administrators, and (f) freedom to explore. He further states, "There's no magic formula for successful collaboration. But . . . teachers know a great deal about what works—and what doesn't" (para. 24). How then do we identify the qualities that take these collaborative conversations to the desired level of transformative learning for teachers and thereby their students? And what if time *is* the major obstacle to effective communication among teachers?

A REMEDY FOR TIME LIMITATIONS: CONVERSATION PROTOCOLS

Engaging in productive conversations with colleagues can be frequently hindered by time. One way to make the best use of allotted time to discuss workplace issues is to use specific formats for structured conversations that allow for a clear, common focus of discourse and provide guidelines for all members' participation. These conversation protocols facilitate a balanced approach, allowing all members to be actively involved in the decision-making process by bringing a diversity of voices and opinions to bear on issues that require it (Garmston, 2007).

Conversation protocols can be very specific in how they guide the course of a discussion by identifying each group member's time frame for speaking and the precise subject matter to be addressed. Staying within the protocol's framework can help assure collaborative partners that each member will be heard and prevent conversations from going off on tangents. Various types of structured conversations can help generate ideas and provide a means for collaborative groups to interact and reflect on their practices. Table 6.2 is an example of a conversation protocol that can be used for co-teaching partners to reflect on their classroom practices.

Even if you have been a collaborating partner, or co-teaching for a long time, each new school year brings new and unique challenges. Teachers change grade levels, retire, are reassigned to other schools, or are no longer employed with the district due to budget cuts. New curriculum and special programs are adopted, or assessment/evaluation methods, government standards, and state regulations are revised. These events and policies lead ELD/ELL teachers to forge new relationships or begin needed conversations with additional colleagues to strategize and plan for EL instruction. Conversation protocols can be a useful tool to further the progress of these important dialogues. Table 6.3 illustrates the many conversation topics that can be facilitated by conversation protocols for newly formed or ongoing collaborative or co-teaching partners.

Table 6.2 Protocol for Collaborative Professional Conversations on Co-Teaching

1.	Co-teachers set aside 20 minutes for this activity. They agree to a set of accepted parameters for this professional conversation.
2.	One co-teacher offers his or her account of successful aspects of the shared co-teaching experience. The other co-teacher is silent and takes notes. (3 minutes)
3.	The same step is repeated with the second co-teacher. (3 minutes)
4.	Each teacher takes a turn to clarify one key element in the other's presentation. (3 minutes total)
5.	Co-teachers start an open discussion to analyze the reasons for their successes and/or identify any other contributing factors that hindered the success. (8 minutes)
6.	The session is concluded with each co-teacher reflecting on the conversation and identifying one specific goal or step for the future. (3 minutes)

Adapted from Easton, L. B. (2009, February/March). Protocols: A facilitator's best friend. *Tools for Schools, 12*(3), 6.

Table 6.3 Conversation Protocol Topics to Enhance Instruction for ELs

Categories	Subareas
1. Use of Teaching Strategies	Lesson structure
	Questions
	Examples
	Teaching aids
	Group learning
	Reinforcement
2. Engagement	Learner attention
	Learner background knowledge and life experiences
	Learner interest
3. Lesson Content	Clearly identified concepts
	Clear distinction between concepts and illustrations
	Appropriate level of complexity
	Alignment to standards
4. Classroom Management	Variety of control techniques
	• Positive and negative
	• Verbal and nonverbal
	Efficiency of class administration
	Use of students in administrative tasks
5. Trial-and-Error Learning	Appreciation of mistakes
	Openness to student correction
	Sufficient repetition
6. Classroom Environment	Joy
	Order
	Best use of facility
7. Language Skills	Clear pronunciation
	Appropriate vocabulary level
	Effective communication
8. Assessment	Formative assessment
	Progress monitoring
	Benchmark assessments
	Differentiated assessment practices
	Adaptations and modification of summative assessments

(Continued)

Table 6.3 (Continued)

Categories	Subareas
9. Evaluation	Modification in lessons based on real-time experience
	Awareness of learners' success or failure
	Assistance to students in need
	Interventions
10. Administrative Issues	Record keeping

Adapted from Allen, D. W., & LeBlanc, A. C. (2005). *Collaborative peer coaching that improves instruction: The 2 + 2 performance appraisal model* (pp. 76–77). Thousand Oaks, CA: Corwin.

WHEN *DO* COLLABORATIVE TEAMS MEET?

According to Nancy Love and her colleagues (2008), teaching can be divided into three parts—lesson planning, delivery, and personal reflection. However, time for planning and reflection, as a part of ongoing practices with colleagues, is minimally scheduled into the school day. Administrators and other stakeholders view student–teacher contact time to be the key for increased academic success among pupils and believe "if teachers are not in front of students, they are not doing their job" (Love, 2008, p. 42). Yet, a growing number of research studies indicating positive relationships between teacher collaboration and increased student achievement (Goddard, Goddard, Kim, & Miller, 2015; Killion, 2015) are beginning to lay the foundation for a change of attitude toward collaborative practices.

In our own discussions with a variety of educators, teachers frequently report that the regular school day is the best time to collaborate with their fellow teachers and that their teaching schedules should reflect formal opportunities to work together. ELD/ELL teachers throughout the United States have shared with us that they conduct most of their planning with classroom teachers informally—in the hallway, in the classroom when children are engaged in an activity, while microwaving their lunch in the teacher's lounge, or waiting to use the restroom. They also reveal that when they have had formal opportunities to collaborate, their efforts have resulted in more successful lesson delivery and higher student achievement in a variety of classroom settings for English learners.

Finding Time During the School Day

Although there may be obstacles that challenge teachers who are interested in exchanging ideas, coordinating their instruction, developing co-teaching lessons for ELs, and so on, the most pressing one is a lack of time to implement ongoing plans for collaboration. When there is no set time for collegial conversations, these discussions may occur at the end of the school day when some faculty meetings are scheduled. Not only are teachers tired from their day's work, but agendas for these meetings may not include planning time for teachers. Not having planned time during the school day can soon quell teacher enthusiasm for coordinated or co-taught instruction and prevent the development of routines, settings, resources, and strategies to benefit ELs. Table 6.4 suggests ways to facilitate scheduled time for collaborative teams to meet.

| Table 6.4 | Creating Opportunities for Teachers to Meet During the School Day |

Adjust school schedules.	• Establish one period per week at the beginning or end of the school day in which students are engaged on the playground or in the auditorium so teachers can meet.
	• Devise a common planning period for teachers.
	   ○ Employ substitute teachers to cover classes.
	   ○ Reduce number of periods teachers have contact with students.
	   ○ Schedule special subjects (art, music, etc.) during same time block.
	• Modify the school schedule to add fifteen minutes per day for four days with early dismissal on day five, leaving one hour each week for collaboration.

Provide incentives.	• Provide extra pay for teachers who formally collaborate during their lunchtime. • Employ school aides to release teachers from lunch or recess duty. • Offer teachers rewards; for example, for the first to obtain the latest technology or for collaborating during personal preparation time.
Use resources more efficiently.	• Have certain teachers (literacy, gifted and talented, etc.) provide special lessons in classrooms to free up the core content teachers. • Redistribute students for one period so that three classes become two. • Invite community members to demonstrate their talents to students. • Consider funding sources and available grant money to fund a collaboration initiative.
Find time during class hiatus.	• Employ staff development days for teaching teams to conduct long-term planning. • Increase the number of days teachers work or decrease the number of days school is in session. • Use faculty meetings before and after school. • Engage older students in community service or younger pupils in in-school tutoring.

Adapted from Love, N. (2009). *Using data to improve learning for all: A collaborative inquiry approach.* Thousand Oaks, CA: Corwin; Villa, R. A., Thousand, J. S., & Nevin, A. I. (2013). *A guide to co-teaching: New lessons and strategies to facilitate student learning* (3rd ed.). Thousand Oaks, CA: Corwin.

EXPECTATIONS FOR TEACHER COLLABORATION

Vignette Revisited

When we revisit the opening vignette, we find Melissa and Jennifer creating an inclusive classroom where all students are valued and engaged with one another in learning. They have well-established routines for students to follow, and they strive to create a learning environment for their students that is innovative, fosters student autonomy, and has an established norm of high expectations for all students. It is apparent from this brief co-teaching partner profile that much lesson planning, program assessment, and ongoing reflection has gone into the development of this multifaceted classroom.

Vignette Reflection

What can we learn from Melissa and Jennifer's co-teaching partnership? First and foremost, both of these teachers have made a strong commitment to collaboration for the sake of teaching ELs, and they value the practice of co-teaching. They regularly engage in the review of research and student data (evidence), offer each other constructive feedback, and reflect on their planning, instructional delivery, and impact on students. Their strong commitment to inclusive practices drives them to meet not only during regular planning periods but also during their lunch break, and they use technology to extend their planning time together. The committed partnership they have created truly demonstrates the need for the two most important ingredients for collaboration to be successful: equity between partners and specific time frames for collaboration to take place.

Equity in Collaboration

Equity—a careful balance between members of a collaborative team, in which everyone has fair and reasonable opportunities to share their ideas, offer feedback, explore alternatives, and even lead discussions—is key to collaboration. To improve this balance in collaborative practice and to solidify both classroom and ELD/ELL teacher expectations for its practice, all participants must have the *DESIRE* to make collaboration work. Consider the following acronym—DESIRE—for setting expectations for collaborative work.

- *Define each member's expertise and purpose in the collaborative process.*
- *Explore topics that meet the needs of marginalized students.*
- *Share your personal expertise with one another.*
- *Identify the desired outcomes.* Partners in the process should have a clear focus on the purpose of both finite and ongoing collaboration.
- *Recognize each member's role within the collaborative team.*
- *Evaluate your efforts.* Let all who have been a part of the collaborative group offer their observations and evaluations of the process to improve collaborative efforts.

When the purpose and expectations for collaboration are set, administrators and teachers can develop the necessary time frames for collaboration to take place. Table 6.5 illustrates various topics for teacher collaboration accompanied by possible time frames to accomplish the task.

Roadblocks to Establishing Time Frames for Collaboration

At times, administrators who want to foster collaborative environments will elicit from their faculty ideas to produce the needed time frames for collaborative practices. Unfortunately, not all teachers view collaboration in a positive light, and some may seek to create impediments to prevent the establishment of specific schedules for meetings to take place. Based on our

Table 6.5   Identifying Time Frames for Teacher Collaboration

Purpose	Type of Collaboration	Time Frame

Examining beliefs and assumptions about ELs	Specific purpose	• Single-meeting framework after school
		  ○ Full-faculty meetings
		  ○ Department meetings

Improving instructional planning for ELLs	Ongoing	• Team meetings during the school day • Voluntary in-person meeting after school • Use of online or Web-based resources beyond the school day
Adapting resources for test preparation	Specific purpose or ongoing	• Congruent preparation periods
Preparing lessons and planning for co-teaching	Ongoing	• Scheduled collaboration period during the school day • Use of online or Web-based resources beyond the school day

Identifying obstacles to collaboration scheduling	Specific purpose	• Single-meeting framework after school
		  ○ Full-faculty meetings
		  ○ Department meetings

Resolving issues in collaborative practices	Ongoing	• Team meetings • Scheduled collaboration periods

conversations with both ELD/ELL and classroom teachers, the following are some of the possible roadblocks to setting collaborative time frames:

1. The idea that the school community does not recognize the value of collaboration between ELD/ELL and classroom teachers during the school day

2. The belief that administrators will not provide the necessary time during the school day for ongoing collaboration

3. The existence of a school culture that overvalues autonomy, individualism, and personal space, time, or possessions

4. The lack of continuous professional development that not only demonstrates the benefits of teacher collaboration but also provides clear instruction with respect to how to effectively collaborate

5. The acceptance and promotion of certain beliefs and opinions not based on current research regarding the education of ELs and how these notions can affect the instruction of ELs and the overall ELD program

TIME FRAMES FOR CO-TEACHING

For a growing number of ELD/ELL and classroom teachers who co-teach or would like to adopt a co-taught or inclusion model of instruction, scheduling is one of the many variables to be addressed for the successful development of language acquisition, literacy, and content-area subjects with English learners within the confines of the same classroom. Adequate time must be designated during the school day to accomplish co-teaching goals. Furthermore, if ELD classes are to be taught using co-teaching models, administrators and teachers must take into account the age of the students, the set-up time each lesson entails, and the time of day for instruction that would most benefit EL students.

Scheduling begins with the building administrator creating a master plan, and the rest often depends on the grade level of the students. For elementary-level teachers, time frames for ELD classes are organized around the daily class schedules that frequently include block time for literacy and mathematics as well as lessons outside the regular classroom in music, art, technology, and other subjects. Many ELD/ELL teachers are responsible for setting up their own schedules and must navigate within the confines of each class's program timetable to arrange their own ELD sessions.

For middle and high school classes, separate ELD instructional periods are usually written into the overall master schedule. However, if co-teaching models are used exclusively, there is no need to schedule separate periods for ELD. We have observed that many school districts take a hybrid approach—having ELs have the benefit of both co-taught and stand-alone classes for ELD. In any case, whether or not ELD co-teaching is conducted throughout the day or used on a part-time basis in combination with a pullout or regularly scheduled periods of ELD instruction, administrative support is essential for co-teaching schedules to be established.

Facilitating Factors for Scheduling Co-Taught Classes

When organizing ELD/ELL lessons or activities in core content classes, the following ideas should be considered before scheduling takes place:

1. *Student clustering.* Co-teaching programs for ELs benefit from thoughtful student placement in core classes classrooms. If ELs are clustered or grouped together into fewer classrooms, more students can be provided extended integrated language and content instruction in their regular classrooms. Clustering, however, may not be possible in schools that have a large percentage of the population designated as ELs.

2. *Teacher volunteers.* When classroom teachers are enthusiastic about co-teaching, minor scheduling glitches, adjustments, and altered routines do not overwhelm willing faculty members.

3. *Class configurations to use co-teaching models.* Adequate classroom size and flexible furniture arrangements assist in successfully accommodating co-taught lessons. These all-important spaces must be available when co-teaching is scheduled.

4. *Full- or part-day ELD/ELL co-teaching.* Decisions must be made in terms of whether the ELD/ELL teacher will

   - remain in one classroom the entire school day,
   - follow the EL group of students from classroom to classroom and co-teach with various content-area teachers,

- co-teach in more than one grade level, or
- provide ELD/ELL services through a combination of co-teaching and stand-alone programs.

Part-Day ELD/ELL Co-Teaching

Co-teaching for English learners can be successfully accomplished using a part-day schedule. In this teaching scenario, the ELD/ELL teacher spends part of the school day co-teaching with one or more classroom teachers, and the rest of the day is devoted to stand-alone or regularly scheduled instruction for ELs outside of the general-education classroom. Table 6.6 identifies a combination co-teaching/stand-alone schedule for an elementary ELD/ELL teacher who is responsible for ELs in Grades 3 and 4.

In our illustrated schedule (Table 6.6), the first period is set aside for collaboration with the different Grade-3- and-4-level teams on alternate days (Monday–Thursday) before the start of daily instruction; the fifth day (Friday) is designated for departments such as ELD/ELL or grade-level teachers to meet as separate teams. Each morning is divided into two periods of back-to-back instruction for each grade level serviced. The afternoon hours are designated for small-group

Table 6.6 Sample Elementary School Schedule: Part-Day Co-Teaching

	Monday	Tuesday	Wednesday	Thursday	Friday
8:10–8:50	Collaborative Team Meeting Grade 4	Collaborative Team Meeting Grade 3	Collaborative Team Meeting Grade 4	Collaborative Team Meeting Grade 3	Department and Grade-Level Meetings
8:50–9:35	Grade 3	Grade 3	Grade 3	Grade 3	Grade 3
9:35–10:15	ELD Co-Teaching	ELD Co-Teaching	ELD Co-Teaching	ELD Co-Teaching	ELD Co-Teaching
10:15–11:00	Grade 4	Grade 4	Grade 4	Grade 4	Grade 4
11:00–11:45	ELD Co-Teaching	ELD Co-Teaching	ELD Co-Teaching	ELD Co-Teaching	ELD Co-Teaching
11:45–12:45	LUNCH AND RECESS				
12:45–1:30	Grade 3 ELs Stand Alone Beginners (Levels 1 & 2)	Grade 3 ELs Stand Alone Beginners (Levels 1 & 2)	Grade 3 ELs Stand Alone Beginners (Levels 1 & 2)	Grade 3 ELs Stand Alone Beginners (Levels 1 & 2)	Grade 3 ELs Stand Alone Beginners (Levels 1 & 2)
1:30–2:15	Grade 4 ELs Stand Alone Beginners (Levels 1 & 2)	Grade 4 ELs Stand Alone Beginners (Levels 1 & 2)	Grade 4 ELs Stand Alone Beginners (Levels 1 & 2)	Grade 4 ELs Stand Alone Beginners (Levels 1 & 2)	Grade 4 ELs Stand Alone Beginners (Levels 1 & 2)
2:15–3:00	Prep Period	Prep Period	Prep Period	Prep Period	Prep Period

instruction in a separate classroom setting with a select group of ELs. The last period of the day is an individual preparation period for the ELD/ELL teacher.

Some ELD/ELL teachers co-teach specific academic subjects in elementary-school classes for part of the school day. Table 6.7 outlines literacy activities that can be co-taught in Grades K–3; it specifies a double, 45-minute period for each integrated co-teaching session; yet individual literacy activities are not 45 minutes long. The schedule additionally suggests co-teaching models to be used by cooperating teachers.

Another part-day schedule configuration involves the ELD/ELL teacher providing instruction by accompanying English learners to their core-subject classrooms. In essence, the ELD/ELL teacher spends most of the day with his or her ELs but co-teaches with different content-area teachers. Table 6.8 identifies a sample middle-school schedule.

Time Management in a Co-Taught Classroom

Co-taught lessons may require additional planning time initially. Teaching teams may spend many hours reviewing assessment data, identifying language and content objectives, selecting and

Table 6.7   Part-Day Co-Teaching Schedule for Specific Content: Literacy

Co-Teaching Schedule for Basic Literacy: Grades K–3					
	Monday	**Tuesday**	**Wednesday**	**Thursday**	**Friday**
Class Activity I	Introduce New Word, Wall Words	Reader's Workshop	Word Wall Activity	Writer's Workshop	Word Wall Activity
Time Frame	40 minutes	40 minutes	30 minutes	40 minutes	30 minutes
Co-Teaching Model	One Group: One Lead Teacher and One Teacher Teaching on Purpose	Multiple Groups: Two Teachers Monitor and Teach	One Group: One Lead Teacher and One Teacher Teaching on Purpose	Multiple Groups: Two Teachers Monitor and Teach	Two Groups: One Teacher Reteaches, One Teaches Alternative Information
Class Activity II	Shared Reading	Guided Reading	Writer's Workshop	Guided Reading	Reader's Workshop
Time Frame	30 minutes	30 minutes	40 minutes	30 minutes	40 minutes
Co-Teaching Model	Two Groups: Two Teachers Teach the Same Content	Multiple Groups: Two Teachers Monitor and Teach	Multiple Groups: Two Teachers Monitor and Teach	Multiple Groups: Two Teachers Monitor and Teach	Multiple Groups: Two Teachers Monitor and Teach
Class Activity III	Debriefing				
Time Frame	20 minutes				
Co-Teaching Model	One Group: Two Teachers Teach the Same Content				

Table 6.8   Middle-School Co-Teaching Schedule: Core Subjects

Seventh-Grade Co-Teaching Schedule Monday–Friday	
Period 1	Science/ELD Co-Teaching
Period 2	Social Studies/ELD Co-Teaching
Period 3	Interdisciplinary Team Meeting: English Language Arts (ELA), ELD, Mathematics, Science, and Social Studies Teachers
Period 4	ELA/ELD Co-Teaching
Period 5	Lunch
Period 6	Lunch Room/Hallway Duty
Period 7	Stand-Alone ELD for Level 1 Students
Period 8	Preparation and Planning

creating appropriate materials and resources, deciding which co-teaching models to incorporate for instruction, and suggesting pertinent learning strategies to use. However, it is as valuable a part of overall planning to jointly develop guidelines for classroom time management to ensure co-taught lessons run smoothly.

Teaching teams must estimate the time that planned learning activities will take and adhere to identified time frames as best as possible. There should be adequate time set aside for instruction, group and individual learning, student evaluation, and debriefing. It also is necessary to be flexible if certain activities take longer than originally anticipated or vice versa and alter allotted time *on the spot.*

Co-teaching partners must identify specific time management parameters and classroom procedures to facilitate co-taught lessons. Some potential topics for discussion with fellow co-teachers are the following:

- Punctuality regarding starting and ending co-taught sessions
- Respect for each other's time by following already agreed-on and planned activities and procedures
- Routines and rituals for beginning, transitioning in and out of, and ending activities
- Classroom rules and classroom management (i.e., who does what and when)
- Student mobility about the classroom
- Appropriate time and procedures for students to take breaks, retrieve materials, sharpen pencils, use the bathroom, etc.
- Strategies for reducing transition time from one activity to another—timers, chimes, music, rhymes, etc.
- Ways and means of offering timely feedback to students and managing student discipline

ADMINISTRATORS' ROLE: SCHEDULING AND SUPPORTING COLLABORATIVE AND CO-TEACHING PRACTICES

We often ask teachers what they would most like their administrators to know about what teachers need to sustain collaboration and co-teaching partnerships. Time and again we hear the same concerns from many different voices:

- I need my administrators to recognize the benefits of co-teaching and to provide the necessary time for collaboration between ELD/ELL and classroom teachers.
- Administrators need to make collaboration a priority and find planning time for us.
- My administrators are aware of our need to collaborate and have committed to make the necessary scheduling changes *next* year, yet they continually change our co-teaching partners, which does not allow for us to grow as a team over time.

Scheduling collaborative practices must begin with identifying an overall plan for collaborative initiatives to take place. Although the majority of teachers may be requesting time to have professional conversations with their colleagues on an ongoing basis, a building principal may not be able to meet that particular request immediately. Additionally, the desire to implement co-teaching as an innovative school practice may exist; yet, administrators may not have all the necessary resources (money, personnel, professional development, time) available to commit to such a long-term plan.

Issues beyond the control of an individual school might first need to be resolved in order for ongoing collaboration to be a part of the regular school day. Contractual and union issues are likely to be negotiated. Whereas several essential opportunities for collaborative practices can be put into place immediately, other initiatives must be developed and implemented over time. It may take years for the desired collaborative practice to be fully developed and instituted. Nevertheless, the most important concerns for administrators to address are the focus on collaboration as a priority, the need to keep the faculty informed, and the necessary efforts to move forward with an overall plan that considers teachers' need for time. The key features for establishing the collaboration time frame for the benefit of ELs are as follows:

1. A strong, articulated commitment to the practice of schoolwide collaboration by collaboratively establishing a timeline for the initiative

2. A comprehensive plan with clearly identified incremental goals for both finite and ongoing collaborative practices to take place

3. Continuous professional-development activities on teacher collaboration for both administrators and teachers to build capacity by expanding the scope of collaborative activities and to improve the quality of teacher collaboration or co-teaching practices

4. Time devoted to evaluate established collaborative practices as they unfold

Summary

In this chapter, we have discussed challenges and presented possible solutions for finding the necessary time for establishing effective collaborative practices. We have outlined specific strategies to manage time constraints by identifying the purposes for collaboration and their related time frames, creating strong team partnerships, and establishing scheduled time for both collaboration and co-teaching activities. We concluded that determining specific time demands along with accompanying resolutions will ensure the institution of regular collaborative practices and co-teaching instruction.

Discussion Questions

1. Watch Video 6.1. What are some ways to make co-planning and teacher collaboration work when there is limited time to plan?

2. With your colleagues, generate a list of ideas detailing when and how you can find time to collaborate and how you can use the time most effectively.

3. Reflect on all the collaborative practices that are ongoing or for specific purposes that you are engaged in this year. Discuss with your colleagues how to enhance your use of the available time frame for each activity.

4. Develop an ideal co-teaching schedule for the grade level(s) you teach. Support your plan with arguments from this chapter or other sections of this book. Present your plan to a colleague or administrator, and negotiate the schedule for the upcoming school year.

5. William Johnston and Tiffany Tsai (2018) found that only 31 percent of teachers have sufficient time to collaborate with others. In addition, 4 percent reported that they have never met their colleagues at school to discuss instructional practices, whereas 43 percent do so weekly. How do these statistics apply to your situation? How can these statistics be improved? Whether you have sufficient time available or not, carefully outline how common preparation time could be used most effectively.

VIDEO 6.1

Co-Planning

http://www.resources
.corwin.com/
CollaboratingforELs

Key Online Resources

Bilingual/ESL/Multicultural Education Resources
http://www-bcf.usc.edu/~cmmr/BEResources.html

Finding Time for Collaboration
www.ascd.org/publications/educational-leadership/sept93/vol51/num01/Finding-Time-for-Collaboration.aspx

The Internet TESL Journal
http://iteslj.org

The Power of Teacher Collaboration (Teaching Channel Blog)
https://www.teachingchannel.org/blog/2014/07/18/power-of-teacher-collaboration-nea

TESL-EJ: The Electronic Journal for English as a Second Language
www.tesl-ej.org/wordpress

University of California Linguistic Minority Research Institute (LMRI)
https://escholarship.org/uc/lmri

7

Where Do Teachers Collaborate and Co-Teach?

The one thing people can't take away from you is your education.

—Michelle Obama

OVERVIEW

Collaborative practices require teachers to share space both inside and outside of the classroom. With twenty-first-century technology, many practitioners also make use of virtual space with online and networked tools for ongoing professional discourse. This chapter will describe the different physical and virtual environments that teachers use to enhance the collaborative process. Our discussion of collaborative and teaching spaces will be placed within the framework of establishing and maintaining a positive, inclusive school culture. We will explore the possibilities of using formal and informal shared spaces for instructional planning and offer strategies to maximize shared classroom space for co-teaching purposes. Organizational tips and suggestions for creative classroom design and classroom management are also presented.

> ### Voices From the Field
>
> Alla Gonzalez Del Castillo, Director of the English for Speakers of Other Languages (ESOL) Bilingual Migrant Program in the Saint Louis Public Schools SLPS, Missouri, shares how collaboration is
>
> *(Continued)*

(Continued)

embedded into strategic initiatives and day-to-day operations within the English Language Learners (ELL) Program.

A typical morning in any school and school district office can be busy. In Saint Louis Public Schools ELL office, Wednesday mornings can be particularly eventful. On Wednesdays, our office staff holds intake sessions for newcomer families. This is a result of our collaboration with a local refugee resettlement agency that shares in our vision of welcoming new Americans.

Collaboration is also taking place within our team as we work together to welcome new English learners (ELs) and support our existing students and families. For example, while our interpreters assist families with enrollment paperwork, other team members assess students to determine their initial language proficiency and recommend program placement. When EL families come to our office with questions, our team not only addresses these questions but also offers families additional services. One such service is a Bilingual Parent Library featuring more than four hundred titles in five languages: Spanish, Arabic, Somali, Swahili, and Nepali. Computer literacy classes are another offering available to EL parents, which resulted from a collaborative effort of our team.

We also provide many professional-development opportunities. This gives our ELD/ELL teachers, classroom teachers, and other district staff an opportunity to enhance their ability to develop students' language and help them advance academically. Collaboration gives us a chance to learn from each other, complement each other's work, and collectively advance our services and support for ELs in Saint Louis Public Schools.

Vignette Reflection

When we more closely examine the complexities of the ESOL Bilingual Program in SLPS, we may wonder about the type of space that is needed to implement the assistance it provides to students, parents, teachers, and staff. Just consider the multiple instructional services it offers to ELs—newcomer center (Grades K–10), co-teaching (Grades K–8), stand-alone ESOL classes (Grades K–12), sheltered instruction classes (Grades 6–12), and mainstream classes (Grades K–12). Additionally, for parents learning English, SLPS provides a bilingual library, computer literacy classes, regularly scheduled meetings and events, and virtual learning spaces. Faculty and staff can avail themselves of multiple professional-development (PD) opportunities—after-school EL PD, co-teaching for ELs, SIOP training, and EL PD on demand. Where does all this activity take place? What physical and virtual spaces might be needed to accomplish all of these programs, trainings, and resources for a school community?

REEXAMINING THE IMPORTANCE OF A POSITIVE SCHOOL CULTURE

We strongly believe that teacher collaboration is essential to all schools' general success and especially for their programs that serve English learners as well as the greater school community. Apart from careful planning to orchestrate the use of available meeting places and to organize classrooms for collaborative or co-teaching teams, the effectiveness of teacher collaboration rests within any school culture. Schools may wish to start by examining their school culture (see Figure 7.1) before implementing plans for teacher collaboration.

Consider each element from Figure 7.1 that comprises a positive school culture—collaborative practices, common goals, teacher input, peer support, professional development, administrative support, respect for diversity, and equal access to resources—and determine to what degree each of these factors is currently present in your school. Which factors are best developed? Which ones need more attention? What factors might be missing from this list? And how do they all relate to addressing policies, programs, and practices for supporting English learners?

Collaboration provides teachers with a common ground for meeting the needs of ELs. It also becomes the vehicle for change and an effective process within a school culture that supports all learners' academic success. Moreover, teachers must believe they each have some input and influence on what is important, useful, and valued within their school organization. In this way, the school culture will reflect not only the common goals of administrators but of teachers as well. If teacher collaboration is recognized as a valuable practice, the necessary resources will likely be made available to make it a reality.

One challenge is that EL populations might feel marginalized by an already established school culture that does not address their particular needs. External factors such as anti-immigrant sentiments in the news might fuel EL students to feel unsure of their place in the greater school community. The very programs that are designed to meet ELs' educational needs might actually be segregating them from their grade-level peers. In fact, some teachers have reported that they sometimes feel marginalized as well, frequently evidenced by statements about their own identities as being "just an EL teacher." All students need to feel as if they belong, and all teachers need to believe they are valued for their own expertise.

Figure 7.1 Elements of a Positive School Culture

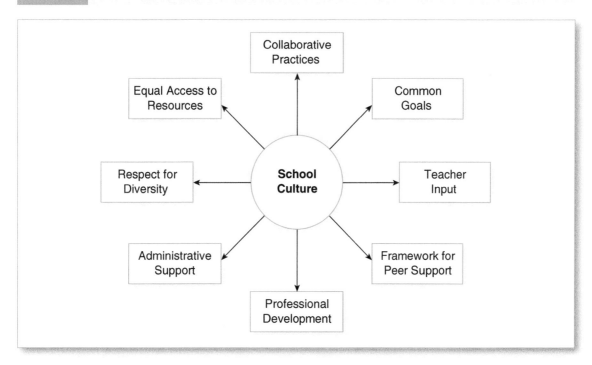

Schools who help to develop a sense of belonging for ELs truly can make a difference. It can affect students' sense of well-being, their feeling of safety and security, as well as their academic growth. Schools can help students to feel accepted as members of the school community by doing the following:

- Creating an environment that is welcoming to all students and their families
- Providing professional learning for teachers and staff about the cultural and religious backgrounds of their students
- Implementing ways to better communicate with families who do not speak English
- Encouraging the entire school community to foster the use of multilingual skills
- Focusing on asset-based practices that capitalize on students' strengths

In addition, the elements of a school culture need to be revisited, reexamined, and revitalized so that no teacher ever feels marginalized and for teacher collaboration to take place most effectively. This most certainly will not happen overnight. It takes much time, patience, and nurturing to develop the necessary trust, understanding, and acceptance for quality teacher collaboration to occur.

SPACES AND PLACES FOR TEACHER COLLABORATION

Teacher collaboration takes many forms, and within a week's time in any school building, teachers will be involved in a number of different collaborative practices. Some of these practices represent the de facto, on-the-fly type. One teacher might see another in the hallway or have a quick chat between regular class sessions. Although a hallway is not the ideal setting for collaborative conversations, informal spaces can play an important role in how and where teachers conduct professional conversations. Formally planned meetings will require a different type of meeting space. So where will grade-level meetings, structured department meetings, professional development or technology workshops, co-planning teams, and general faculty meetings be held? And will they all be in the same place?

Physical Spaces

Schools across the country vary in size, shape, layout, and building capacity. Some school campuses have the capability of accommodating large student populations, which often translates to having the facilities that enable faculty and staff members to meet regularly. Faculty rooms, staff cafeterias, all-purpose rooms, and department offices can all be put to good use for collaboration. Unfortunately, some schools are overcrowded and have difficulty supporting their student populations let alone being able to provide readily available meeting space for teachers.

Informal Spaces

The following spaces are usually available for casual conversations that take place throughout the school day:

- School entrance and exit areas
- Hallways
- Main office
- Playground
- Recess area
- Water cooler or coffee pot
- Teachers' lounge
- Teachers' cafeteria

These informal areas limit the types of professional conversations that can take place. One must be careful when discussing individual students or confidential matters in public or shared spaces. In addition, the physical size of the school building may be a deterrent to informal conversations between faculty members. Large urban schools that house several thousand students generally have multiple floors and hallways in which some pairs of teachers might rarely cross paths.

Formal Spaces

Areas of school buildings that do not house students are precious commodities. How these faculty-only spaces are used often indicates what is valued by the school culture. One school whose administrators and staff are concerned with health and well-being may have a fitness room occupy an available space, whereas another may have a teacher's lounge filled with comfortable sofas, a lending library of popular novels, and a seemingly bottomless pot of coffee. Similarly, if members of a particular district value collaboration, mechanisms will be in place for it to occur regularly. One such way to provide access to teacher collaboration is through formal meeting spaces.

One School's Vision: The Literacy Suite

Ms. Angela Hudson, elementary school building principal, had a particular vision for a specialized literacy location where teachers would be able to find classroom resources to assist their literacy lesson planning and be able to have regular meetings with the district's literacy coach. Both her vision and the hard work of several teachers produced the Literacy Suite, a room filled with leveled, guided reading material, big books, reader's theater scripts, and professional literature. However, the Literacy Suite not only became an excellent place to find classroom resources, it blossomed into a centralized meeting place for teachers to collaborate.

The Literacy Suite is half the size of a regular classroom, and it originally housed the office of the school's superintendent. In more recent years, it served as two small classrooms for the school's remedial reading program. Its renovation into a teacher meeting spot was realized through numerous donated items and time spent planning. For its décor, items such as window curtains added visual appeal. Teachers also contributed materials for student learning in the form of class packs of novels, expository text sets, professional books and journals, and portable technology. Other materials for the lending library were purchased with budgeted funds. In addition, school personnel chipped in to buy a state-of-the-art beverage maker that brews individual servings of coffee and tea.

Whether it's during their prep periods, lunch breaks, or time before and after school, teachers frequent the Literacy Suite to "shop" for new materials, get quick advice from the literacy coach, or grab their favorite hot beverage. It is a place where groups of teachers eat lunch together, share ideas, and help each other plan lessons.

Another School's Vision: The Book Room

The Cordello Avenue School in Central Islip, New York, has a special place called the Book Room. As Yanick Chery-Frederic showed us around, she explained, "When you peek in, you see neatly organized floor-to-ceiling book shelves all around the perimeter of the room. The shelves contain literacy, content-based, and ESOL resources on all grade levels taught in the building. The Cordello Book Room was established in 2001, as a mandate of our Literacy Collaborative Initiative."

The Book Room is accessible to all teachers and has an organized policy for borrowing books. Specific needs of the EL community are addressed via a book selection that simultaneously acknowledges language needs as well as the importance of providing culturally rich and diverse literature.

There are numerous volumes of leveled books for implementation of small-group instruction. There is a large selection of shared reading books and recommended read-alouds for beginner ELs. Grade-appropriate texts of different genres are also available. In addition, a variety of teacher resources that support EL curricula occupy a section of the Cordello Book Room. Also obtainable are units of study for different writing genres—including poetry, personal narratives, how-to writing, nonfiction, fiction, memoirs, essays, and more. These units invariably consist of components that can be differentiated to specifically target EL student writing curricula. The resources have been carefully collected, organized, and reviewed over the years by a committee to make sure all subject matter content and essential skills are supported with multiple and varied instructional resources. The Book Room is not just a professional place for teachers to pick up workbooks or browse teacher guidebooks; it is also a meeting place where important professional conversations about students' needs and best practices to respond to those needs may also take place.

A Third Example of Shared Space: A High School Study Center

Susan Dorkings, the study skills/ESOL department chairperson at the William A. Shine Great Neck South High School in New York describes a unique place for ELs and teacher collaboration. About twenty years ago, the administrators of South High School decided to create a Study Center where various academic labs throughout the building were centralized in one location. Over the years, the Center evolved to a program staffed by eleven qualified teachers and teaching assistants. The teachers rotate through a schedule designed to provide support in math, science, social studies, and English each period throughout the day and before and after school. In addition, two reading teachers and two ESOL teachers are part of the team. They share the same workspace with students, creating an atmosphere where serious academic work takes place. For this reason, collaboration among Center teachers and communication with classroom teachers, guidance counselors, administrators, and other support staff is an ongoing process. This collaboration, both formal and informal, is key to the success of this program.

Many students are assigned to the Study Center program as part of their schedules. Others take advantage of the support provided and drop in for help when they need it. During a period, students can receive help in one academic area or in multiple subjects. Study Center teachers, who have access to students' progress reports and grades, direct students to the teacher who can best address their needs.

Study Center teachers collaborate formally and informally to develop strategies that engage all students in the school—including the EL population. Although the focus of instruction is directed toward each student's coursework, teachers are aware that many students need to build their basic skills in reading, writing, listening, speaking, and studying. Therefore, the collaboration of academic specialists with reading, ELD/ELL, and special-education teachers allows for a team approach toward the development of strategies that address those skills. Each member of the department brings his or her expertise, experience, dedication, and enthusiasm to the Center each day. Students respect the knowledge of the teachers and feel welcomed and supported.

Virtual Spaces

More and more, people are using virtual spaces to communicate with one another. A Gallup poll revealed the most common form of communication between people younger than fifty is texting (Newport, 2014). Even if all teachers might not be digital natives, for the most part, all educators have adapted to using the latest technologies. Typically, all teachers own at least one device that gives them easy access to the Internet—smart phones, tablets, laptops, desktop computers, and so on. For this reason, faculty members who do not have the time or the available space to meet with one another during the school day are increasingly collaborating using virtual spaces.

In addition to common forms of communicating such as texting and e-mail, there are websites where you can access virtual tools to conduct meetings on the Web; some are available at no cost. Anyone with access to a device with Internet access easily can connect to a virtual meeting location. Some websites even offer secure meeting sites so that confidentiality is ensured. These virtual meeting spaces allow participants to present information, share documents, and collaborate in a way that can be equally as effective as a face-to-face meeting.

A quick search for free Web-based chat rooms will yield many options for teachers to explore virtual collaboration at no cost to the user. Simple, private chat rooms, found on websites such as Chatzy, E-Chat, and TweetChat, allow anyone to create a chat room of their own. Google Hangouts is another free service that can provide teachers the ability to initiate and engage in text, voice, or video chats, either as a simple pair of teachers or a larger team meeting. Other websites, such as GoToMeeting, Cisco Webex, and Zoom, provide additional features such as video conferencing for a fee. With these tools in place, colleagues can identify a convenient time to conduct their meetings from their personal devices.

Apart from general apprehension about or lack of experience with certain technology, there are other difficulties teachers may face when trying to engage in collaborative conversations using Web-based tools. In spite of being sufficiently tech savvy, some teachers resist scheduling meetings, even virtual ones, outside the school day. They may feel these meetings intrude on their own personal time, while others are obligated to follow local teacher-union guidelines regarding contractual work hours and extracurricular activities. See Table 7.1 for a summary of some of the most prevalent advantages and challenges of using Web-based technology for teacher collaboration.

Table 7.1 Pros and Cons of Virtual Collaboration

Collaboration and Web-Based Technology	
Pros	**Cons**
• Teachers can collaborate from separate locations. • Virtual environments allow real-time communication. • Meaningful interactions such as idea sharing and problem solving can occur between participants. • Collaborative writing projects can be facilitated. • Collaborative learning and professional development can take place.	• Teachers sometimes resist using new technology. • Technology tools may be unreliable or difficult to use. • There may be resistance to scheduling regular group meetings outside the school day. • A lack of up-to-date personal technology may be an issue.

Using an online tool to submit feedback or give input about an issue requires little time and commitment on the part of group members, yet most participants can contribute to the process within the confines of the school day. This strategy provides opportunities for a variety of staff members to offer their suggestions and advice to those who may have special concerns and can engage faculty members who are only available on a part-time basis. See Figure 7.2, which offers a sample template for documenting staff feedback. Consider using this strategy by posting the template on Google Drive and inviting others to participate in its completion.

Meetings that do not require a face-to-face presence by their participants can be an essential form of collaboration to benefit ELs. Teachers with little or no experience with the special needs of ELs can ask for help and receive advice within a short period of time from a variety of practitioners. ELD/ELL teachers who are struggling to find solutions for ELs who have difficulties outside English language learning can seek help from their colleagues specializing in K–5 classroom teaching, content-area subject matters, or special education.

In the past, the responsibility of assisting the classroom teacher or problem solving for ELs rested solely on the shoulders of the ELD/ELL teacher. However, through the use of technology and other forms of collaborative practice, classroom teachers can be guided by the expertise of different members of the school community, of which the ELD/ELL teacher is an essential member. In addition, ELD/ELL teachers will be more capable of remedying the situation at hand with the assistance of their colleagues. All forms of collaboration can assist the entire school community to move from a "your kids" to an "our kids" mentality.

COLLABORATION INSIDE THE CLASSROOM

The school day begins with most teachers entering the school building, visiting the main office, performing a few clerical duties, offering some brief morning greetings, and proceeding to their separate hallways. From the moment the morning bell sounds, these practitioners remain isolated

Figure 7.2 Feedback Form

Feedback Form

Your input is valuable to our school. Please take a few minutes to share any ideas, suggestions, or advice about the following concern.

Team members' names:	
Date:	Team member initiating discussion:

Concern:

Summary of the issue:

Your feedback:

Please return this form by _____ to _____.

You will receive a copy of all team members' feedback. Thank you for your time and attention to this matter.

---

online resources — Available for download at resources.corwin.com/CollaboratingforELs

in their classrooms away from their peers, left alone with the students in their charge to meet the day's challenges.

Teachers, generally speaking, are accustomed to having their classrooms as their sole domains and take comfort in the modicum of control they hold in their workspace. They set their own class routines, arrange student seating to suit their own lesson ideas, and generally decide what to teach, where to teach it, and when activities will take place within school policy guidelines. However, when ELD/ELL and general-education teachers work together and share the same classroom, there is a different dynamic. Deciding where and how instruction occurs involves careful planning, negotiation, practice, assessment, reflection, and adjustment between those responsible for a co-taught classroom.

Sharing Classroom Space

Teacher collaboration can have a tremendous influence over the way instruction is conceived, decided on, delivered, and assessed for ELs. It most certainly can have a great impact on how these students are regarded—understanding what they already know, what skills they already bring, and what they are capable of learning. It involves sharing student information, lesson ideas, teaching strategies, and, with certain programs for ELs, classroom space. Yet, many factors must be considered when two teachers work so closely together.

Co-teaching requires many teachers to move out of their comfort zones and into unknown territory. Space is not only the final frontier, as a voice from a popular 1960s television series told us, but for some teachers, it is the only frontier. Classroom space is a closely and carefully guarded commodity. Some people, generally speaking, need more control over personal space than others in order to feel sufficiently relaxed and confident to meet the school day's challenges. Concerns about classroom space and how it is best used can bring about a great deal of anxiety and cause conflict between those who must share it.

Examine the behavior of colleagues when they hear someone is changing their position in the district or retiring, and you will observe many of them vying for the soon-to-be vacated space, particularly if it is a plum spot. With overcrowded classrooms and schools bulging at their seams, no wonder teachers need all the courage they can muster to open their doors and share their classrooms. On the other hand, some teachers do not always understand what the fuss is all about. Many ELD/ELL teachers, special educators, literacy specialists, and others spend most of their careers in small, divided classrooms, shared office spaces, all-purpose rooms, borrowed classrooms, hallways, or even spare closets. Some teachers have never had the joy of classroom "ownership," and so they may not understand a classroom teacher's concerns over the matter.

One Classroom Versus Two Classrooms

Programs for ELs generally are established according to the student population, assessed needs, available faculty and personnel, funding, and resources. Some ELD/ELL teachers have the flexibility to select from a variety of program models to deliver instruction, whereas others are restricted to one particular model. In many cases, a program coordinator, building principal, an administrator at the district level, a combination of school leaders, or state-level policies determine the choice of models for EL programs. Some programs establish separate, stand-alone classroom settings for EL instruction, whereas others prescribe a shared environment. Let's take a look at some program models that incorporate collaborative practices to enhance instruction for ELs.

- *Stand-alone/Pull-out programs*: Even though general-education and ELD/ELL teachers maintain their own separate rooms for instruction, co-planning efforts and the use of a parallel teaching model—where the content, skills, and strategies being taught in one class are coordinated with another—can yield positive learning environments for ELs in both class settings. The ELD/ELL teacher incorporates grade-level curriculum with language acquisition instruction in the stand-alone/pull-out classroom while the general-education teacher is teaching the same content material in the grade-level classroom. Collaboration efforts can also help general-education teachers identify, include, and assess language objectives for ELs alongside content objectives when these students are learning mainstream curriculum content.

- *Push-in programs*: ELD/ELL teachers provide instruction for a group of ELs by pulling them aside yet remaining in grade-level classes. This shared-space arrangement can benefit ELs with the right amount of joint planning and the use of a parallel teaching or a multiple-group model, which uses small groups and learning centers; however, we recognize the many challenges and limitations of this approach and do not tend to recommend it. When we have observed this approach, we noted that the two teachers can teach the same content to two different groups of students, or multiple groups can be assigned to centers, with the ELD/ELL teacher assisting ELs to complete various center activities. Having established a common set of learning objectives, each teacher has the freedom to choose the best resources to meet their students' needs. When this model is used without any joint planning, it reduces its effectiveness and may lead the ELD/ELL teacher into being more of a teacher aide or "helper" than an experienced specialist.

- *Co-teaching programs*: Teachers carefully coordinate instruction for ELs and determine which co-teaching models will provide the best lesson delivery for all students. Some co-teaching teams may settle on one or two program models to incorporate into their teaching routines, whereas others prefer to select co-teaching models according to what is being taught. We often recommend the latter. Co-taught classrooms require a great deal of cooperation as well as careful planning not only of lesson content but also of classroom management and the equitable use of available space for student learning to take place.

Shared Space Versus Personal Space

Every teacher needs his or her own personal space. In a co-teaching situation, classroom space needs to be carefully planned and negotiated. A good place to start is to have a conversation with your co-teaching partner or team in order to answer the following general and specific questions:

1. What will our co-teaching arrangement look like inside the classroom?

2. Which co-teaching models will we use to meet the needs of our students and match our own teaching styles?

3. What are our expectations for shared classroom space?

4. What are each teacher's "non-negotiables"—anything necessary for each teacher to function within the same class?

5. If we use multiple models for instruction during one teaching session, how will the classroom's overall design accommodate their use?

6. Where will teaching resources be kept for easy access for all co-teaching partners?

7. Which resources might both teachers comfortably share, and which ones might be off limits?

8. Which areas of the room will be designated as shared spaces?

9. How will one classroom accommodate each individual's need for personal space?

The Importance of Personal Space

When ELD/ELL teachers enter a general-education classroom for one class period or part of the school day, it is important that they have a "go to" area as soon as they walk in the door. It may be a table in the back of the room, a small desk set aside for their own use, or a designated wall space with their own materials and supplies and an adjacent chair. Having a specific spot for the co-teacher when she or he arrives will lessen classroom interruptions, keep students who are already engaged in learning on task, and prevent awkward moments that can occur. When the co-teacher's entrance is smooth, it eliminates the feeling that one is an "intrusion" teacher instead of an "inclusion" teacher.

Benefits of Shared Space

The benefits of sharing classroom space are endless. It not only benefits students and teachers, but it can also send subtle messages about the school's learning culture to the community at large. Here is a sample of the possible advantages and ideas brought about by teachers who share classroom space:

- All students are a part of the same learning community.
- Students can learn from the experience of two or more teachers.
- Students can gain different perspectives and guidance.
- Low-achieving general-education students and former limited English proficient (FLEP) students all benefit from the use of strategies for ELs.
- The use of various co-teaching models helps to meet individual students' learning style needs.
- Teachers learn different techniques by observing each other's teaching.
- Staff development through in-class coaching or mentoring can readily be addressed in a co-taught classroom.

CLASSROOM DESIGN FOR CO-TAUGHT LESSONS

In your mind's eye, travel back in time to the middle of the twentieth century and enter a classic American schoolroom. What you most likely are picturing is a large teacher's desk sitting front and center, accompanied by rows of stationary, wooden student desks. The classroom walls are covered with chalkboards and bulletin boards. There is little room for students to move about the classroom if they were allowed to do so. Now in the same way, picture a typical twenty-first-century classroom. What do you see? In many classrooms, there are movable pieces of furniture, tables and chairs instead of individual desks, carpeted areas, a bank of computers, personal, portable tablets (e.g., iPads or Chromebooks), increased space, and areas for small-group instruction. Classroom design has changed to some extent and in many ways is more conducive to co-taught classes.

Get Organized

Anxiety may often be the first reaction some teachers feel when they must leave their personal class domains and enter another teacher's space to deliver instruction for ELs. They wonder how they will be able to conduct lessons when their materials and resources are housed elsewhere. Being organized is essential for teachers to successfully meet the needs of ELs in general-education classrooms. There are several ways to arrange the necessary resources so that they are readily available. The following steps should be considered when getting materials organized for co-taught lessons:

Step 1: Establish Where Your Materials Will Be Housed

This will depend on the amount of space available in the general-education classroom and the willingness of the classroom teacher to share his or her space. From our own teaching experiences, there is generally little, if any, classroom space available to share. Classrooms are usually overcrowded with students and further crowded with textbooks, reference materials, classroom libraries, and so on. Most ELD/ELL teaching material will be kept elsewhere and transported to the general-education classroom.

Try to use nearby spaces creatively to house materials if there is no other option available in the co-taught classroom. An ample-sized hallway might hold a tall cabinet where materials can be kept. In addition, storage closets, hidden nooks under stairways, or extra shelf space in the school library might just do the trick.

Step 2: Determine How Materials Will Be Transported

There are a variety of ways that materials can be transported to and from classrooms if needed. One of the best ways is to have a set of wheels that can move resources from place to place. Teacher carts, commercially available in a variety of shapes, sizes, and styles, can provide more than adequate transport.

The goal of using a cart is to create a mobile station of resources for teaching ELs. To make sure the cart is functional, the following planning and preparation is needed:

- At the beginning of each school day, the cart should be reviewed and materials matched with planned lessons.
- Checklists can be developed to aid with the cart's organization.

- When preparing traveling carts, consider how many classrooms will be visited within a single school day.
- Always include complete class rosters, individual EL student folders, and student assessment information on the cart for reference.

When a cart is not available or a school has multiple floors that would make a cart impractical, a large, sturdy bag can be used to carry materials. Totes, canvas carryalls, or even backpacks with various pockets and slots to separate items can be a portable solution for getting materials to and from different classrooms. Some teachers even have converted rolling suitcases into efficient, organized, and easily portable containers for materials.

Step 3: Negotiate Who Will Provide the General Classroom Supplies

Most classroom teachers are allowed a limited number of supplies (e.g., chart paper, erasers, markers, pencils, etc.), and as the school year comes to a close, those items become in short reserve. Yet, ELD/ELL teachers cannot always carry all the needed supplies from class to class. It would be most wise for co-teachers to discuss which classroom materials all can use and what additional materials are needed. For special projects, the co-teachers can pool their resources to provide the required materials.

Step 4: Predict "Teachable Moments" and Have Resources Available

This step is a tall order and one that requires a good deal of practice. When ELD/ELL teachers co-teach, they may not have their instructional resources at their fingertips—as they would if they were in their own classroom. When students ask questions that create opportune teaching moments, ELD/ELL teachers like to rely on certain materials to enhance their explanations: bilingual dictionaries, globes, literature, manipulatives, maps, photographs, textbooks, and workbooks.

EL/ELL teachers often need to travel light and cannot depend on having all the necessary resources handy for teachable moments. However, most classrooms have some available technology for use, and teachers can avail themselves of the Internet, which can be a great virtual substitute for traditional resources.

Becoming technological savvy is imperative. Teachers should practice searching for general websites that contain maps, photographs, and other useful information for ELs. It can be helpful to maintain a list of suitable sites to use in co-taught classrooms and be able to retrieve information on the spot without prior planning, allowing them to make the most of teachable moments. We certainly recognize that despite filters and security measures, teachers still need to be wary about the appropriateness of the information retrieved from the Internet and make sure unsuitable websites are not used for instructional practices.

Rethinking Teaching Spaces

A classroom designed for one instructor might not be adequate for co-teaching situations. Therefore, co-teachers must plan and manage the teaching space in a way that enhances lesson instruction and corresponds with the selected co-teaching model. (See Table 7.2 for a summary of the seven co-teaching models we introduced in Chapter 4 aligned to specific space requirements and recommended suggestions.)

Table 7.2 Co-Teaching Models and Organizing Classroom Space

Co-Teaching Models	Space Requirements	Suggestions to Consider
One group: one leads, one teaches "on purpose"	Space for students to work in small groups	• Desks or tables arranged in clusters • A carryall bag for resources and supplies for "on-purpose" teaching
One group: two teach same content	Room sufficient to divide students into two groups	• Separate teaching spaces • Chart easel, whiteboard, etc. • Place to house resources and materials • Seating arranged in horseshoe or circle • May be situated in different rooms
One group: one teaches, one assesses	Area for whole class to gather together	• Carpeted area • Chart easel, whiteboard, etc. • Place to house resources and materials
Two groups: two teach same content	Whole-group seating area	• Carpeted area • Chart easel, whiteboard, etc. • Interactive whiteboard • Computer with projector • Seating arranged in horseshoe or circle
Two groups: one preteaches, one teaches alternative information	Small- and large-group seating arrangements	• Separate teaching spaces • Hands-on materials • Computers/interactive whiteboards • May be situated in different rooms
Two groups: one reteaches, one teaches alternative information	Small- and large-group seating arrangements	• Separate teaching spaces • Hands-on materials • Computers/interactive whiteboards • May be situated in different rooms
Multiple groups: two monitor/teach	Areas designated for small groups and center or station learning	• Establish areas of the room for each learning station • Have baskets for needed materials • Provide portable box or folder-type centers that can be easily adapted to different classroom spaces

Vignette Revisited

The ESOL Bilingual Program in SLPS has many program components that serve the greater school community. For this reason, they have a variety of designated spaces so that their program components can function at their optimum. Their newcomer center—The Nahed Chapman New American Academy— is housed in its own building and serves K–8 newly arrived English learners. To support the development of the whole child as well as incorporate aspects of the students' home cultures, the district, in cooperation with a dozen sponsors, created a state-of-the-art soccer field at the newcomer center, using soccer as a vehicle to develop English language skills. For this reason, we recognize the importance of examining all spaces, both inside and outside the classroom, as potential learning zones.

THE IMPACT OF CLASSROOM DESIGN

What Research Says

Many educators (e.g., Bauscher & Poe, 2018; Earthman, 2013; Uline, Tschannen-Moran, & Wolsey, 2009) have been investigating the impact of school facilities on student learning. When classroom design is the specific focus, many educational facility planners, architects, and school administrators note the trend of replacing individual student desks to create new opportunities for learning. The following elements are frequently identified features of a well-designed classroom that accommodates a range of varied learning needs:

- An individual space or research space where students complete individual work without being distracted by the rest of the class
- A reading nook or learning center where one-to-one instruction and make-up work can be scheduled; may feature a bookcase, comfortable chairs, and a rug
- Common areas where presentations and community meetings may take place
- A cooperative learning space where various small-group instructional activities occur
- A teacher center where individual testing, conferencing, or meetings are scheduled to take place

An extensive body of literature supports the importance of school and classroom climate. For example, Ming-Te Wang and Jessica Degol (2016) conclude that "school climate is predictive of student academic, behavioral, and psychological outcomes" and there is a documented "link between positive features of school climate and optimal student outcomes across academic, behavioral, and psychosocial domains" (p. 343). Building on social cognitive theorists, Nancy Van Note Chism (2006) suggests that "environments that provide experience, stimulate the senses, encourage the exchange of information, and offer opportunities for rehearsal, feedback, application, and transfer are most likely to support learning" (p. 2.4). When two or more teachers share the responsibility for creating such a stimulating learning space for their students, they have the opportunity to do the following:

- Redefine the teaching–learning process: Break the mold of the one-teacher-one-class model and allow for multiple educators to interact with students.
- Promote student engagement through varied approaches to teaching.
- Reduce the teacher–student ratio and increase attention given to individual students.
- Foster both collaborative learning and student independence: Based on the lesson goals, design activities that invite students to work cooperatively or independently while teachers monitor and facilitate such learning.

What Practitioners Suggest

In addition, researchers and practitioners also addressed the importance of classroom design to better respond to varied learning needs of students. Carol Ann Tomlinson (2017) recommends that flexible grouping arrangements allow teachers to move away from creating tracks (separating students into low- and high-achievement groups) within the class and, instead, group students in different ways at different times. In such a differentiated classroom, ELs are sometimes grouped together for instruction, whereas at other times they are placed with their more proficient English-speaking classmates. As Tomlinson proposes, teachers should consider differentiating for content, process, product, and learning environment based on their students' readiness level, interest, and learning profile.

When you are deciding on grouping configurations, use the following guiding questions:

1. Which students are ready linguistically to work with the target content and language objectives?

2. Which students are ready academically (have solid background knowledge) to work with the target content and language objectives?

3. Which students share common interests (or shared background experiences) regardless of their academic readiness or language proficiency levels?

4. Which students share similar learning-style strengths or multiple intelligence profiles?

5. Which students share similar work habits or other learning tendencies (source of motivation, need for adult guidance, tendency to get distracted if not supervised, etc.)?

6. Which students are able to complete the task independently, with peer support, with written teacher scaffolds, or with direct teacher assistance?

7. Which students work well together for no particular reason?

What Co-Teachers Need: Shared Classroom Management

To be successful in redesigning the traditional, transmission-type classroom model—in which one teacher spends much of his or her instructional time in front of the entire class—it is important to establish class routines and rules of behavior that both teachers in the co-taught classroom adhere to and enforce. These rules and behavior management strategies can change from classroom to classroom and between different co-teaching teams. There are some basic guidelines that should be followed when establishing classroom management practices.

Rules and Routines

Here are some tips for jointly establishing an effective learning atmosphere:

1. With the students, create a set of written class rules that are easily visible. Add visuals or bilingual translations so ELs clearly understand expectations.

2. Keep students engaged via classroom activities that are meaningful and accessible to them.

3. Be consistent with both praise and necessary consequences.

4. ELD/ELL teachers may defer to general-education teachers in all matters that have not been previously negotiated.

ADMINISTRATORS' ROLE: SCHOOL ORGANIZATION AND LOGISTICS

The building administrator's role is to create physical and virtual spaces that support the collaborative team's planning and instruction for ELs. This can be accomplished in a variety of ways.

Focus on Sustained, High-Quality, Meaningful Teacher Collaboration

1. Secure and create inviting, functional, professional rooms as places for teacher collaboration, including spaces for small- and large-group meetings.

2. Establish and continuously update the school's professional library, where teacher resources may be stored, reviewed, and discussed.

3. Create and support physical and virtual spaces for teachers to share their lesson plans, teacher-created instructional materials, and assessment tools.

4. If feasible, enhance opportunities for collaboration by placing ELD/ELL teachers' desks in a teachers' workroom (if they share one).

5. If feasible, set up ELD/ELL offices and classrooms in close proximity to those of their general-education colleagues.

Focus on Teacher Assignments and Student Placement

1. Carefully develop EL placement policies and consider their implications. Cluster ELs based on your local population and demographics.
   - Saint Paul Public Schools (SPPS) has used the following formula:
     ○ Cluster ELs in one or two classrooms, when less than 30 percent of students are ELs.
     ○ Cluster, but be sure ELs do not exceed 50 percent of any class roster, when 30–50 percent of students are ELs.
     ○ Distribute ELs among all classrooms, but group by need or language level, when 50 percent or more of students are ELs.
   - Katherine Fearon (2008) reports a similar ratio developed for a team teaching pilot program in a New Jersey public school:
     ○ The number of ELs should not exceed nine students or 50 percent of the class.

Although we concur with the fundamental ratio of students provided in Fearon's report, we recognize that there are schools which contain large percentages of ELs—60 percent or greater—that would make such a distribution of students not feasible.

   - George Theoharis and Joanne O'Toole (2011) report on district policy that required ELs not to exceed 60 percent of the class. In reality, the schools they studied created inclusive EL classes with 10 to 30 percent ELs, or "not overloading any one classroom and to maintain close to the natural proportion of the school" (p. 672), which was 18 percent. In addition, language clusters were created to further support peer interaction in students' home languages.

- Saint Louis Public School's policy indicates that if the school has less than 30 percent ELs, they will be clustered into one or two classrooms. If the percentage falls between 30 and 50, students will be clustered in one or two classrooms, but no more than 50 percent of any class will comprise of ELs. If a schools demographics exceed 50 percent ELs, the students will be distributed evenly among all classrooms and ELs will be clustered by need and language proficiency level.

2. Assign ELs to general-education classroom teachers at the elementary level and content teachers at the secondary level who demonstrate the highest levels of knowledge and skills regarding second language acquisition, cultural responsiveness, and ELD methodologies, and who volunteer to be selected for such a task (thus also demonstrating the necessary professional dispositions and positive attitudes toward linguistically and culturally diverse student populations).

3. Assign teachers to work together who complement each other's knowledge base, skills, and competencies and who are willing to engage in collaborative practices.

Most of all, create a school culture that respects both an inclusive and safe learning space for all ELs and teacher collaboration spaces that inspire and support teachers in their efforts to work together.

Summary

Creating and sustaining real and virtual spaces for teachers to collaborate responds not only to the essential Maslowian need for "shelter" but also for the need for "safety and security" (Maslow, 1970). Despite the critical shortage of available space in many schools, teachers will only be able to collaborate and co-teach successfully if real and virtual space is provided for planning, delivering, and assessing effective instruction and for being engaged in job-embedded, continued professional development.

Discussion Questions

1. Watch Video 7.1 How do schools foster a positive culture?

2. Prakash Nair (2014) argues that classrooms and schools must be redesigned into collaborative spaces that better support student-centered learning. In what ways do your classroom and school spaces support these ideals?

   a. Reflect on the patterns of instructional and noninstructional events that keep happening in your classroom or school. What are the most common teaching–learning activities that recur? How does the physical space support you in these endeavors?

   b. Review the patterns of space in your classroom or school building: In what way do the patterns of space impact on the patterns of events that take place?

3. Revisit Figure 7.1 depicting the elements of a positive school culture. With your colleagues, discuss which of the elements presented in this figure appear to be most essential to support the education of ELs.

VIDEO 7.1

School Culture

http://www.resources
.corwin.com/
CollaboratingforELs

4. What are the attributes of a collaborative school environment? Consider both what you have read in this chapter and your own experiences. Generate a list of key characteristics you would like to see further developed in your school.

5. How does the teaching–learning environment help teachers develop collaborative practices? In what ways may it hinder such practices?

6. Sketch a floor plan of an ideal classroom where co-teaching could take place most effectively. Consider the need for changing the floor plan to accommodate various co-teaching models. Draw in as many details as possible. Share and discuss your drawing with your co-teacher or other co-teaching teams for additional input.

Key Online Resources

Classroom Architect

http://classroom.4teachers.org

Differentiating Instruction

www.caroltomlinson.com

Multiple Intelligences

www.howardgardner.com

School Improvement Research Series at Education Northwest

http://educationnorthwest.org/resource/825

8

What Next? Reviewing and Evaluating Integrated, Collaborative Service Delivery for ELs

Everything that can be counted does not necessarily count; everything that counts cannot necessarily be counted.

—William Bruce Cameron

OVERVIEW

The goal of this chapter is twofold: It is designed (1) to help create a framework for reflection on the process and outcomes of collaborative practices designed specifically to support English learners (ELs) and (2) to offer tools to conduct both formative and summative evaluations of an integrated, collaborative service delivery for ELs. We offer guidance on introducing reflective practices to be used among teachers and share several self-assessment tools to aid reflective, collaborative practitioners in their effort to improve their instruction.

Voices From the Field

Sarita Amaya, Assistant Administrator for Multilingual Programs for the Beaverton School District, Beaverton, Oregon, reflects on her experience with implementing an integrated, collaborative service delivery for ELs districtwide.

I served in the role of Assistant Administrator for Multilingual Programs in the Beaverton School District, Oregon from Fall 2016 to Summer 2018. Having experienced success with the implementation of collaborative co-teaching at Elmonica Elementary during my time there as assistant principal, I was confident I would be able to do the same districtwide. At Elmonica, principal Cynthia Lam-Moffett was able to be creatively innovative with funding to ensure one English language development (ELD) teacher at each grade level. As assistant principal, my task was to provide the professional development and support for each grade-level team to collaboratively, plan, teach, and assess alongside the ELD teacher. As a team, we embarked on this effort together, fostered a spirit of collaboration among teachers, and successfully increased student achievement for English learners (ELs) that year.

I had high hopes for rolling out similar efforts districtwide. Beaverton School District is the second largest school district in the state of Oregon with a population of a little over 40,000 students, 13 percent of whom are ELs. Beaverton School District is representative of over 100 different languages and is one of the most culturally and linguistically diverse districts in the state. During the 2016–2017 school year, many supports were in place. Principals and educators had received co-teaching training throughout the year, a district collaborative co-teaching guide for implementation had been developed, and collaborative co-teaching schools were able to access up to eight hours of collaborative planning time each month to support school building efforts.

There are a total of twenty-five schools that are implementing the co-teaching model in Beaverton School District: fifteen elementary schools, two K–8 schools, four middle schools, and four high schools. All schools have unique needs and have co-teaching set up in very different ways. For most schools, one ELD teacher at each grade level is not sustainable. With limited staffing in many schools, it was not realistic. Nonetheless, school leadership worked diligently to find ways for there to be an integration of language learning and mastery of grade-level content knowledge and skills through collaboration and co-teaching. In the 2017–2018 school year, the first co-teaching training-of-trainers cohort was created to build more capacity districtwide. Teams attended school visits to see the different co-teaching models in action; they used early-release Wednesdays for collaborative planning and assessment and accessed additional hours to attend conferences and plan outside of their regularly scheduled workdays. The commitment and dedication were evident.

Questions continued to linger in my mind. What is the impact of all these efforts on student achievement? How were students doing on the English Language Proficiency Assessment for the 21st Century (ELPA21)? How were they doing on the Smarter Balanced Reading and Math Assessments (SBAC)? How do we know for sure the increase in language proficiency and academic achievement was a result of the collaboration and co-teaching program model?

Vignette Reflection

In the vignette, Sarita Amaya described a districtwide initiative and understood the need to assess the impact of a collaborative approach to EL services. It is clearly evident that the school district provided systematic and sustained professional development on collaboration and co-teaching to guide teachers on how to implement new program strategies. It is also apparent that capacity building was a priority and realistic goals were set across the school district. In addition, the Beaverton School District Team recognized that decisions had to be made regarding what measures would be used to determine the value of the new initiative and its power to affect learning for ELs.

REFLECTIVE PRACTICES

How do we know how we are doing in the day-to-day business of collaboration? Do we stop and reflect often enough to see if we are still accomplishing what we have set out to do? Are we documenting both our personal and collective reflections, and are we using these data to further evaluate or assess our practices? How do we connect our collaborative practices with student progress, and why is reflection a worthwhile process to gather valuable program data?

Reflective practice entails the periodic consideration of one's teaching methods and their effects on learning outcomes. Although sharing one's thoughts about teaching can be conducted informally with friends and colleagues over coffee, developing a structure for formal reflection and assessment can enhance decision making and help render judgments regarding classroom practices that positively affect student learning. Simple, yet powerful measures can be established to guide teachers to examine and confirm their use of the best approaches with their students.

Historical Perspectives on Teacher Reflection

The importance of reflection has been documented for generations in and outside teacher education (Boyle-Baise & Sleeter, 1996; Dewey, 1933). John Dewey (1933, 1938) suggests that teachers grow in their practice when they avoid coming to fast conclusions and, instead, consider dilemmas through studying them, developing new understandings, and then making sound decisions. We often encourage our preservice and inservice teachers to take the time to reflect for the very reasons Dewey suggests—to truly examine the issues and not jump to any hasty conclusions. This recommendation is critical when working with English learners due to the complex nature of this population of students and the types of challenges teachers encounter that may not have simple or easy answers.

Kenneth Zeichner and Daniel Liston (1996) celebrate teachers who are aware of and question the beliefs and values they bring to teaching. Through reflective practices, they encourage all educators to examine their experiences and solve problems in a constructive manner. As Donald Schön (1990) states, reflective practitioners engage both in *reflection in action* (while being engaged in a classroom experience with students) and *reflection on action* (through action research and lifelong learning). Both types of reflective practice—reflection in action and reflection on action—provide teachers opportunities for professional learning. For this reason, we often identify collaboration and co-teaching as the *dynamic duo* of professional development. First and foremost, these practices are, for the most part, embedded in the school day. Through co-teaching partnerships (i.e., teachers working together in the same classroom), vast amounts of rich data can be gathered for on-the-spot reflection as well as further review in collaboration with others outside the classroom—closely examining the data more extensively to jointly make decisions that will drive instructional improvement as well as enhance personal learning.

Teachers develop scientific or technical knowledge in their teacher preparation programs, but experiential learning takes place once they are practicing in the classroom and are *learning by doing*. Peter Airasian and Arlen Gullickson (1994) claim that "it is the constant cycle of experience, reflection, and improvement that marks a teacher's growth and development; teachers do learn by doing, but only if they also reflect on, critique, and base future actions on knowledge gained from past actions" (p. 195). Robert Tremmel (1999) explains simply yet expressively what reflection means for teachers: It is "using such abilities as feeling, seeing, or noticing to examine what it is you are doing; then learning from what you feel, see, or notice; and, finally, intelligently, even intuitively, adjusting your practice" (p. 89). We regularly advise teachers to take risks and think outside of the box. Risk taking can only be most effective when teachers have reflected on their instructional practices and personal experiences in the classroom—observing students as individuals and teams, listening to questions and answers, recognizing the levels of engagement and participation, checking for understanding, supporting task completion, and even intuitively gauging the level of positive energy in the room. By reflecting on day-to-day instruction, teachers can better identify what works and what needs to be fine-tuned.

The common theme among all these descriptions of reflective practices is the importance of contemplating the practical knowledge and experience teachers gain in the classroom and the changes they make to their own practice based on what new understandings they have gained. Yet, these characterizations should also express the idea of co-reflection—when teachers join together to examine their beliefs and values, consider solutions to identified issues, engage in collaborative inquiry, and overall examine what they are doing and the impact it might have on the students they teach. It is the concept of co-reflection in addition to individual reflective practices coupled with systematic assessment that we advocate for here.

Reflective Practice Today

Teacher reflection continues to be a powerful notion often connected to preservice and inservice teacher education and data-driven decision making. One of the most renowned experts in the field of teaching English to speakers of other languages (TESOL) teacher education with a specific focus on reflective teaching is Thomas S. C. Farrell (2015), who defines reflection as "a cognitive process accompanied by a set of attitudes in which teachers systematically collect data about their practice, and, while engaging in dialogue with others, use the data to make informed decisions about their practice both inside and outside the classroom" (p. 123). The dialogic approach is especially appreciated because this book is dedicated to advocating for collaborative practices in service of ELs.

Teachers naturally tend to be data gatherers and problem solvers, "always shifting the level of scaffolds they provide to balance support with rigor, foster independence, and engage every learner every time" (Singer, 2015, p. 16), which is the ultimate goal of engaging in reflection. More specifically, we also build on the work of Karen Osterman and Robert Kottkamp (2015), who define what reflective practice for educators is as follows:

> Reflective practice is a meaningful and effective professional development strategy. Even more, it is a way of thinking that fosters personal learning, behavioral change, and

improved performance. Through systematic inquiry and analysis, it is a way for individuals to create meaningful and enduring change by changing themselves. It is a way to address problems rather than symptoms. (p. 1)

To further support the importance of reflection in the context of collaborative teaching practices, we adapted Osterman and Kottkamp's (2015) outline of reflective practice developed for professional development and applied it to collaborative instructional practices. Figure 8.1 represents the purpose and context of collaborative reflective practices, assumptions underlying such practices, and strategies used to engage in reflections. As you review Figure 8.1, consider ways you might use this protocol or modify it to better correspond with your own needs.

Figure 8.1   Reflective Practice for Collaborative Endeavors

Reflective Practice

Purpose
To understand our own and colleagues' teaching

To build our own and shared competencies regarding ELs

To understand our impact on students' language development and content mastery

Assumptions
Learning is personally and interpersonally meaningful.

Learning is holistic.

Knowledge is a shared tool.

Learning is co-constructed.

Context
Job-embedded learning

Experiential, classroom-based knowledge construction

Strategies
Reflective journals or logs

Collaborative conversations

Collaborative inquiry

Peer coaching and mentoring

Collaborative action research

Integration of experiential and formal knowledge about ELs

Adapted from Osterman, K. F., & Kottkamp, R. B. (2015). *Reflective practice for educators: Professional development to improve student learning.* New York, NY: Skyhorse.

How to Get Started With Reflection

What happens when you reflect on your teaching practices alone? You develop a deeper understanding of your own actions, a firmer grasp on the processes that take place in your classroom, and stronger problem-solving skills. When reflection becomes a shared experience, you gain additional insights into the teaching–learning process through a second (or third or more) set of lenses.

As Mary Zabolio McGrath and Beverley Holden Johns (2006) suggest,

> We encourage you to view the events of your school day as they unfold. In so doing, we challenge you to not only fully involve yourself in each day's events, but also to look for occurrences that call for reflection, events that challenge you to redirect your teaching strategies, and dynamics in your day that give you inspiration. (p. vi)

A similar practice of paying attention to as many details as possible may be considered capturing a snapshot or a *slice of life* (Tremmel, 1999). For our purposes, we would like to invite you to reflect on both the processes and the outcomes of the various collaborative practices and co-teaching endeavors in which you are currently participating and try to capture a slice of your collaborative life for the sake of ELs. Such efforts will be well aligned to what Osterman and Kottkamp (2015) value about reflective practice as "a collaborative search for answers rather than an effort to teach a predetermined response to a problem" (p. 17).

One of the most powerful ways to engage in reflection is to initiate a dialogic process (Mann & Walsh, 2017). Consider differentiating between private and public dialogic reflections, the former suggesting interactions between the teacher and reflection tools and the latter referring to interactions between individuals. Jim Knight (2016) reminds us that "the goal of dialogue . . . is to have a conversation where all parties understand, hear, shape, and are shaped by each other's thoughts" (p. 69). We are also inspired by William Isaacs's (1999) words in *Dialogue and the Art of Thinking Together*, who calls for "energy, possibility, and safety" (p. 244), without which we are unlikely to experience dialogue. In our context, dialogic processes are at the cornerstone of collaboration and co-teaching, which in turn, provide a strong context for co-constructing meaning out of individual or shared teacher experiences while also examining the impact on student learning. One place to begin your shared reflection is to consider whether or not you have an asset-based shared philosophy. (See Figure 8.2 for a reflection tool.)

We encourage you to not only search for answers jointly as a team but also design your own collaborative reflective framework. We like to call it *Collaborative Professional Reflections*, or the CPR of collaboration. It works by following these steps:

1. Decide on how much time you will devote to collaborative reflection (5–10 minutes per session will suffice).

2. Generate a few manageable, yet critically important, reflective questions that best fit your collaborative practices (see Table 8.1 for ideas).

3. Establish simple yet effective ground rules (one voice at a time; respect and reflect before resent and repent).

Figure 8.2   Sharing an Assets-Based Perspective

Reflection Question	Yes	Sometimes	No	Question or Idea to Strengthen an Asset-Based Perspective
1. Do we view students' cultural backgrounds as a valuable source of knowledge and skills that we can build on in our lessons?				
2. Do we view diverse perspectives as a beneficial resource for all students and look for ways to incorporate these diverse perspectives into our co-teaching?				
3. Do we recognize and appreciate that our students' families may contribute to their children's educations in varied and sometimes unseen ways?				
4. Do we hold all our students to the same high standards?				
5. Do we recognize that students who are struggling in our class may be doing so because they need additional forms of support that they are not currently receiving?				

Adapted from Staehr Fenner, D., & Snyder, S. (2017). *Unlocking English learners' potential: Strategies for making content accessible.* Thousand Oaks, CA: Corwin.

 Available for download at resources.corwin.com/CollaboratingforELs

Table 8.1 Key Reflective Questions

What?	How?
• What is my role in this collaborative situation? • What are my strengths and major contributions to this partnership? • What works in our collaborative practice? • What do we do well? • What can we improve?	• How do I contribute to the collaborative partnership? • How do I support my colleagues? • How do my colleagues support me? • How do we impact our students' language acquisition and academic, social, and affective development? • How do I make a difference? • How do we, collaboratively, make a difference?

Consider the list of reflective questions in Table 8.1 to get you started on your collaborative search for answers.

Setting a Course for Ongoing Reflection

As you begin to consider how your reflective practices will take shape, you may wonder what types of strategies are needed to make ongoing reflection a success. Stephen Brookfield (2017) suggests that we view what we do and how we form assumptions about the teaching–learning process that takes place in our classrooms through four different lenses:

The students' eyes:

- What are the students seeing and experiencing?

Our colleagues' perceptions:

- What are our colleagues seeing and experiencing?

Our own personal experiences:

- What have we experienced in the past that is similar or different?

Relevant theory and research:

- What do related educational theory and research have to say about these experiences?

Because it is a multidimensional process, it cannot be a single event or irregular occurrence. Instead, Brookfield (2017) advises regular, disciplined, critical reflection. We invite you to try out the four-lens approach to reflection or devise different approaches to support your efforts with your collaborative team members and co-teaching partners in order to fully integrate your reflective inquiry into your teaching practice. For reflection to be continual, its documentation needs to be easily and readily accomplished.

As you and your collaborating teachers make reflection an integral part of your practice, keep in mind the importance of creating a reflective framework and using protocols

(Murawski & Lochner, 2017). The use of a framework allows teaching partners to reflect on the same topics in a nonjudgmental way. Using protocols or structured reflection guides will help refine the process of reflection whether you engage in it alone or with your co-teachers. The use of these concrete devices can reveal more specific information about teaching practices and student learning. We also affirm that a framework for thinking about a range of different types of teacher collaboration and engaging in regular, professional dialogues with colleagues benefits everyone. We educators need opportunities to share our stories of success and our challenging moments; we must express our frustrations, offer our words of wisdom, and request help or suggestions.

Strategies for Ongoing Reflection

Here are some ideas to help foster continuing reflection through self-examination of practices as well as in concert with your colleagues.

Strategy 1: Daily Deliberations

When reflecting on everyday practices, try using a simple log format that encourages you and your collaborative partners, both individually and collectively, to keep track of what works and what could be done better. A log may be used in varied contexts of collaborative activities and co-teaching settings (see Tables 8.2 to 8.4).

Strategy 2: Weekly Wonders

Once a week, reflect on your successes. Select one outstanding event, activity, or moment that made you stop, pause, or even *wonder*. Take a mental snapshot of the best moments of the week and reflect on them. Even consider taking an actual photo of an event or activity and share your reflection with your colleagues. Another way to implement Weekly Wonders is by engaging in collaborative conversations and identifying one area for improvement. As you reflect on the week with your colleagues, try to finish the sentence stem *I wonder if we . . .* or *I wonder what would happen if . . .* You might also choose to brainstorm new questions and directions you might have or new strategies you might try that will help you achieve your goals.

Strategy 3: Monthly Milestones

Once a month, set aside time to recognize and celebrate milestones and accomplishments. During that time, identify at least one new step you took together toward building a stronger collaborative relationship or a more effective co-teaching partnership. Document these milestones and share them with colleagues, administrators, parents, and students in appropriate formats.

Reflective Practice for School Improvement

In a broader context, Jennifer York-Barr, William Sommers, Gail Ghere, and Jo Montie (2016) identify four levels of reflective practice to improve schools. When transferred into the collaborative English language development/English language learning (ELD/ELL) context, the four levels

Table 8.2 A Basic Collaboration Log

Date	Collaborative Activity	Successes	Challenges

Table 8.3 A Reflective Log Template for Co-Teaching

Date	What Worked for Us Today	What We Could Improve Next Time

Table 8.4 A Co-Teaching Log Template to Include Detailed Notes

Guiding Questions	Notes
What was our goal today?	
How did we approach the goal?	
What did we do well?	
What do we want to do better?	

online resources   Available for download at resources.corwin.com/CollaboratingforELs

Table 8.5 Four Critical Steps for Reflective Questions

1. What happened? (Description)	2. Why? (Analysis, interpretation)
• What did I do? What did others (e.g., co-teachers, students, adults) do? • What was my effect at the time? What was their effect? • What was going on around us? Where were we? When during the day did it occur? Was there anything unusual happening?	• Why do I think things happened in this way? • How might the context have influenced the experience? • Are there other potential contributing factors? • What are my hunches about why things happened the way they did?
3. So what? (Overall meaning and application)	4. Now what? (Implications for action)
• Why did this seem like a significant event to reflect on? • What have I learned from this? How could I improve? • How might this change my future thinking, behavior, or interactions? • What questions remain?	• Who should be actively included in reflecting on this event? • Next time a situation like this presents itself, how do I want to behave? • How can I set up conditions to increase the likelihood of productive interactions and learning?

Adapted from York-Barr, J., Sommers, W. A., Ghere, G. S., & Montie, J. (2016). *Reflective practice for renewing schools: An action guide for educators* (3rd ed. (p. 128)). Thousand Oaks, CA: Corwin.

serve as critical guides for improving interpersonal and communication skills, as well as productivity. The contents of Table 8.5 are organized around the four overarching questions for reflection (What happened? Why? So what? Now what?).

SELF-ASSESSMENT TOOLS

As a form of reflection, self-assessment focuses your attention both on your own individual and collaborative practices. Checklists, rubrics, scoring guides, and other measurement tools often help collaborating teachers to gather more systematic data about their interactions, their effectiveness during the teaching–learning process, and their impact on their students' learning. The next two tables contain a self-assessment checklist for collaboration (Table 8.6) and for co-teaching (Table 8.7), whereas Figure 8.3 offers a self-assessment template for co-teaching that requires additional descriptive or narrative input from teachers completing it.

How to Use Self-Assessment Tools

Self-assessment checklists or other tools may be collaboratively developed as the outcome of reflections and professional dialogues, thus making the development of a self-assessment tool a creative, collaborative activity in and of itself.

Table 8.6   A Collaboration Self-Assessment Checklist

Yes	No	Factors Impacting Collaboration
		1. Communication: Our collaboration has open and clear communication.
		2. Goal Setting and Evaluation: Our collaboration has established goals, and we collect data to measure how we meet our goals.
		3. Climate: The school environment supports teacher collaboration through shared decision making.
		4. Resources: Our collaboration has access to needed resources.
		5. Leadership: Our school leadership facilitates and supports team building and capitalizes on diversity and individual, group, and organizational strengths.

Adapted from Borden, L. M., & Perkins, D. F. (1999). Assessing your collaboration: A self-evaluation tool. *Journal of Extension, 37*(2). Retrieved from http://www.joe.org/joe/1999april/tt1.php

 Available for download at resources.corwin.com/CollaboratingforELs

Table 8.7   A Co-Teaching Self-Assessment Checklist

Yes	No	In Our Co-Teaching Partnership
		We decide which co-teaching model we are going to use in a lesson based on the benefits to the students.
		We share ideas, information, and materials.
		We identify each other's resources and talents.
		We are aware of what our co-teacher(s) is (are) doing even when we are not directly in one another's presence.
		We share responsibility for deciding what to teach.
		We agree on the curriculum standards that will be addressed in a lesson.
		We share responsibility for deciding how to teach.
		We share responsibility for deciding who teaches what in each lesson.
		We are flexible and make changes as needed during a lesson.
		We identify student strengths and needs.
		We share responsibility for differentiating instruction.
		We include other people when their expertise or experience is needed.
		We share responsibility for how student learning is assessed.
		We can show that students are learning when we co-teach.
		We agree on discipline procedures and carry them out jointly.
		We give feedback to one another on what goes on in the classroom.
		We make improvements in our lessons based on what happens in the classroom.
		We communicate our concerns freely.
		We have a process for resolving our disagreements and use it when faced with problems and conflicts.
		We have fun with the students and with each other when we co-teach.
		We have regularly scheduled times to meet and discuss our work.
		We use our meeting time productively.
		We can effectively co-teach even when we don't have enough time to plan.
		We explain the benefits of co-teaching to the students and their families.
		We model collaboration and teamwork for our students.
		We are both viewed by our students as their teachers.
		We depend on one another to follow through on tasks and responsibilities.
		We seek and enjoy additional training to make our co-teaching better.
		We can use a variety of co-teaching models.
		We communicate our need for logistical support and resources to our administrators.

Adapted from Villa, R. A., Thousand, J. S., & Nevin, A. I. (2013). *A guide to co-teaching: New lessons and strategies to facilitate student learning* (3rd ed.). Thousand Oaks, CA: Corwin.

 Available for download at resources.corwin.com/CollaboratingforELs

| Figure 8.3 | Co-Teaching Self-Evaluation |

School _____ Name _____

Grade/Content Area _____ Date _____

Role _____ (general educator, ELD/ELL specialist, paraprofessional, administrator, other)

Share strengths (*Shine*) and suggestions or concerns (*Refine*) for each of the following:

Planning (Use of scheduled time, creative ways of finding time to cooperate and communicate, clarity and articulation of content and language goals or objectives, preparation of differentiated learning activities, collection of supplementary materials, sharing of ideas)

Shine	Refine

Instruction (Flexible, interchangeable roles; implementation of specially designed, differentiated learning activities; appropriate use of a variety of co-teaching approaches; flexible grouping configurations; effective use of modified instructional materials)

Shine	Refine

(Continued)

Figure 8.3 (Continued)

Assessment (Use of informal and formal assessment tools, offering informal and formal feedback, shared responsibility for student assessment and evaluation, focus on both academic and linguistic development, grading)

Shine	Refine

Additional Factors (Sharing all responsibilities, joint use of available resources, shared accountability, dispositions toward collaboration, professional growth, commitment and enjoyment)

Shine	Refine

Once a self-assessment tool is selected, adapted, or developed, several approaches may be chosen to implement the tool. For example, if you decide to use one of the previously presented self-assessment checklists, you can choose any of the following approaches to apply them:

1. Complete the self-assessment checklist in cooperation with your colleagues at the beginning of the year and set it aside for a designated period of time (three months, a semester, or even an entire year), after which you will reassess. Compare the results. Identify necessary courses of action and appropriate modifications to your collaborative practices.

2. Complete the self-assessment checklist independently at the beginning of the year. Periodically reassess yourself to reveal areas in need of improvement and areas of effectiveness.

3. Complete the self-assessment checklist independently at the beginning of the year and then periodically throughout the year. Each time you meet with your teaching team members, compare your answers through collaborative conversations. Identify shared concerns, chart your joint progress, and set new, attainable goals based on the results.

Benefits of Self-Assessment

What are some documented benefits of teacher self-assessment? Self-assessment leads to professional growth by shaping teachers' concept of excellence in teaching and by enhancing their ability to recognize outstanding teaching–learning experiences that lead to student mastery of new content (Ross & Bruce, 2007). Self-assessment practices also help teachers define their own professional-development goals by helping them grasp the difference between desired and actual teaching practices. Finally, self-assessment tools not only facilitate communication among teachers, they may also serve as a menu of choices for future action.

ONGOING (FORMATIVE) COLLABORATIVE PROGRAM ASSESSMENT

When teachers, administrators, and other stakeholders are fully committed to a collaborative ELD/ELL service delivery model, ongoing (formative) collaborative assessment practices must be initiated. Many school district administrators and teachers not only are interested in examining the research behind particular collaborative practices but also understand the need to evaluate initiatives that have been undertaken on a local level.

Among others, John Norris (2016) recognizes the growing interest in language program evaluations. He notes that "program evaluation enables a variety of evidence-based decisions and actions, from designing programs and implementing practices to judging effectiveness and improving outcomes" (p. 169), all which are critical when implementing collaborative integrated ELD/ELL services. The ultimate question is: How do we know that our collaborative approach to serving ELs is working? To gauge the effectiveness of your ELD/ELL service delivery model, there are several formative-assessment techniques you and your colleagues may use, including the following:

 a. Engaging in regular collaborative conversations

 b. Participating in peer observations

 c. Monitoring students' language development content attainment

 d. Designing and initiating a collaborative inquiry framework

 e. Forming a program review-and-assessment committee that meets regularly to evaluate formative-assessment data

Quick Tips on How to Get Started With Formative-Assessment Practices

Professional Conversations

Start by regularly engaging in professional dialogues about your practices with your collaborative colleagues. Share your lesson plans and unit plans, explore your classroom dilemmas, and offer support and input to your fellow teachers.

Peer Observations

Teachers who collaborate regularly but do not have the opportunity to co-teach miss out on the opportunity to see each other in action. Visit your collaborative team members and observe each other teaching the English language learners for whom you share responsibility. Try to split your attention between (a) teacher watching (determining the best practices and successful techniques your colleagues are using with ELs) and (b) student watching (establishing how ELs respond to the instruction). Keep in mind what Russell Quaglia and Lisa Lande (2017) so aptly state: "There is perhaps no greater compliment and motivational tool than the praise received from an individual who understands, values, and is committed to the same profession" (p. 86). And remember to compliment your colleagues every day!

Monitoring Student Performance

In Chapter 4 we discussed various protocols for collaborative assessments of student work. We revisit that approach here for program assessment purposes. Regularly review student work, in a collaborative fashion, to document the impact collaborative practices (including co-teaching) have on student learning. Analyze the outcomes of formal and informal learning and performance assessments. Prepare and review case studies of students whose linguistic, academic, or social-emotional learning (acculturation) is cause for concern.

Collaborative Inquiry

Among so many others, in their seminal work, John Goodlad, Corinne Mantle-Bromley, and Stephen John Goodlad (2004) recommend that teachers engage in a process of inquiry that consists of four cyclical, ongoing steps: dialogue, decision making, action, and evaluation focused on a shared purpose. They claim that such collaborative inquiry is "the single-most important vehicle for school renewal" (p. 110). For formative-assessment purposes, we suggest adapting Goodlad et al.'s four-step framework to your local context:

1. *Dialogue*: Regularly engage in preplanned professional dialogues about key instructional issues and ELs' academic and linguistic development and performance.

2. *Decision making*: Collectively decide what collaborative practices you wish to initiate, develop, continue, or discontinue.

3. *Action*: Based on the collaborative decisions, actively engage in initiating, developing, continuing, or discontinuing certain practices.

4. *Evaluation*: Regularly collect and analyze both informal and formal data about both your teaching practices and EL student learning.

Collaborative inquiry can be a powerful approach to increasing student achievement on standardized tests as well as improving school culture through the ongoing reflection and sharing of its members (Donohoo & Velasco, 2016; Love, 2009). One way to examine the extent to which collaborative practices are in place in your school is to conduct a survey.

Administrators may use the following survey (see Figure 8.4) to determine how teacher collaboration already is being used in their schools. In this way, principals and other building administrators can hone in on the specific needs of their faculty and devise particular initiatives to help make collaborative practices successful. Additionally, this same survey can assess to what degree collaborative initiatives have been achieved after they have been operational for a period of time.

Periodic Program Review-and-Assessment Meetings

To review key aspects of the collaborative ELD/ELL program, set up an assessment committee to meet periodically. Schedule meetings with a clear and concise agenda and well-defined roles. Manage the logistics of the meetings by identifying a facilitator who will set the topic, goal, or purpose for each meeting and create an agenda with specific time slots and allotted discussion times for each item. This type of organization will help the flow of the meeting and ensure that each topic is addressed. Program review-and-assessment meetings may address the agenda items presented in Table 8.8 throughout the year.

Several different formats may be used to capture the essence of each meeting. In addition to more traditional meeting minutes, we suggest you try the SNAPS template in Figure 8.5. *SNAPS* stands for the following:

- *Successes* the team has experienced related to the agenda item are discussed first, to start the meeting on a positive, welcoming note.
- *New approaches*, initiatives, or suggestions recommended by a committee member are discussed and recorded next.
- *Appreciative comments* allow for staff recognition.
- *Problems* then are discussed related to the topic.
- *Solutions* are brainstormed by the team to end the meeting productively.

Figure 8.4   Evaluation Survey

Evaluation Survey

Collaboration and Co-Teaching for ELs

Directions: Use the following statements to identify the successes and challenges of co-teaching or collaboration activities in your school. Circle a number from 1 to 5 for each statement (1 = strongly disagree, 2 = somewhat disagree, 3 = neither agree nor disagree, 4 = somewhat agree, 5 = strongly agree).

Leadership and Collaboration

District and building administrators value teacher collaboration.	1	2	3	4	5
Building administrators encourage and support collaboration efforts between ELD/ELL instructors, teachers, and other specialists.	1	2	3	4	5
Professional development is provided to train teachers in collaborative planning and decision making.	1	2	3	4	5
Teachers are provided scheduled time to collaborate with other teachers.	1	2	3	4	5
Teacher recommendations derived through collaboration are given serious consideration.	1	2	3	4	5

Teacher Collaboration

ELD/ELL and general-education teachers maintain ongoing conversations about the teaching and learning of ELs.	1	2	3	4	5
Teams of faculty members, along with others in the school community, work together to identify and solve ELs' learning difficulties.	1	2	3	4	5
ELD/ELL and general-education teachers converse across grade levels and content areas to promote understanding of ELs and to share teaching strategies.	1	2	3	4	5
Teachers experiment with new ideas they learned through teacher collaboration in their classrooms.	1	2	3	4	5
Teachers collaborate with each other after school hours.	1	2	3	4	5

Shared Values for the Education of ELs

The school community has established a common vision for the education of ELs.	1	2	3	4	5
EL student learning is the responsibility of all teachers.	1	2	3	4	5

Shared Values for the Education of ELs					
Formal and informal communication practices for the benefit of ELs have been established between faculty and staff members.	1	2	3	4	5
Parents of ELs and other community members have had formal opportunities to share their ideas and concerns about the education of ELs.	1	2	3	4	5
Teachers have had input in the decision-making process for the education of ELs.	1	2	3	4	5
School Support for Teacher Collaboration					
All teachers and staff members are perceived as valuable members of the school community.	1	2	3	4	5
Adequate time is provided for teachers and staff to meet and discuss EL issues.	1	2	3	4	5
Conversation protocols have been established to make optimum use of collaborative meeting time.	1	2	3	4	5
Teachers serve on committees to select new teachers, administrators, and other staff members.	1	2	3	4	5
Extracurricular activities are planned for faculty and staff to promote camaraderie and reduce isolation.	1	2	3	4	5
Shared School Practices					
Faculty and staff both individually and collectively reflect on their practices with ELs.	1	2	3	4	5
Teachers are able to determine their own professional-development needs with regard to ELs.	1	2	3	4	5
Parents of ELs are offered workshops on a regular basis throughout the school year.	1	2	3	4	5
Administrators participate in professional-development activities along with teachers.	1	2	3	4	5
Regularly scheduled collaborative team meetings are conducted by teachers to benefit the instruction of ELs.	1	2	3	4	5

Adapted from Roberts, S. M., & Pruitt, E. Z., (2009). *Schools as professional learning communities: Collaborative activities and strategies for professional development* (pp. 27–29). Thousand Oaks, CA: Corwin.

online resources — Available for download at resources.corwin.com/CollaboratingforELs

Table 8.8 Year at a Glance: Program Review-and-Assessment Meeting Agendas

Month	Key Agenda Item
September	Program Initiation, Goal Setting, Logistics
October	Partnerships and Implementation Needs
November	School Context
December	Strategies for Ongoing Collaboration
January	Administrative and Teacher Leadership
February	Professional-Development Practices
March	Resources
April	Teacher Evaluation/Satisfaction
May	Student Performance Data
June	Planning for Next Year

PROGRAM EVALUATION

Formal evaluations are often conducted by outside agencies or highly trained program evaluators working in specially designed district offices. Yet, looking at the impact of how your school or district serves ELs might begin with a collaborative examination of what works and what can be done to improve the services. Daniel Stufflebeam and Chris Coryn (2014) claim that evaluations must look beyond whether a particular program met its objectives and what the outcomes were. Instead, they also need to "examine a program's objectives, structure, and processes especially if the evaluation is to contribute to program improvement or adoption or adaptation by other service providers" (p. 7).

The American Evaluation Association (2018) suggests that educators observe the five essential principles presented in the following textbox when they conduct program evaluations.

Five Essential Principles of Evaluation

1. *Systematic Inquiry*: Evaluators conduct systematic, data-based inquiries.

2. *Competence*: Evaluators provide competent performance to stakeholders.

3. *Integrity*: Evaluators display honesty and integrity in their own behavior and attempt to ensure the honesty and integrity of the entire evaluation process.

4. *Respect for People*: Evaluators respect the security, dignity, and self-worth of respondents, program participants, clients, and other evaluation stakeholders.

5. *Common Good and Equity*: Evaluators work for the common good and help advance an equitable and just society.

Adapted from American Evaluation Association. (2018). *American Evaluation Association guiding principles for evaluators.* Washington, DC: Author. Retrieved from http://www.eval.org/p/cm/ld/fid=51

Figure 8.5	Meeting-Minutes Template (SNAPS)

Successes:

New approaches:

Appreciative comments:

Problems:

Solutions:

online resources   Available for download at resources.corwin.com/CollaboratingforELs

Essential Questions Aligned to the Five Evaluation Principles

We developed essential questions to consider for each principle of collaborative ELD/ELL program evaluation following the inquiry stance we established earlier in this book.

1. Systematic Inquiry

   a. What steps are we going to take to perform a useful evaluation?

2. Competence

   a. What skills and resources are needed to complete the program evaluation?

   b. How are we going to ensure that evaluators demonstrate not only all the necessary knowledge and skills but cross-cultural competence as well?

3. Integrity

   a. How are we going to ensure that the evaluation process yields valid and reliable information?

4. Respect for People

   a. Who will be affected by the evaluation process and how?

5. Common Good and Equity

   a. How will transparency be ensured?

   b. Who will be informed about the outcomes of the evaluation?

We encourage our readers to devote additional time and effort to respond to the guiding questions presented here while being aware of what Joellen Killion (2018) refers to as distinguishing between black-box and glass-box approaches to evaluation. Black boxes appear "when shortcomings occur either in the program design or in the evaluation" (p. 31), which indicates that there is insufficient information about how the program works. On the other hand, glass-box program designs or evaluations "reveal the transformative process that a program initiates" (p. 31). To measure the impact and effectiveness of a program, it is important to understand how the various components and activities interact with each other to yield the results. One way to achieve success with program evaluation is to begin with a theory of action plan according to Killion (2018), which includes the following key components:

1. The program resources or inputs;

2. The actions or strategies program designers plan to use to produce the results (theory of change);

3. The outputs each action produces, if any;

4. The outcomes of the actions, both short and long term;

5. The goal of the program; and

6. The context of the program. (pp. 60–61)

Another approach is to use the five guiding principles set by the American Evaluation Association, which may serve as the foundation for planning an evaluation. Roger Kaufman, Ingrid Guerra, and William Platt (2006) suggest a four-phase evaluation action plan, which we adapted to better respond to the context of ELD/ELL service delivery. In our adaptation, we matched each phase with an appropriate, broad purpose and aligned each purpose with three essential questions to guide educators in the process of planning a systematic program evaluation (see Table 8.9).

Select Tools to Use for Program Evaluation

Questionnaires and Surveys

Open-ended questionnaires allow program stakeholders, including students and their parents, to share their ideas (along with positive and negative experiences, needs, concerns, and problems) in

Table 8.9 Evaluation Plan for Collaborative ELD/ELL Services

Evaluation Plan	Alignment and Direction	Selection of Evaluation Methods	Results	Action and Adjustment
Purpose	To ask the right questions and to plan the evaluation process	To determine an approach for collecting valid and useful data	To compare what was accomplished with the program goals	To determine what to keep and what to change
Key questions related to collaborative ELD/ELL services	1. What collaborative practices have been implemented to meet our program goal? 2. What aspects and outcomes of our collaborative practices are we going to evaluate? 3. What are the desired outcomes?	1. What information are we going to collect? 2. What tools and instruments do we need to collect the data? 3. Who is going to collect what type of data? Where, when, and how?	1. Did the outcomes match our original goals and intentions? 2. What trends and patterns are observed in student achievement and teacher performance? 3. What factors contributed to the outcomes and how?	1. What steps should we take to improve our program? 2. What practices should we retain, adjust, or eliminate? 3. What are the intended and unintended outcomes of our collaborative practices?

Adapted from Kaufman, R., Guerra, I., & Platt, W. A. (2006). *Practical evaluation for educators: Finding what works and what doesn't* (p. 3). Thousand Oaks, CA: Corwin.

broad terms. As a follow-up, more structured questionnaires or surveys are often developed to focus on select concerns using multiple choice and true-or-false formats or three- to seven-point scales to solicit various degrees of agreement or disagreement with the statements. Such structured data gathering and evaluation tools guide respondents to address a limited number of purposefully included, critical items related to the ELD/ELL program.

Focus Group Discussions

Focus group discussions are also called group interviews and usually include eight to twelve teachers (or other stakeholders meeting in their own groups) who explore a predetermined set of questions that focuses on their shared experiences. Focus groups offer an effective format for gathering rich, authentic data about group members' perceptions of underlying issues and concerns as well as their actual and intended action. Student and parent focus group discussions may also yield valuable data about the services ELs receive.

Interviews

Interviews are usually defined as one-on-one (face-to-face or telephone) interactions between the evaluator and the interviewee. Individual interviews with representative members or randomly selected members of each constituency group offer further insights into the data collected through questionnaires, surveys, and focus group discussions.

Formal Observations

Observations planned for program evaluation purposes usually focus on (a) teacher activities in and outside the classroom, such as during professional-development settings or while participating in a range of collaborative practices and (b) student activities while engaged in learning in the classroom, extracurricular programs, or other interactions.

Student Progress and Achievement Data

To measure the impact a program or service delivery model has on student learning, it is wise to collect student data as well. Two types of student data may be considered valuable: One set of data will reveal student progress, and the other set will document student outcomes. Monitoring student growth in the areas of academic, linguistic, and literacy development allows the team to track short-term changes and whether or not students meet interim benchmarks. On the other hand, using multiple measures of student learning outcomes, including standardized assessment data, will reveal patterns of student achievement.

Vignette Revisited

In the chapter-opening vignette, we shared the Beaverton School District's journey under the leadership of Sarita Amaya. Here is what the district did to assess the outcomes of the three-year co-teaching initiative:

During the 2014–2015 school year, the state of Oregon replaced previous state tests in reading, writing, and math with the new Smarter Balanced assessments in English language arts and math. During the 2015–2016 school year, Oregon replaced the previous state test in English language proficiency with the new ELPA21 assessment that is aligned to current state standards. At the same time during the 2015–2016 school year, under the leadership of Administrator for Multilingual Programs, Toshiko Maurizio, the Beaverton School District Multilingual Department embarked on a three-year English learner program model evaluation and study. Our study provided detailed information about the effectiveness of the seven program models currently being implemented across the district, including the collaborative co-teaching model.

Education Northwest, in conjunction with the Beaverton School District Multilingual Department, conducted the data analysis and concluded that co-teaching has a positive impact on student learning. More specifically, when students only received co-teaching services implemented with fidelity (including co-planning and co-assessment), students performed higher on a range of literacy assessments (ELPA21 reading, writing, listening, and Smarter Balanced English language arts) when compared with students who also participated in pull-out and push-in services (defined as in-class instruction without collaborative planning).

ADMINISTRATORS' ROLE: LEADING EFFECTIVE ASSESSMENT PRACTICES

Reflection and Self-Assessment

Reflection and self-assessment tools not only are helpful for teachers but also will aid administrators in their quest for developing a method for ELD/ELL program evaluation. Inspired by Ronald F. Ferguson's (2006) work on effective staff development, we have designed the following self-assessment or reflection questions as a tool for administrators:

1. Did I introduce the concept of an integrated, collaborative ELD/ELL program in ways that foster trust (feelings of security) and interest?

2. Did I assign responsibilities to teachers and manage accountability for collaborative practices in ways to achieve a balance of leadership control and teacher autonomy?

3. Did I plan, initiate, and monitor implementation of the integrated, collaborative ELD/ELL program in ways that inspire ambitious goals and commitment?

4. Did I support ongoing implementation of the integrated, collaborative ELD/ELL program in ways that motivate sincere, continued commitment and hard work, despite setbacks and inevitable challenges?

5. Did I recognize, celebrate, and reward accomplishments in ways that sustain and strengthen positive changes?

Assessing the Level of Collaboration

Assessing the level of collaboration within a school or, more specifically, within an ELD/ELL program, may be challenging. Using the assessment tool presented in Figure 8.6 will allow

Figure 8.6 Assessing an Integrated, Collaborative Model to Serve ELs

Rate the following activities on a scale of 1 to 5, with *1* indicating that it never takes place and *5* indicating that it is a common practice.

1 = Never	2 = Rarely	3 = Sometimes	4 = Frequently	5 = Always or almost always

1. Interdisciplinary, cross-specialization conversations

   a. to discuss students' linguistic and academic development   1 2 3 4 5

   b. to consider ELs' changing curricular and instructional needs and appropriate adaptations   1 2 3 4 5

   c. to explore extracurricular opportunities for ELs   1 2 3 4 5

   d. to examine student work   1 2 3 4 5

   e. to enhance parental involvement   1 2 3 4 5

Other:

2. Common planning opportunity

   a. to compare and align lesson objectives   1 2 3 4 5

   b. to design or modify instructional materials   1 2 3 4 5

   c. to adapt instructional strategies   1 2 3 4 5

   d. to adapt curriculum   1 2 3 4 5

   e. to align curriculum   1 2 3 4 5

   f. to engage in curriculum mapping   1 2 3 4 5

Other:

3. Shared classroom experiences

   a. classroom visits to observe each other's best practices   1 2 3 4 5

   b. classroom visits to observe ELs' participation in various instructional settings   1 2 3 4 5

   c. classroom visits to peer coach (such as using the 2 + 2 model)   1 2 3 4 5

d. co-teaching to deliver instruction collaboratively	1	2	3	4	5

Other:

4. Reflection and inquiry

a. working in well-established teacher teams	1	2	3	4	5
b. participating in collegial circles	1	2	3	4	5
c. participating in teacher study groups	1	2	3	4	5
d. sharing professional readings (sharing literature on collaboration and ELD/ELL topics)	1	2	3	4	5
e. conducting collaborative action research	1	2	3	4	5
f. engaging in lesson study	1	2	3	4	5
g. offering internal staff development for colleagues (on collaboration and ELD/ELL topics)	1	2	3	4	5

Other:

5. Administrative support and feedback

a. offering instructional leadership (being knowledgeable about both ELD/ELL and collaborative practices)	1	2	3	4	5
b. establishing logistical support for all levels of collaboration	1	2	3	4	5
c. securing necessary materials and resources	1	2	3	4	5
d. offering ongoing professional-development opportunities that foster collaboration	1	2	3	4	5
e. creating a professional learning community	1	2	3	4	5

Other:

online resources 🔒 Available for download at resources.corwin.com/CollaboratingforELs

administrators to gain insight into the types of collaborative activities that take place or should take place. By closely examining the following key areas, they can maximize the effectiveness of ELD/ELL programs and can more fully address the linguistic, academic, and cultural needs of English language learners through collaboration.

1. Interdisciplinary, cross-specialization conversations
2. Common planning opportunity
3. Shared classroom experiences
4. Reflection and inquiry
5. Administrative support and feedback

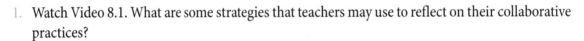

Summary

An effective collaborative ELD/ELL program model must have a carefully designed assessment component. A range of formal and informal approaches to assessment are available to support reflective, collaborative practices among ELD/ELL specialists and their general-education colleagues. The ultimate goals of assessment and reflection are to enhance the effectiveness of all teachers' classroom instruction and to ensure improved student achievement.

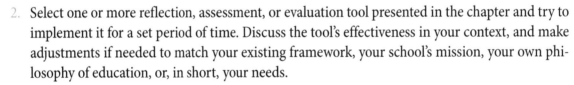

Discussion Questions

VIDEO 8.1

Reflection

http://www.resources
.corwin.com/
CollaboratingforELs

1. Watch Video 8.1. What are some strategies that teachers may use to reflect on their collaborative practices?

2. Select one or more reflection, assessment, or evaluation tool presented in the chapter and try to implement it for a set period of time. Discuss the tool's effectiveness in your context, and make adjustments if needed to match your existing framework, your school's mission, your own philosophy of education, or, in short, your needs.

3. Rebecca Gajda and Christopher Koliba (2008) offer systematic recommendations to administrators on improving teacher collaboration at the secondary level. Without any specific reference to English learners, they assert the importance of ensuring that teachers work in teams. Specifically, they describe high- and low-functioning teams this way:

> Teachers in high-functioning teams will systematically collect and analyze both quantitative information (such as summative test scores or tallies from observational checklists) and qualitative information (such as notes taken during a classroom observation of a colleague and student written work), whereas low-functioning teacher teams tend to rely on anecdotes, hearsay, and general recollections to inform their dialogue and decision-making. (p. 146)

Reflect on this quote and generate a list of quantitative and qualitative data sources—relevant to your teaching situation—that would be useful to inform your decision making about a collaborative ELD/ELL program.

4. Consider the following three levels of assessment. How would you collect relevant data for each of them to inform all stakeholders about the effectiveness of your collaborative ELD/ELL program model?

   - Teacher perception: What do teachers really think of collaborative practices? Do they value them? What do they gain from them?
   - Instructional practices: As a result of collaboration, do teachers enhance or change their teaching practices? Are their instructional strategies appropriate for ELs? Observations by the principal, peers, or interviews may be used to collect data.
   - Student learning: Does collaboration have an impact on ELs' language development and overall student learning?

Key Online Resources

American Evaluation Association (AEA home page with links to evaluation organizations, training programs, and Internet resources)

www.eval.org

ELL Program Road Maps: Collaborative Coteaching, Beaverton School District, Oregon

https://www.cosa.k12.or.us/sites/default/files/images/program_roadmaps_cc.pdf

Joint Committee on Standards for Educational Evaluation

www.jcsee.org

Learning Forward

www.learningforward.org

National Science Foundation, *User-Friendly Handbook for Project Evaluation*

www.nsf.gov/pubs/2002/nsf02057/start.htm

Self-Assessment Checklists From Scholastic

http://teacher.scholastic.com/professional/selfassessment/checklist/index.htm

Teaching Diverse Learners: Assessment (The Education Alliance at Brown University)

https://www.brown.edu/academics/education-alliance/teaching-diverse-learners/assessment

Web Center for Social Research Methods

www.socialresearchmethods.net

Portraits of Collaboration

None of us is as smart as all of us.

—Ken Blanchard

OVERVIEW

This chapter is unlike the previous eight you have just finished reading. Here we present seven new case studies that depict the context of collaboration, the key collaborative practices that take place in each case, what challenges the collaborating teachers have faced, and how they have overcome them to reach success. It is our hope that these case studies will help to bring together the many ideas, strategies, and approaches to collaboration and co-teaching presented in this volume in authentic contexts. The case studies include some parting thoughts (or words of wisdom) from the collaborating team and some of their teacher-created resources as well.

DISTRICTWIDE CASE STUDY

Who: The West Hempstead English as a New Language (ENL) Department is comprised of ten teachers who are certified in teaching English to speakers of other languages (TESOL) and at least one additional subject area. Under the leadership of Faith Tripp, we serve approximately two hundred active English language learners (ELLs) and eighty-five former ELLs in a district of just over two thousand students.

(Continued)

(Continued)

What: West Hempstead provides integrated ENL and stand-alone ENL services for students in Grades K–12 in both general-education and special-education classes.

Where: At the elementary level, we have stand-alone classes and a minimum of two integrated ENL classes per grade level that use the co-teaching model. At the secondary level, we provide sheltered content-area, integrated co-taught, and stand-alone ENL classes. We also have a students with interrupted formal education (SIFE) program in the high school that utilizes the Bridges to Academic Success curriculum.

When: Our ENL program is fully implemented five days per week. Elementary teachers have at least one common free period per six-day cycle as well as a shared professional period once per day. Secondary teachers do their best to meet during a common free time that may be a free period, study hall, or hall duty.

Why: We have found that the students experience the most academic and social-emotional success when they receive instruction consistently, every day. Elementary ENL teachers service one or two grade levels so that they can become experts at the curriculum and limit the number of co-teaching partnerships that must be nurtured. At the secondary level, the teachers concentrate on a particular content area that they hold additional certification in or are passionate about.

Context of Collaboration

West Hempstead has experienced a fairly significant change in demographics over the past decade. In the past five years, the number of ENL teachers in the district has doubled from five to ten. Over the past two years, the ENL teachers' schedules have changed significantly to create time for collaboration and allow for a greater balance of resources at the elementary and secondary levels. Five teachers now service one to two grade levels in the elementary schools, and five teachers focus on specific content areas in the secondary schools. There is a designated classroom in each building that serves as a shared space for the ENL teachers to collaborate with one another, access materials, and conduct their stand-alone classes. ENL teachers' schedules are carefully designed to include time for collaboration with their co-teachers, and partnerships are created with teacher input and honor requests whenever possible. We strive to maintain and support productive co-teaching teams by providing ongoing coaching sessions that occur during the school day and focus on best practices for working with ELLs in co-teaching settings. In addition, we provide professional development after school for the ENL teachers and their co-teachers that focus on using thinking routines (Ritchhart, Church, & Morrison, 2011) and project-based learning (Larmer, Mergendoller, & Boss, 2015) as scaffolds for ELLs. ENL teachers also attend monthly department meetings that provide an opportunity to collaborate with their ENL colleagues in the district. Finally, we manage a successful ENL Department Twitter page that serves as a professional learning network (PLN) where we connect with ENL educators across the country.

Collaborative Practices

In the past, the ENL Department was under the umbrella of the English Department and did not have an identity. Two years ago, the West Hempstead ENL Department became its own entity and the rest is history. We immediately began building a team that worked together, supported one another, and had a shared goal: the success of all students. We collectively got to work advocating for ourselves and for our students. It did not take long for our colleagues both in the district and those around New York to see the amazing things that were happening in the West Hempstead ENL Department.

In the 2016–2017 school year, the ENL Department participated in multiple professional-development sessions on the use of thinking routines. While their co-teachers were not mandated to attend these sessions, they were encouraged to do so in order to establish a common language and shared strategies that could be implemented to support ELLs in their classrooms. The ENL teachers immediately began to implement the strategies and protocols in their stand-alone classes, and the students' opportunities to read, write, speak, listen, and view began to grow, as did their confidence! As the ENL teachers became more adept at incorporating thinking routines into a variety of contexts, they suggested adding them to lessons in their integrated ENL classes. As the teams experimented with various thinking routines, the classroom teachers became excited at the heightened level of engagement and participation from both the ELL and non-ELL students. To celebrate the students' learning, the ENL teachers made it a habit to tweet examples of student work that highlighted thinking routines. Between lunchtime conversations, sharing examples of student work, and Tweeting, the success of thinking routines spread like wildfire and attendance at the after-school professional-development sessions increased. With the tremendous success of thinking routines for both collaboration and student learning, the ENL Department began to share their work by presenting at conferences such as NYS TESOL, Long Island ESOL, the Long Island Teachers' Institute, and NYSABE. Thinking routines have given our ELLs a voice. Classroom teachers are less intimidated by having ELLs in their class because they have a toolbox of strategies that they can use to engage all students in learning. Finally, the ENL teachers and ELL students are being recognized for the incredible work that they do and for the amazing contributions they make to the district.

The ENL Department has also led the way with using technology as a scaffold for learning. Some of our favorite resources include Twitter, Flipgrid, Buncee, Quizizz, RecapThat, and Kahoot! Once again, the ENL teachers incorporated these tools into their stand-alone classes and slowly introduced them to their co-teachers. As the collaborative relationships continue to grow, the teams are taking more risks and trying new things. The use of technology has also allowed the students' families to become better informed and more involved in their children's education.

In the 2017–2018 school year, we focused on project-based learning in the integrated classes. The ENL teachers and their co-teachers attended professional development on project-based learning that was presented by the coach working with the district. The after-school professional development was designed as an opportunity for teachers to explore and plan projects for their integrated classes. The teachers developed projects that incorporated thinking routines and technology. When the coach was visiting, she observed the PBL lessons and provided feedback and support. Aligning the after-school professional development with the coaching sessions proved to be a valuable experience for the teachers and the students.

Thinking routines, project-based learning, and technology have started a whole new conversation in the West Hempstead School District. The ENL teachers can often be found leading the integrated classes because of the level of trust that has developed between the partners. As a department, we are proud that our work has inspired a more collaborative culture across the district.

Challenges and Successes

We continually reflect on the successes and challenges we face, and we adjust our schedules and curriculum accordingly. One of our greatest successes has been incorporating Project Zero thinking routines into our stand-alone and integrated ENL classes. Reducing the number of co-teaching partnerships by clustering the students and narrowing the teachers' focus to specific grade levels or content areas have also led to positive outcomes. Nurturing successful co-teaching relationships by continuing the "marriages" has also been a great benefit to the teachers and the students. Providing coaching and after-school professional development to support the co-teaching teams has allowed teachers to take risks and grow as partners.

The challenges we face are not unlike other districts that are implementing integrated services for ELLs. Although schedules are designed to allow for some shared planning time, we still struggle with finding sufficient time to plan, assess, and reflect. Although classroom teachers are volunteering to teach the integrated ENL classes, there are still many "arranged marriages" across the district. Like many ENL directors, I wear many hats, and I rely on the ENL teachers to manage many of the day-to-day operations in their buildings. In the near future, I hope to have a bilingual guidance counselor at the high school who is tasked with working with the ELLs. I am very grateful for the professionalism and dedication of each member of the ENL team who graciously takes on the role of advocate, teacher, counselor, and friend to our students every day.

Words of Wisdom

This is cliché, but it is important to include all stakeholders in the decision-making process. Do your best to assign the ENL teachers to grade levels or content areas that they are passionate about, and limit the number of co-teachers they have to work with. When teachers volunteer to be partners, make it happen! Keep good teams together! Remember that it takes time and experience to grow and nurture strong collaborative relationships. Consider using a coach to support the co-teaching teams. Expand your PLN, and celebrate the amazing work of the teachers and students, by creating a department Twitter account. Finally, approach every situation, whether it involves teachers or students, with compassion, patience, and a sense of humor.

ELEMENTARY SCHOOL CASE STUDY #1

Who: Allyson Caudill, English as a second language (ESL) teacher; Ashley Blackley, first-grade teacher; John Cox, second-grade teacher

What: Co-teaching for English learners (ELs) in the general-education classroom

Where: Barwell Elementary School, Wake County Public Schools, Raleigh, NC

When: During the literacy block (approximately two hours per day in each classroom: 9:15–11:00 a.m. in John's second-grade classroom, 12:15–2:15 p.m. in Ashley's first-grade classroom)

Why: To us, best practice is not to remove language learners from the mainstream classroom, but instead to provide them the support they need to be successful within that environment. Our goal is to foster an environment where responsibility is shared and value for one another is high in order to advance our mutual cause: providing the best education possible for our students.

Context of Collaboration

We teach at Barwell Road Elementary, a preK–5 Title 1 school in Wake County Public School System (WCPSS). WCPSS is a huge school district, with 183 total schools and average student enrollment hovering around 160,000. It is the largest school system in the state of North Carolina and the fifteenth largest in the nation (as of 2016–2017). Barwell operates on a year-round calendar, which is 190 student days divided into four quarters with a break at the end of each quarter. With a little over 700 students, 175 of whom are identified as limited English proficient (LEP), our ESL population makes up about 25 percent of our student body. There are twenty-three languages represented, with Spanish being the most common home language.

For our purposes, ELs are intentionally grouped within Grades 1 and 2. Administrative support was key to cluster the ELs with emerging language skills with a handful of model native English-speaking students. The result is a class roster of roughly 50 percent ELLs, 25 percent native English-speaking model students, and 25 percent randomly selected. These rosters allow for highly targeted language instruction and support for the ELL population within the context of the mainstream classroom. This is in line with the district's revised vision of ESL instruction as a collaborative practice.

A unique aspect of our co-teaching dynamic is that Allyson (ESL), Ashley (first grade), and John (second grade) function as a triad. We plan, assess, and reflect together as a collaborative team. Allyson (ESL) serves Grades K–2, but co-teaching occurs only in Grades 1 and 2. Allyson (ESL) co-teaches daily with Ashley (first grade) and John (second grade). Both classes of students will come together at the end of a quarter to share in a reader's theater performance. Kindergarten and any comprehensive, or beginning level, English learners (ELs) have scheduled ESL class, in an isolated setting with Allyson (ESL). The foundation of both co-taught classrooms is parity. Our goal is to be seen as equals in the eyes of both our students and their parents.

Collaborative Practices

To maximize our co-teaching time and provide the most effective instruction for our students, we co-plan every lesson. Allyson (ESL) has dual ownership of every lesson with either Ashley (Grade 1) or John (Grade 2). Sometimes this means meeting before or after school or even on Sundays to unpack the standards, plan dynamic learning experiences, and ensure dual ownership of every lesson. This planning also helps instruction go uninterrupted even if unexpected events occur. Both teachers in the classroom have a clear, consistent understanding of the daily objectives, lesson activities, and assessment. To guarantee that time is not wasted, the team has developed a lesson plan format. The team approaches co-planning in a consistent order. First, the team reviews all standards and sets daily objectives. Next, the team develops an assessment that addresses the objectives and standards. Then lesson activities are selected that stem from the expectations of the assessment. The very last piece of the planning process is the selection of a co-teaching approach. The team makes it a priority not to stick with one approach, as the approach should meet the need of the lesson and the students.

The process of collaborating together as a team has changed what daily instruction looks like for Allyson (ESL), Ashley (first grade), and John (second grade). Allyson spends the entire literacy block (105–150 minutes depending on the day) with John in the morning and then the entire literacy block with Ashley in the afternoon. When Allyson arrives in both classes, instruction begins with a strong sense of urgency. The lesson has already been carefully planned as a team, and the lesson activities begin in a style that is unique to the pairing of Allyson and Ashley or Allyson and John. There is never a moment that having two teachers in the classroom is underutilized. If there is an interruption, the strong parity and intensive planning process ensures that instruction does not miss a beat. The team has found that the explicit language instruction and scaffolding with supports benefits all students in each classroom. Many students who are proficient with the English language, yet are below grade level on benchmark testing, rely on the supports to guide their thinking. As a result, Ashley and John have taken to using these supports outside of the reading block. Teaching content vocabulary using the strategies from the co-teaching block has become the new normal in their classrooms. Other teachers within the school have taken notice and frequently ask the team to share these strategies. Empowered by these requests, Allyson has begun offering after-school seminars on the use of the supports. Both classrooms in this triad have also been identified as model classrooms for the school district and have hosted educators from all over the district in their classrooms. Footage has been taken of each co-teaching team in action to be used for in-district training purposes and is the proof of how effective this team's instruction has become.

Taking time to reflect on what went well and what did not has become the most important practice for Allyson (ESL), Ashley (first grade), and John (second grade). A level of trust has developed between each team member to allow for candid conversations to occur. Each co-teacher feels comfortable bringing up concerns if a particular lesson did not go well, an assessment did not fit with the activities, or if an entire unit needs to be reworked. The knowledge that all three teachers are solely focused on what is best for the students is what drives daily instruction to evolve and improve. At times this can actually happen during instruction. If one member of the team feels it necessary, he or she can pivot the lesson in a way to ensure student comprehension and engagement. Frequently these moments yield dynamic debriefing conversations focused on the improvement of daily instruction.

Challenges and Successes

- **Challenge: Time**

    Finding time to co-plan, review student data, and reflect on student progress and our own effectiveness can be challenging. Not to mention, it's not just your time, you also have to work around another person's schedule. At first, this was a struggle and we often found ourselves underprepared. Last school year, it was not possible for us all to have mutual planning time built into the school day. So, to compensate, we met after school and on Sundays. Fortunately, after emphasizing the importance of common planning time and presenting end-of-year data (literacy growth percentages and state and district test results) showing the effectiveness of what we were doing, our administration allowed us to build in common planning time this year!

Challenge: Scheduling

Allyson (ESL) serves grade levels K–2 and approximately eighty students in the building. Therefore, every year it is a challenge to create a schedule ensuring she is serving all her students while also having two co-teaching blocks and common planning time. Not to mention, the schoolwide schedule (when each grade level has specials, recess, lunch, etc.) cannot be altered. Truly, it is like a puzzle. Often it will take multiple drafts and plenty of changes before the schedule is set. Each year, for the first few weeks of the school year at least, it is understood that there may be adjustments, and flexibility is key. However, the puzzle is worth it! Even the ELs not in the co-taught classes benefit from the knowledge Allyson gains from collaborating so closely with the classroom teachers. She is able to integrate more content into her scheduled ESL class(es) as well as prepare students better for what they might experience in those classes because she is always informed about what standards and skills are being taught, the routines and expectations, as well as the academic language needed to be successful at any given moment.

Success: Parity

We take pride in the parity we have established in our classrooms, and visitors often say, if they didn't already know, they wouldn't be able to tell which one of us was the classroom teacher and which one of us was the ESL teacher. Our students feel comfortable coming to either of us for anything. Equally as exciting is that the parents feel the same way. They might get a phone call from Allyson (ESL) or a Class Dojo message—an application used to privately communicate between parents, teachers, and students—sent home from the classroom teacher (John and/or Ashley). They treat us as equals and know what one says the other agrees. Both teachers are in our class pictures, and we even present awards at our academic awards assemblies as a team. It is Mr. Cox and Ms. Caudill's class and Mrs. Blackley and Ms. Caudill's class. Never one or the other.

We have also developed cross-classroom parity within our triad. Cross-classroom parity means we provide opportunities for both classes to get to know each other and the other teacher. The close collaboration between the three teachers and two classes fosters consistency and vertical alignment to the point where when Ashley and Allyson's first graders move up to John and Allyson's second-grade class, a lot of the routines and expectations are already in place. It is evident that the co-planning and sharing between the team allows for a smoother transition and increased opportunity for student success.

Success: Student growth

We keep detailed data on all of our students. These range from district test scores to performance on formative and summative assessments to quick exit tickets to anecdotal notes in small group. Through consistent collaborative practice and co-teaching, our students have shown exceptional growth! It is not uncommon for students in the co-taught setting to grow seven or eight reading levels in one year. We set our expectations high, and our students rise to the challenge!

Words of Wisdom

Change your vocabulary: With co-teaching, it is no longer YOUR classroom, and they are no longer YOUR students. If you truly want to make co-teaching work, you have no choice but to accept that as fact. Try saying this more often: OUR classroom, OUR students.

Communication: Don't be afraid to share your thoughts, feelings, and opinions with your co-teacher. Co-teaching is like a marriage, and it will fail if you do not create a safe environment for open communication. Make a deal never to get offended or upset but, instead, to always keep an open mind. There will be times you feel overwhelmed. Support each other. There will be times you disagree. Compromise. There will be times you feel upset, disappointed, or worried. Talk about it. Remember, you succeed and fail together.

Prove it's working: Administrative support can be difficult to obtain. Here is our advice: Come prepared and back it up with data. When you approach your administration about co-teaching, bring research from the field, proposed schedules, and a clear plan. We discovered they are much more likely to say yes if you bring a solid proposal and you show you have thought it through. Then, if you get the go-ahead, track everything. Bring them more data. Show them it's working by highlighting students' growth. Before you know it, they may just be inviting people to come see co-teaching in action!

Sample Materials

Sample Material #1: Co-Teaching Schedule

Caudill (ESL), Cox (Grade 2), Blackley (Grade 1)

2018–2019

Time	Type
9:15–11:00 W–F 9:15–11:45 T–Th	Co-teach in Grade 2 (Cox)
Co-Plan W–F 11:00–12:15 (Grade 1, Blackley) T–Th 11:45–1:00 (Grade 2, Cox)	
12:20–1:30 W–F 1:00–1:30 T–Th	Co-teach in Grade 1 (Blackley)
1:30–2:00	Scheduled ESL (K)
2:00–3:40	Co-teach in Grade 1 (Blackley)

Sample Material 2: Co-Teaching Meeting Agenda

I. 2018–2019 Co-Teaching Schedule
   A. For how long and at what times will the co-teaching blocks occur?
   B. Set consistent co-planning times

II. Meet the Teacher/Staggered Entry
   A. Info packets for families: Include info on co-teaching
   B. Welcome letters: Introduce both teachers, write and sign together
   C. Photo/video releases
   D. How will co-teachers split their time between classes?

III. Reflection
   A. What did we do well last year?
   B. What needs improvement?
   C. Analyze data: What does last year's data tell us, and how will we use it to inform our teaching this year?

IV. Collaborative Goal Setting
   A. Co-teaching goals
   B. Professional practice goals
   C. Student performance goals

Sample Material 3: Collaborative Goal Setting

1. Co-teaching (CT) goals
2. Professional practice (PP) goals
3. Student performance (SP) goals

Sample Goals

- This week we will try two new co-teaching approaches. (CT goal)
- This quarter we will work on trying to understand each other's perspectives more through active listening and clarifying questions. (CT goal)
- During the 2018–2019 school year, we will use "exit tickets" to assess student learning of daily lesson targets for each unit, provide immediate intervention for students who don't achieve learning targets and reassess student learning. (PP goal)

(Continued)

(Continued)

- By the end of the school year, at least 80 percent of our students will be reading on grade level (Level J) as measured by the mCLASS Text Reading Comprehension (TRC) assessment. (SP goal)

   Resources, videos, and more can be found on our blog at www.readysetcoteach.com. We are always updating and adding more!

ELEMENTARY SCHOOL CASE STUDY #2

Who: Nicole Fernandez (English as a new language [ENL] teacher) and Danielle Youngs (Grade 1 teacher)

What: All-day co-teaching integrated first- and second-grade classes

Where: Rocky Point Union Free School District (UFSD), Rocky Point, NY

When: Eight years of co-teaching

Why: Based on the success of an earlier pilot program of co-teaching for two periods a day, the team was given the opportunity to cluster students and expand co-teaching into an all-day partnership.

Context of Collaboration

As an ENL teacher at Rocky Point School District, I (Nicole) have been teaching there for about thirteen years. When Danielle and I first started to work together in a K–2 elementary school building, we only had a pull-out English as a second language (ESL) program. At that time, we had approximately twenty students in the school. Over the past fourteen years, our numbers have doubled to about forty students. Most of our English learners (ELs) are at the entering or emerging level when they start in kindergarten and often continue to receive services when they leave our school. When we first started, we found that no matter how much I talked to the classroom teachers and no matter how much I worked with the children, they were not making the progress that we hoped they would. There was always a disconnect between what the students knew and were able to do in the pull-out class compared with how they performed in the general-education classroom.

Collaborative Practices

Our more formal collaboration began in 2008, when I started pushing in to Danielle's second-grade classroom for one period each day. I intentionally say "pushing in" because we weren't co-teaching. I was just trying to help in the classroom and do what turned out to be a little bit more like homework help. From there it progressed to where I would contribute more to the lessons, such as reading aloud and discussing a story. Initially, we did not have common preparation time, so we faced lots of challenges with planning. We always knew what our goals and objectives would be, but we had to make a lot of on-the-spot decisions.

During the first couple of years, I would be only in Danielle's classroom for one or two periods a day, and, again, by the time I finished reading and discussing a story, my time in the classroom was over, and I had to leave. We didn't see enough progress from the students, so we knew we had to further change our collaborative practice. In the following year, we were given permission to cluster all the second-grade ELs into Danielle's classroom; we secured common planning time, and I was able to spend three periods a day with the students co-teaching reading, writing, and math. Our program became very successful as determined by the progress of all of our students.

Since 2017, I have been spending four to five periods in Danielle's classroom, and we truly co-teach all the core subject matters. In the classroom, we have about 50 percent ELs, but all the students (and their parents) can contact either of us. Both of our names are on the door, on the board, on letters home to parents, and on just about everything. Both of us support all of the students with schoolwork, homework, and learning strategies, and it really seems to be helping our ELs. To further strengthen our collaborative practice and to offer more continuous support to our ELs and their families, we have begun to loop from first to second grade in order to work with the same group of children for two years.

Successes and Challenges

We carefully document our students' language and academic development and share our success with our administrators every year to get board approval for continuing the co-teaching program. We have seen so much growth this current school year: We have five students who were at the entering level when they started; they were not communicating in English at all and did not have any literacy skills. By mid-year, they were talking and had become social and comfortable in the class; they knew their letters and were reading on Level A or almost Level B. They still lack more complex academic vocabulary, but they have the pieces that they need to be successful. We found that for our students it is all about building background, expanding their vocabulary, and embedding language into everything they do throughout the day. All activities that our ELs do are modified so they can learn alongside their peers.

It's not always easy. There are lots of challenges each year. We have to find something different to try to do with our kids, whether it be scheduling, prep time, planning, or just learning to work with students that are difficult to reach. Every year we work together it gets a little easier because we know each other better. At this point, the class can just flow even when I'm not there because it's set up in a way that our class works likes a machine. We have set routines, and our students understand what we expect them to do. The students have made more progress than we have ever seen before. Most have made more than one year's progress in literacy development, and they have increased their language proficiency level as well.

Words of Wisdom

Just keep at it. When you have two teachers in the room and one has the content background and the other understands that the academic language might not be understood, they can give two different kinds of lessons at the same time, and it is really helpful to meet all students' needs.

MIDDLE SCHOOL CASE STUDY #1

Who: Andrea Calabrese (English language learner [ELL] teacher) and Mike Garguilo, middle school science teacher

What: Seventh-grade science

Where: Sleepy Hollow Middle School, Public Schools of the Tarrytowns, Sleepy Hollow, NY

When: Since 2016–2017 school year

Why: To increase support for English learners (ELs) through project-based learning in a science classroom

Context of Collaboration

Mike and I co-teach one 45-minute period per day every day in a seventh-grade sheltered science class in Sleepy Hollow Middle School, which is in the Public Schools of the Tarrytowns, that serves approximately 2,900 students, 23 percent of whom are English learners. The dominant language of ELs is Spanish, which is seen as a strength of the district. Our district webpage (https://www.tufsd .org/domain/10) states:

> All elementary students will benefit from our Foreign Language in the Elementary Schools (FLES) program, which in its second year of implementation, provides Spanish language instruction to students in grades K–2 and will be expanding annually to include all K–5 students. Our long-standing and successful Dual Language Program is offered in grades K–4. In this program, classes are organized to contain equal proportions of native English and native Spanish speaking students. Fifty percent of the instruction is in English and fifty percent of the instruction is in Spanish to support the development of biliteracy in all students.

Our ELs receive a lot of support. Based on New York State regulations, they receive stand-alone English as a new language (ENL) classes, and a 90-minute English language arts (ELA) block, for 45 minutes of which the ELA teacher co-teaches with the English language development/English language learner (ELD/ELL) teacher. The students also have a bilingual math teacher and bilingual social studies teacher, and they also receive native language instruction.

In our co-taught class, we have eleven ELs with their English-speaking classmates, and we also have a bilingual paraprofessional. The curriculum is the same as in all the other seventh-grade science classes, but the delivery is different. Our district switched to taking the Regents Living Environment Examination in eighth grade the year before we started co-teaching, and we found that our ELs were not doing well on this New York State assessment. The plan was to offer additional support to ELs through co-teaching (and, if feasible, through summer school), and our students were doing much better on the assessments as a result of our work.

Collaborative Practices

Mike introduced project-based learning in his science class the year before we began to collaborate to make the content more accessible. Three years ago when we started to co-teach, my initial role was to help bridge the language gap. Even when the traditional curriculum was replaced with the project-based approach, our students continued to struggle with comprehending the science content and using academic language. My role was to help mitigate the learning of ELs and bridge that gap.

The entire seventh-grade science curriculum is laid out for the year in a shared folder on our school network. Mike uploads the science content, and I transfer it to a shared Google Drive where I work on adapting the material. We constantly communicate, send the lesson plans and adapted materials back and forth, and I often ask him: "Is this what you are saying?" to clarify the content. I am not a certified science teacher, so I try and get the essence of what the lesson is about and remove the obstacles to the language for ELs. Mike's study notes and materials are on grade level and very complex, so I add images or more white space to his materials; I color-code key words, if needed, and I also insert Spanish translations in a different color. I try to use cognates where possible and often create a storyboard out of the key concepts we teach to make the context in which the word is used more real.

We collaborate a lot virtually—via text messages, Google Docs, and e-mails. We meet face-to-face only on an *as-needed* basis because we have been teaching together for three years; we have fully developed a differentiated, project-based science curriculum, and we know each pretty well.

Challenges and Successes

At the beginning of our collaboration, we participated in a grant-funded program that supported us with resources and after-school planning time. Now we no longer get those hours, so it is a bit challenging. Because we are both experienced in our fields, we can plan without meeting with each other for three hours at a time.

Our biggest success is that the kids enjoy the class, one reason being that they are able to access concepts that they weren't able to before. My own success story is that now my co-teacher, Mike, is able to see that ELs can learn science through the methods we have been using together that make the content more approachable. He now is using the strategies that he learned from me in his other classes as well.

Words of Wisdom.   The biggest thing is communication. You need to be open and honest with each other. You need to be willing to point out to the other person what you see as the challenges, keeping in mind that it is not about hurting your partner's feelings. It's best to honestly reflect together about how students should be taught and the best ways to reach them. Some co-teachers don't say anything to each other because they want to avoid confrontation. That type of avoidance won't build relationships or improve teaching practice. Talk to each other and be willing to listen to figure out what is the best way to proceed. And remember, it is going to be a lot of work; it's not going to be just an extra ten minutes a day to modify your lessons. There is so much work that goes into co-teaching and making content comprehensible for ELs. That is why Mike and I are always texting or e-mailing one another, and why I am always working.

MIDDLE SCHOOL CASE STUDY #2

Who: Brittany Schmidt (English as a second language [ESL] teacher) and Ashley DeKoch (eighth-grade English language arts [ELA] teacher)

What: Co-teaching for English language learners (ELLs)

Where: Greenville Middle School, Hortonville Area School District, Greenville, WI

When: During the last literacy block of the day, 1:42–3:12 pm

Why: We believe co-teaching is best practice not only for ELL students. Our collaboration benefits instruction for all students, and also pushes our own teaching to new levels. We are more easily able to differentiate instruction for all levels of learners.

Context of Collaboration

Ashley and I co-teach eighth-grade ELA at Greenville Middle School, a Grade 5–8 middle school in the Hortonville Area School District, in Greenville, Wisconsin. This school district has a total of seven schools, including one charter school. Greenville Middle School had a total of 608 students for the 2017–2018 school year. There were 33 students identified as English learners this year at Greenville Middle School, and a total of 102 in the district. The majority of ELL students speak Spanish as their first language.

We began co-teaching last year when Ashley was teaching fifth grade. In our fifth-grade co-taught math class, ten out of our thirty students were identified as ELLs. We planned targeted learning stations based on the needs of our students, and we were extremely successful in raising our students' math scores. Ashley moved up to eighth-grade ELA this year, and because of the ELL needs in eighth grade for the 2017–2018 school year, we grouped the ELL students together in Ashley's last block of the day so that we could continue co-teaching. In addition to the five ELL students in our class, over 80 percent of our class was below grade level in reading, and many students required specific behavioral and learning plans.

Collaborative Practices

We have one set co-planning day a week for about 30 to 40 minutes when we look at lessons for the following week. This time usually consists of discussing what is planned for Ashley's first two blocks and determining what changes or modifications need to be made for our block. We also determine which co-teaching model will best meet all of the students' needs on a given day. The most utilized co-teaching model in our block is definitely team teaching—two teachers teach the same content to the whole class. We are very comfortable bouncing off of each other's thinking in order to provide clarification and comprehension during lessons. When we are not team teaching, we are parallel teaching; that is, Ashley and I each take a group, and we teach the same content or skills. We make these decisions based on what our students are coming in with and how prepared they are for the lesson. For ELA, there is obviously some reading that students need to do to participate in a lesson.

Due to the many needs in our block, there are days where only two or three students have done the assigned reading and are ready to continue with the next lesson. This is where flexibility comes into play. After determining the level of preparation for students, sometimes we split the class. Those who are prepared stay with one teacher and continue with the planned lesson, while the other half go with the other teacher to catch up with reading and do a modified lesson. Station teaching—where multiple groups of students work together to complete a task—is also a regular model in our class. It usually takes place after a team-taught mini-lesson. The following is an example of how we set up a lesson that begins with team teaching and then shifts into station teaching:

In the beginning of our persuasive writing unit, we focused on persuasive language. To introduce our lesson, we had our learning target and a video clip that showed U.S. propaganda about Japanese internment camps. Ashley introduced the video with some background information, and after the students viewed it, I shared what I noticed about the language being used while Ashley scribed. After we modeled how to pick out specific language, we showed a video of Ashton Kutcher accepting a Teen Choice award, and students discussed with partners what persuasive and engaging words and phrases he used.

After the mini-lesson, we introduced four different learning stations students would be rotating to during the remainder of the block. Two of the stations were teacher-led, one was group work, and the last was independent work using technology. The two teacher-led stations were purposeful: One focused on reading and the other on vocabulary. The variety of work at these stations provided students with higher-order thinking skills, collaboration, close-reading skills, technology integration, new vocabulary, and movement all in one lesson.

Something we have tried this year is modifying writing rubrics to reflect the English proficiency levels of our ELLs. All of our ELL students in our block are at a Level 3 for writing. Using the WIDA can-do descriptors and the WIDA writing rubric, we adapted writing rubrics for our informational and memoir writing units. We adapted the informational writing rubric designed by Lucy Calkins to use with ELLs (see Table 9.1).

Our relationship as co-teachers has grown so much, and we are at a comfortable place in terms of collaboration and execution of ideas. We have equal roles in our block and are both seen as ELA teachers.

Challenges and Successes

One challenge we face is the complex student needs in our block. There are many different needs we take into consideration when planning our lessons, which becomes overwhelming at times. There are days when the students leave after class, and we just need to take some deep breaths and remind ourselves that tomorrow is another day. Keeping all of the diverse needs in mind on a daily basis, however, has made both of us stronger teachers.

Another challenge we tackle is when academic struggles lead to behavior problems. There are many distractions that cause disruptions on a daily basis, which has pushed us to make our lessons as engaging as possible while also maintaining high expectations for all students. Because of all the scaffolding of instruction that we do, sometimes we feel we may be giving them extra support when it might not be needed. Students are comfortable in our classroom and are willing to share but at times become too dependent on our thinking and modeling.

Table 9.1 Rubric for Information Writing: Eighth-Grade ELL

STRUCTURE					
	Not yet	**Near Mastery**	**Mastery**	**Exceeds**	**Comments**
Overall	The writer conveyed ideas and information about a subject in a well-structured text.	The writer brought together ideas and information about a subject in a text that develops a subtopic and/or an idea.	The writer discussed key concepts within a topic and made it clear why these concepts are important. Provided examples with relevant information.	The writer discussed complex concepts, presenting information in an engaging manner. Used a variety of text structures and formatting.	
Lead	The writer wrote an introduction. Subtopics to be addressed may be missing.	The writer explained the topic's significance. Subtopics to be addressed are clear.	After hooking the reader, the writer provided context and introduced a focus/main idea.	The writer wrote an engaging lead that explained the topic's significance and mentioned key issues to be discussed.	
Transitions	Transitions are missing from the text.	The writer used some transitions to help connect ideas and information (using words such as *specifically, for instance, related to, just as, on the other hand, however*).	The writer used transitions throughout the text to link concepts with related information (using words such as *specifically, for instance, related to, just as, on the other hand, however*).	The writer used transitions to lead readers across parts of the text (using phrases such as *just as, returning to, as we saw earlier, similarly to, unlike*, and *yet*).	
Ending	The conclusion is missing final insights or implications for the reader to consider.	The writer wrote a conclusion in which he or she restated the important ideas and offered a final insight or implication for the reader to consider.	The writer reinforced and built on the main point(s) in a way that made the entire piece a cohesive whole. The conclusion may have restated the main points, responded to them, or highlighted their significance.	In the conclusion, the writer suggested implications, built up the significance of the main points, and/or alluded to potential challenges.	

STRUCTURE					
	Not yet	**Near Mastery**	**Mastery**	**Exceeds**	**Comments**
Organization	The writer chose a focused subject, but the subject does not continue throughout the writing. The writing lacks a logical order.	The writer focused on a subtopic or a particular point or two. The writer produced descriptive paragraphs centered around a central idea. The writer shows developing organization in the expression of an expanded idea.	The writer focused on key concepts within the topic. The writer produced descriptive paragraphs centered around a central idea. Concepts and examples were introduced in a logical fashion. The writer shows developing organization in the expression of an expanded idea.	The writer's organization structure introduced and layered key concepts and information. The writer described relationships between details or examples and supporting ideas. The writer shows an organized expression of ideas with emerging cohesion.	
DEVELOPMENT					
	Not Yet	**Near Mastery**	**Mastery**	**Exceeds**	**Comments**
Elaboration	The writer used one kind of information.	The writer used more than one kind of information. The writer used trusted sources and gave the sources credit. The writer worked to make information understandable and interesting.	The writer included varied kinds of information such as facts, quotations, examples, and definitions. The writer consistently incorporated and cited sources. The writer worked to make the topic compelling as well as understandable.	The writer brought out the parts of the topic that were most significant to the audience. The writer analyzed the relevance of information and made sure the information supported the major concepts. The writer incorporated trustworthy and significant sources.	

(Continued)

Table 9.1   (Continued)

DEVELOPMENT					
	Not Yet	**Near Mastery**	**Mastery**	**Exceeds**	**Comments**
Craft	The writer is missing concrete details, comparisons, and/or images to explain information and keep the reader engaged. General vocabulary is used when more specific language is needed.	The writer supported readers' learning by using a teaching tone and a formal style, as appropriate. Possible usage of general vocabulary where more specific language is needed. The writer used concrete details, comparisons, and/or images to explain information.	The writer used words purposefully to affect meaning and tone. The writer's vocabulary usage attempts to fulfill the writing purpose. The writer used metaphors, anecdotes, images, or comparisons.	The writer intended to affect the reader in different ways and chose language to do that. The writer varied the tone to match different purposes of the different sections. The writer's vocabulary usage generally fulfills the writing purpose.	
CONVENTIONS					
	Not Yet	**Near Mastery**	**Mastery**	**Exceeds**	**Comments**
Spelling, Punctuation, and Sentence Structure	Possible use of some conventions. Comprehensibility is impeded by errors.	The writer uses repetitive sentence and phrasal patterns and grammatical structures used in social and instructional situations or across content areas. The writer demonstrates a variable use of conventions.	The writer uses a developing range of sentence patterns and grammatical structures common to content areas. The writer demonstrates a developing use of conventions to convey meaning.	The writer uses a range of sentence patterns and grammatical structures characteristic of the content areas. The writer demonstrates generally consistent use of conventions to convey meaning.	

Our greatest success has grown out of a challenge we faced. Our co-taught lessons are highly engaging. We plan all of our lessons out in great detail, equipped with video clips, differentiation, groupings, stations, and enrichment ideas. There is never a "boring" or "typical" day in our classroom. This variety of instructional strategies keeps students on their toes and interested in what each day will bring. Here is an example of how we use video clips to enhance our learning target:

During our narrative nonfiction unit, students were to infer how setting affects characters. To introduce this thinking, we showed two different movie trailers, *Boy in the Striped Pajamas* (Heyman, 2008) and *Everest* (Kormákur, 2015). We included some guiding questions to push students' thinking about the setting further than the obvious.

Boy in the Striped Pajamas

- What do you notice about Bruno's emotions when he is at home in the beginning?
- How do his emotions change when he gets to his new home?
- How does the setting affect Bruno and Shmuel's friendship?

Everest

- How does the setting challenge the characters?
- How does the setting prove that teamwork is important?

After discussions about the movie trailers, we transferred that thinking to reading by modeling using our read-aloud mentor text, *How They Choked: Failures, Flops, and Flaws of the Awfully Famous* (Bragg, 2016). Ashley modeled an inference that would be at mastery level, and I modeled an inference that would show what exceeding mastery would like so that students were clear on what they needed to include.

Another big part of engagement being such a success in our classroom is the fluidness of our co-teaching roles. We are able to model much more effectively what mastery looks like and what they need to be able to do. We have also documented the percentage of our students who met or exceeded mastery on a number of essential standards by the end of the year (see Table 9.2).

Words of Wisdom

Be flexible! No matter how much you plan, you need to meet your students where they are. If they are not ready for what you have planned, you need to be able to adapt the lesson to their needs. Also be flexible in the models you choose to use on a given day. If team teaching isn't going so well, change it right there in the moment. If both teachers are confident in that change, students will be as well. For example, we were reading the book *Unwind* (Shusterman, 2009) as a whole class during our dystopian unit. One day, we began making characterization maps of two of the main characters. At the end of class, we told students they needed to have read the next chapter for tomorrow before our lesson on point of view. The following day, only four of our sixteen students were caught up with the reading. I took those four students into my room and continued with the planned lesson, while Ashley read aloud to the rest of the class, catching them up, and modeling how to post direct

Table 9.2 English Learners' Year-End Progress: Select Standards

Standard	Percentage of Students at Mastery or Exceeding
RI.8.1: Cite the textual evidence that most strongly supports an analysis of what the text says explicitly as well as inferences drawn from the text.	88
RI.8.2: Determine a central idea of a text and analyze its development over the course of the text, including its relationship to supporting ideas; provide an objective summary of the text.	93
RL.8.2: Determine a theme or central idea of a text and analyze its development over the course of the text, including its relationship to characters, setting, and plot; provide an objective summary of the text.	81
W.8.7: Conduct short research projects to answer a question (including a self-generated question), drawing on several sources and generating additional related, focused questions that allow for multiple avenues of exploration.	93
W.8.8: Gather relevant information from multiple print and digital sources, using search terms effectively; assess the credibility and accuracy of each source; quote or paraphrase the data and conclusions of others while avoiding plagiarism and following a standard format for citation.	88
RI.8.8: Delineate and evaluate the argument and specific claims in a text, assessing whether the reasoning is sound and the evidence is relevant and sufficient; recognize when irrelevant evidence is introduced.	88
W.8.1: Write arguments to support claims with clear reasons and relevant evidence.	81
SL.8.4: Present claims and findings, emphasizing salient points in a focused, coherent manner with relevant evidence, sound valid reasoning, and well-chosen details; use appropriate eye contact, adequate volume, and clear pronunciation.	88

Note: Students not at mastery have all moved from "Not Yet" on the preassessment to "Near Mastery," and we continue to work with these students at Extended Learning Time and/or during class to get to mastery.

and indirect character traits. By the end of the day, all students were where they needed to be, and we were ready to move on. Flexibility is key to meeting student needs.

You both need to be excited about and 100 percent on board with co-teaching. Students will notice if one teacher isn't giving 100 percent. If that excitement is not there from the start, your co-teaching partnership will not be successful. This blog post about preparing for honeymoon phase of co-teaching and beyond (https://oscarworthyteaching.wordpress.com/2018/04/06/the-co-teaching-act/).

Keep an open mind. You now have two experts in the classroom. Your co-teacher will have great ideas that you haven't thought of, and vice versa. Be open to suggestions and new ideas! Some of them may take you outside of your comfort zone, but that is usually what sparks the most successful lessons. An example of this would be when we were struggling to get students to think more deeply about theme. I went to Ashley with the idea of trying a Socratic seminar with two different texts but the same universal questions for both groups. Although Ashley was a little hesitant and not familiar with the strategy, she agreed to give it a try. With the right scaffolds and supports, student dialogue exceeded our expectations, and students proved to themselves they could think deeper about theme.

Our universal questions included the following:

- What important theme does this literary work convey?
- What do the characters do or say to help illustrate the theme?
- How does the setting help determine the theme?
- What events take place to help illustrate the theme?

HIGH SCHOOL CASE STUDY #1

Who: Rachel Ogimachi (English language learner [ELL] and English language arts [ELA] teacher) and Patricia Beltran (ninth-grade ELA teacher); their success story documented by Thad Williams, Multilingual Curriculum Developer

What: Ninth-grade English language arts

Where: Sammamish High School, Bellevue School District, Bellevue, WA

When: 2016–2017 and 2017–2018 school years

Why: To increase support for emergent bilingual students in an inclusive environment and develop teacher capacity to teach emergent bilingual students in general-education English language arts

Context of Collaboration

Sammamish High School is a Grade 9–12 neighborhood school with approximately 1,121 students representing over forty-six different languages. Sammamish High School is located in the Bellevue School District, a large and diverse suburb on the east side of Seattle, Washington. The school has a diverse ELL population of about 116 students, including students from many countries in Asia, Central America, Mexico, and parts of Europe. The ELL population consists of students with interrupted formal education backgrounds, students new to English, and students with differing levels of literacy in their first language and developing English language and literacy. Sammamish High is a diverse and innovative school, with administrators and teachers who have grown the focus on co-teaching and collaboration as a way to support all students in learning and develop teachers' skills in teaching all students, specifically ELLs. One example of this is the increase in co-teaching partnerships across all content areas. A second example is how administrators align the master schedule to create common planning periods and provide opportunities for teachers to collaborate during one of their two planning-periods.

In this co-teaching partnership, Rachel co-teaches one ninth-grade ELA class with Patricia, and each teaches the same curriculum in a ninth-grade ELA class that is not co-taught. Both teachers draw heavily on the curriculum that Patricia developed for the other four sections of ninth-grade ELA. They utilize co-planning to support both the class they teach together and the classes they are teaching individually. Rachel and Patricia's classes are comprised of ninth-grade general-education, special-education, and ELL students. The ELL population they teach can be further broken down into the proficiency-level designations of newcomer, beginner, intermediate, advanced, recently transitioned, and bilingual students. A few students are dual-qualified in special education and ELL. Rachel is in her seventh year of teaching, and Patricia is in her twentieth year of teaching. As the multilingual curriculum developer, I support both teachers in curriculum development, adaptations, instructional coaching, and co-teaching.

Collaborative Practices

Rachel and Patricia engage in formal collaborative practices as well as many informal practices. Rachel and Patricia initially committed to meeting once a week on a common planning period. They realized this was not enough time, so they agreed to meet twice a week during their common planning period. During this time Rachel and Patricia engage in the following practices to foster collaboration and growth, as well as to focus on student needs and learning:

1. Talk through how past units worked and the needs for specific scaffolds based on the language demands, standards, or content skills being developed. They refer to this process as *mapping* and engage in it as one way to align student language development with English Language Proficiency (ELP) Standards (see Mapping Tool in textbox).

2. Look at student work together and discuss as a way to stay student-centered and to inform their thinking about where students are and need to be and areas for scaffolds or increased expectations.

Additional strengths that both teachers bring to the teaching context are a background in English language arts and multiple years of teaching experience. Additionally, Rachel is ELL endorsed and contributes this perspective and expertise to the co-teaching partnership. As Rachel puts it, "Co-teaching is really about melding our mainstream teaching styles together with all student needs in mind . . . One powerful practice has been seeing how we each create and use scaffolds in practice during class time." This observation gives them something to reflect on, process the student growth or lack thereof, and then make plans for the next steps in supporting student learning. This co-teaching partnership and the chance to co-plan creates more bandwidth as well. It allows them to create more scaffolded reading experiences for the variety of texts they use, differentiate for beginner ELLs, and still work as a team during the instructional time to monitor and draw all students into participation and learning.

Collaboration for the sake of ELLs in this partnership focuses on three specific areas: (a) teacher–student and student–student relationship building, (b) developing language scaffolds, and (c) formative assessment. The opportunity to have two teachers in the same physical classroom space is a tremendous benefit, but without clear areas of focus, roles, and purpose, it can become a challenge. In their first year of partnering as co-teachers, Rachel and Patricia found that focusing on these three areas gave them the chance to team-teach and provide a challenging yet supportive environment for students at different places in their language and content skill development. Both teachers operate from a pedagogical stance that embraces culturally responsive teaching, specifically the "Four R's" (relationships, rigor, relevance, realness; Hammond, 2015). Collaborating for the sake of ELLs embraces the importance of relationship-building with students, which in turn creates trust, a low-affective environment, and students' willingness to take risks in using language. Rachel and Patricia also spend much of their time during co-planning and during the actual class time developing language scaffolds. This includes, but is not limited to, developing scaffolded reading experiences and texts, writing prompts and sentence frames, and a variety of structured talk activities that give students multiple opportunities and partners to practice speaking and listening. The third area is formative assessment. Rachel described it as "checking in and assessing where students are and need to be." This is a collaborative practice that they plan and design for in some lessons. In other lessons, the "checking-in" happens between one of the teachers and students, and they do this by prompting about student work, progress, and goal setting. Rachel summed up her reflection on collaborative practices by saying, "It is personally and professionally refreshing to feel like you have a partner in what you are trying to do."

Challenges and Successes

One of the biggest challenges that Rachel and Patricia face in their co-teaching partnership is navigating decision making. Rachel shared that "the process of giving up autonomy of having your 'own' classroom is challenging." This stemmed from Rachel and Patricia trying to cultivate a strong partnership, working relationship, and team, yet also trying to figure out how and when to push for an instructional decision, scaffold, or strategy that one felt like she would do if in her individual classroom. One example of this was around the use of daily warm-ups as a writing routine and how much time to spend on this activity. Something like this can easily drive a wedge in the partnership, so it must be discussed openly and regularly and with the students at the center of the conversation. With regard to this example, Rachel shared, "I realized it was an important part of class for her," so it was a place to start by acknowledging the value it had for one partner and then moving to discuss its purpose and having flexibility for the sake of students and objectives of the lesson.

An additional challenge that Patricia and Rachel have experienced in their first year is managing how students perceived their roles as co-teachers. Although being aware of a few ways to overcome this challenge—such as using specific co-teaching models consistently, making physical changes such as having both names listed on the door and in the online gradebook, and creating shared and equal teacher work space—they have struggled to accomplish these things, and it has left their roles unclear to students at times.

The successes from this partnership are many. Rachel shared that the opportunity to work so closely with another colleague is personally and professionally enriching. They also shared that the real successes are about the benefits to the English learners and the progress they have seen students make. These benefits ranged from the social dynamics of the class, increased language arts skills and general language development, stronger peer models, increased attention from two teachers, and the ability to offer two or three check-ins per class period with the beginner-level students and other students as needed.

Words of Wisdom

As a team working as co-teachers and curriculum partners, we learned it is easy to get overwhelmed at the secondary level in a co-teaching partnership because of pacing expectations, curriculum demands, and a wide range of student needs. Remember that it is a multiyear process. The second year will look a lot different and hopefully feel a lot better. Give yourself and your partner grace in the first year. Each co-teaching partnership will likely be different, so be proactive about checking in with how each other is feeling about the partnership and the classroom. It is always okay to find or make time and ask: "How are you feeling about this?" "Here is what I was thinking and why I did that. What do you think?" We focus on relationships with students a lot. It is important to focus on relationships with our co-teaching partners, too!

Sample Material

Mapping Tool

Content Area _____ Freshman Composition _____ Grade Level _____ 9 _____

Practice: EP1 – Support a range of analysis of grade-level complex texts

What ELP standard(s) did it bring you to? ELP Standard 6: Analyze and critique the arguments of others orally and in writing.
    Summarize the language behaviors at Language Proficiency Levels 1, 3, and 5.

Level 1	Level 3	Level 5
Identify a point an author or a speaker makes. Student might do this by pointing, underlining, or highlighting.	Identify the main argument an author or speaker makes. Identify one reason an author or a speaker gives to support the argument. Cite textual evidence. Student might do this by rephrasing the argument and reason or writing it out with or without the support of sentence frames.	Analyze and evaluate the reasoning and use of rhetoric in persuasive texts. Cite specific textual evidence to support the analysis. Student might do this in an academic classroom conversation, in a writing response, or by analyzing multiple text and writing examples.

HIGH SCHOOL CASE STUDY #2

Who: The English as a new language (ENL) teachers of West Hempstead High School. There are four of us—Madeline Valencia, Lisa McCarthy, Lili Ferguson, and me (Nick DiBenedetto). Our department chair, Faith Tripp, is also the principal at one of our elementary schools (see Elementary Case Study #1).

> *What:* We share English language development/English language learner (ELD/ELL) resources with one another, collaborate in the creation of mini-units, and assist one another in preparing materials for our content classes. Finally, we discuss specific students and support each other on a regular basis.
>
> *Where:* West Hempstead High School, West Hempstead, NY
>
> *When:* We collaborate to some degree daily and weekly. All of this collaboration is informal.
>
> *Why:* Our department at the high school works together to share best practices and provide the best instruction possible for our students.

Context of Collaboration

The West Hempstead High School population is 43 percent White, 29 percent Hispanic, 29 percent Black, and 7 percent Asian. 38 percent of the population is considered low-income. The ELL population has grown significantly over the past few years, and there are about fifty-nine ENL students at the high school. We also have eleven monitored students and fifteen students that are declassified as ELLs. The high school as a whole has around six hundred students. We have four ENL teachers at the high school. Our department chair works in a different building, so teachers and administrators often come to us for assistance with matters concerning our ELL population.

Collaborative Practices

This year is the first year that we have had four ENL teachers at the high school level. Each of us for the most part co-teaches in classes where we are either certified in that content area or have a passion. Madeline works with our science teachers and students, Lili works with our English teachers and students, Lisa works with our math students and teachers, and I work with our social studies teachers and students. When students come for extra help, the students have a good understanding of who is going to best be able to assist them with their content needs.

In addition to having specific contents that we usually work with, all of us teach stand-alone classes, and we do our best to use similar mini-units where it is appropriate. Basic concepts in the units are the same, and we then modify them to work with the English language proficiency levels that we are working with. Typically, we sit down as a group once every two weeks and discuss what we are doing with our stand-alone classes. We then pool our resources and create shared Google folders that all of us can access and edit. This makes it easy for us to modify the resources to make them appropriate for our teaching styles and groups of students.

We also sit down as a group to discuss student placement when there are concerns about particular students and their schedules. Three out of the four of us use the same room as a "home base," making all of this collaboration a little bit easier. We use this room for extra help, and it contains resources for all of the content areas. In this sense, our students do not have to go looking around for assistance, as they know that they can find at least one of us in that room at any given time.

Challenges and Successes

One of the most successful aspects of collaboration within our department is our ability to share our ideas with other teachers. As a department, following the district's initiative, we have been using thinking routines in our own classrooms, and other teachers have started using them after they have seen us posting about them on social media. We are also successful at collaborating with people in our own department; we share lessons, ideas, and generally are very supportive of one another. We have all made an effort to maintain a professional learning network on Twitter, and this further helps us by allowing us to not only share our own ideas but also reach out for assistance from other professionals in our field of work.

Although we have a great deal of success within our department, it is often difficult to collaborate with teachers who are outside of our department. Whereas some teachers are open to implementing some strategies that we use as a department, others are reluctant to do things differently. That being said, as a group we continue to be supportive of one another, and when we are having difficulties working with co-teachers, we always have someone who is willing to listen and provide feedback and advice.

Words of Wisdom

1. Be an advocate for your students; they often do not feel comfortable standing up for themselves, and it is often the job of an ENL department to be the voice of these students. In a sense, we are often playing roles as surrogate parents, and we should take that responsibility seriously and approach all topics with a sense of compassion.

2. Develop relationships with students; we have found that our students are relationship driven. They respond well to teachers who show that they care. On any given day, someone walking into any of our rooms will notice that our classroom environments are extremely nurturing.

3. Learn about your students; we have taken the time to learn about our students' countries of origin. Students are almost always surprised when a teacher takes the time to learn about what makes their country unique. We take time out of our instruction to ask questions and learn things that will continue to make us better educators.

Summary

Though the seven case studies we introduced in this chapter represent a range of collaborative practices, they demonstrate a shared commitment and passion for working with others to create more effective and equitable learning opportunities for English language learners. The experiences and contexts in which the teachers' daily instructional and collaborative practices take place vary greatly. Each story is unique, yet many of the challenges and the successful outcomes are similar. We hope the words of wisdom they offered help everyone who reads them.

Discussion Questions

1. After watching Video 9.1, ask yourself how schools might collect their own data in cooperation with teams who collaborate and co-teach

2. Compare the context of collaboration in select case studies to your own context. Which of the seven situations is most like your own?

3. Select one of the seven case studies for closer analysis. What are two examples of collaboration that most intrigued you? What are at least two possible ways the collaborative practices could be further enhanced?

4. Examine the case studies from an administrative point of view. What role did the school administrator play to make the collaboration work? What could the administrator plan as viable next steps to further enhance collaboration?

5. Develop a case study of your own by interviewing a colleague or documenting your own practice. Turn the four case study headings—context of collaboration, collaborative practices, challenges and successes, and words of wisdom—into interview questions.

VIDEO 9.1

Case Studies

http://www.resources
.corwin.com/
CollaboratingforELs

References

Airasian, P. W., & Gullickson, A. (1994). Examination of teacher self-assessment. *Journal of Personnel Evaluation in Education, 8*, 195–203.

Allen, D. W., & LeBlanc, A. C. (2005). *Collaborative peer coaching that improves instruction: The 2 + 2 performance appraisal model.* Thousand Oaks, CA: Corwin.

American Evaluation Association. (2018). *American Evaluation Association guiding principles for evaluators.* Washington, DC: Author. Retrieved from http://www.eval.org/p/cm/ld/fid=51

ASCD. (2014). *Whole child, whole school, whole community.* Retrieved from http://www.ascd.org/ASCD/pdf/siteASCD/publications/wholechild/wscc-a-collaborative-approach.pdf

Bauscher, R., & Poe, E. M. (2018). *Educational facilities: Planning, modernization, and management* (5th ed.). Latham, MD: Rowman & Littlefield.

Beninghof, A. M. (2012). *Co-teaching that works: Structures and strategies for maximizing student learning.* San Francisco, CA: Jossey-Bass.

Beninghof, A., & Leensvaart, M. (2016). Co-teaching to support ELLs. *Educational Leadership, 73*(5), 70–73.

Berger, J. G., Boles, K. C., & Troen, V. (2005). Teacher research and school change: Paradoxes, problems, and possibilities. *Teaching and Teacher Education, 21*, 93–105.

Blase, J., & Kirby, P. C. (2009). *Bringing out the best in teachers: What effective principals do* (3rd ed.). Thousand Oaks, CA: Corwin.

Blythe, T., Allen, D., & Schieffelin Powell, B. (2015). *Looking together at student work* (3rd ed.). New York, NY: Teachers College Press.

Borden, L. M., & Perkins, D. F. (1999). Assessing your collaboration: A self-evaluation tool. *Journal of Extension, 37*(2). Retrieved from http://www.joe.org/joe/1999april/tt1.php

Boyle-Baise, M., & Sleeter, C. E. (1996). Field experiences: Planting seeds and pulling weeds. In C. A. Grant & M. L. Gomez (Eds.), *Making schooling multicultural: Campus and classroom* (pp. 371–388). Englewood Cliffs, NJ: Merrill/Prentice Hall.

Bragg, G. (2016). *How they choked: Failures, flops, and flaws of the awfully famous.* New York, NY: Bloomsbury.

Brookfield, S. (2017). *Becoming a critically reflective teacher* (2nd ed.). San Francisco, CA: Jossey-Bass.

Calderón, M. E., & Slakk, S. (2018). *Teaching reading to English learners, Grades 6–12* (2nd ed.). Thousand Oaks, CA: Corwin.

Cohan, A., & Honigsfeld, A. (2006). Incorporating "lesson study" in teacher preparation. *Educational Forum, 71*(1), 84–93.

Collier, V. P., & Thomas, W. P. (2002). Reforming education policies for English learners means better schools for all. *State Education Standard, 3*(1), 30–36.

Collier, V. P., & Thomas, W. P. (2007). Predicting second language academic success in English using the prism model. In C. Davison & J. Cummins (Eds.), *International handbook of English language teaching* (Part 1, pp. 333–348). New York, NY: Springer.

Colton, A., Langer, G., & Gott, L. (2016). *Collaborative analysis of student learning: Professional learning that promotes success for all.* Thousand Oaks, CA: Corwin.

Conderman, G., Bresnahan, V., & Pedersen, T. (2009). *Purposeful co-teaching: Real cases and effective strategies.* Thousand Oaks, CA: Corwin.

Crawford, J. (2008). *Advocating for English learners: Selected essays.* Clevedon, UK: Multilingual Matters.

Csikszentmihalyi, M. (1990). *Flow: The psychology of optimal experience.* New York, NY: Harper & Row.

Cummins, J. (2001). *Negotiating identities: Education for empowerment for a diverse society.* Los Angeles: California Association for Bilingual Education.

Danielson, D. F. (2016). *Talk about teaching! Leading professional conversations* (2nd ed.). Thousand Oaks, CA: Corwin.

Darling-Hammond, L. (2010). America's commitment to equity will determine our future. *Phi Delta Kappan, 91*(4), 8–14.

Darling-Hammond, L., & Burns, D. (2014, December). *Teaching around the world: What can TALIS tell us.* Retrieved from https://edpolicy.stanford.edu/library/publications/1295

Davison, C. (2006). Collaboration between ESL and content area teachers: How do we know when we are doing it right? *International Journal of Bilingual Education and Bilingualism, 9*(4), 454–475.

Deal, T. E., & Peterson, K. D. (1999). *Shaping school culture: The heart of leadership.* San Francisco, CA: Jossey-Bass.

DeFlaminis, J., Abdul-Jabar, M., & Yoak, E. (2016). *Distributed leadership in schools: A practical guide for learning and improvement.* New York, NY: Routledge.

DelliCarpini, M. (2008). Teacher collaboration for ESL/EFL academic success. *Internet TESL Journal, 14*(8). Retrieved from http://iteslj.org/Techniques/DelliCarpini-TeacherCollaboration.html

DelliCarpini, M. (2009, May). Dialogues across disciplines: Preparing English-as-a-second-language teachers for interdisciplinary collaboration. *Current Issues in Education* (Online), *11*(2). Retrieved from http://cie.ed.asu.edu/volume11/number2/

Dewey, J. (1933). *How we think: A restatement of the relation of reflecting teaching to the educative process.* Boston, MA: D. C. Heath.

Dewey, J. (1938). *Experience and education.* New York, NY: Macmillan.

Donohoo, J. (2013). *Collaborative inquiry for educators: A facilitator's guide to school improvement.* Thousand Oaks, CA: Corwin.

Donohoo, J., & Velasco, M. (2016). *The transformative power of collaborative inquiry: Realizing change in schools and classrooms.* Thousand Oaks, CA: Corwin.

Dove, M. G., & Honigsfeld, A. (2018). *Co-teaching for English learners: A guide to collaborative planning, instruction, assessment, and reflection.* Thousand Oaks, CA: Corwin.

DuFour, R. (2005). What is a professional learning community? In R. DuFour, R. Eaker, & R. DuFour (Eds.), *On common ground: The power of professional learning communities* (pp. 31–43). Bloomington, IN: Solution Tree Press.

DuFour, R., DuFour, R., Eaker, R., & Many, T. W. (2016). *Learning by doing: A handbook for professional learning communities at work* (3rd ed.). Bloomington, IN: Solution Tree Press.

Earthman, G. (2013). *Planning educational facilities: What educators need to know* (4th ed.). Latham, MD: Rowman & Littlefield.

Easton, L. B. (2009, February/March). Protocols: A facilitator's best friend. *Tools for Schools, 12*(3), 6.

Echevarria, J., Vogt, M. E., & Short, D. (2016). *Making content comprehensible for English learners: The SIOP model* (5th ed.). Upper Saddle River, NJ: Pearson.

Eells, R. J. (2011). *Meta-analysis of the relationship between collective teacher efficacy and student achievement* (Doctoral dissertation). Loyola University Chicago, Illinois. Retrieved from http://ecommons.luc.edu/cgi/viewcontent.cgi?article=1132&context=luc_diss

Elmore, R. F. (2000). *Building a new structure for school leadership.* Washington, DC: Albert Shanker Institute. Retrieved from http://www.ashankerinst.org/Downloads/building.pdf

Ermeling, B. A., & Graff-Ermeling, G. (2016). *Teaching better: Igniting and sustaining instructional improvement.* Thousand Oaks, CA: Corwin.

ESSA definition of professional development. (2015). Retrieved from https://learningforward.org/who-we-are/professional-learning-definition

Farrell, T. S. C. (2015). *Promoting teacher reflection in second language education: A framework for TESOL professionals.* New York, NY: Routledge.

Fattig, M. L., & Taylor, M. T. (2007). *Collaboration, lesson design, and classroom management, Grades 5–12.* San Francisco, CA: Jossey-Bass.

Fearon, K. (2008). *A team teaching approach to ESL: An evaluative case study* (Master's thesis, No. AAT 1456437). Kean University, Union, NJ.

Ferguson, R. F. (2006). Five challenges to effective teacher professional development: School leaders can improve instruction by addressing these issues. *Journal of Staff Development, 27*(4), 48–52.

Ferlazzo, L., & Hull Sypnieski, K. (2018). *The ELL teacher's toolbox: Hundreds of practical ideas to support your students.* San Francisco, CA: Jossey-Bass.

Fernandez, C., & Chokshi, S. (2002). A practical guide to translating lesson study for a U.S. setting. *Phi Delta Kappan, 84,* 128–134.

Fizell, S. G. (2018). *Best practices in co-teaching and collaboration: The HOW of co-teaching—Implementing the models.* Manchester, NH: Cogent Catalyst.

Fogel, L. W., & Moser, K. (2017). Language teacher identities in the southern United States: Transforming rural schools. *Journal of Language, Identity and Education, 16*(2), 65–79. doi:10.1080/15348458.2016.1277147

Foltos, L. (2018, January 29). Teachers learn better together [Blog post]. Retrieved from http://www.edutopia.org/article/teachers-learn-better-together

Fradd, S. H. (1992). *Collaboration in schools serving students with limited English proficiency and other special needs.* Retrieved from ERIC database. (ED352847)

Freeman, Y. S., & Freeman, D. E. (2016). *ESL teaching: Principles for success* (2nd ed.). Portsmouth, NH: Heinemann.

Friend, M. (2005). *The power of 2.* DVD. Greensboro, NC: Marilyn Friend, Inc.

Friend, M. (2008). *Co-teach! A handbook for creating and sustaining classroom partnerships in inclusive schools.* Greensboro, NC: Marilyn Friend, Inc.

Friend, M. (2013). *Co-teach! A handbook for creating and sustaining effective classroom partnerships in inclusive schools* (2nd ed.). Greensboro, NC: Marilyn Friend, Inc.

Friend, M. (2017). *Special education: Contemporary perspectives for school professionals* (5th ed.). New York, NY: Pearson.

Friend, M., & Cook, L. (2013). *Interactions: Collaboration skills for school professionals* (7th ed.). Boston, MA: Pearson.

Friend, M., & Cook, L. (2016). *Interactions: Collaboration skills for school professionals* (8th ed.). Upper Saddle River, NJ: Pearson.

Fullan, M. (2014). *The principal: Three keys to maximizing impact.* San Francisco, CA: Jossey-Bass.

Fullan, M. (2015). *The new meaning of educational change* (5th ed.). New York, NY: Teachers College Press.

Gajda, R., & Koliba, C. J. (2008). Evaluating and improving the quality of teacher collaboration: A field-tested framework for secondary school leaders. *NASSP Bulletin, 92*, 133–153.

García, O. (2009). *Bilingual education in the 21st century: A global perspective.* Malden, MA: Wiley-Blackwell.

García, O., & Kleifgen, J. A. (2018). *Educating emergent bilinguals: Policies, programs, and practices for English language learners.* New York, NY: Teachers College Press.

García, O., & Li, W. (2014). *Translanguaging: Language, bilingualism, and education.* New York, NY: Palgrave Macmillan.

Garmston, R. (2007). Balanced conversations promote shared ownership. *Journal of Staff Development, 28*(4), 57–58.

Gately, S., & Gately, F. (2001). Understanding co-teaching components. *Teaching Exceptional Children, 33*(4), 40–47.

Genesee, F. (1999). *Program alternatives for linguistically diverse students* (Educational Practice Report No. 1). Washington, DC, & Santa Cruz, CA: Center for Research on Education, Diversity, & Excellence.

Genesee, F., & Lindholm-Leary, K. (2013). Two case studies of content-based language education. *Journal of Immersion and Content-Based Language Education, 1*, 3–33. doi:10.1075/jicb.1.1.02gen

Gibbons, P. (2015). *Scaffolding language scaffolding learning: Teaching English language learners in the mainstream classroom.* Portsmouth, NH: Heinemann.

Glickman, C. D. (1998). *Renewing America's schools: A guide for school-based action.* San Francisco, CA: Jossey-Bass.

Goddard, R., Goddard Y., Kim, E. S., & Miller, R. (2015). A theoretical and empirical analysis of the role of instructional leadership, teacher collaboration, and collective efficacy beliefs in support of student learning. *American Journal of Education, 121*, 501–530.

Godwin, P., & Gross, K. (2005). Education's many stakeholders. *University Business, 8*(9), 48–51.

Gonzalez, V. (2017). Responsibilities of an ESL teacher [Blog post]. Retrieved from https://elementary englishlanguagelearners.weebly.com/blog/responsibilities-of-an-ESL-teacher

Good, T., & Brophy, J. (2008). *Looking in classrooms* (10th ed.). New York, NY: Pearson.

Goodlad, J. I., Mantle-Bromley, C., & Goodlad, S. J. (2004). *Education for everyone: Agenda for education in a democracy.* San Francisco, CA: Jossey-Bass.

Goodman, D. J. (2015). Oppression and privilege: Two sides of the same coin. *Journal of Intercultural Communication, 18*, 1–14.

Gottlieb, M. (2016). *Assessing English language learners: Bridges to educational equity.* Thousand Oaks, CA: Corwin.

Gottlieb, M., & Honigsfeld, A. (2017). *Co-assessment* as, for, *and of learning: The power of collaboration.* Paper presented at the annual WIDA Conference, Tampa, FL.

Hammond, Z. L. (2015). *Culturally responsive teaching and the brain: Promoting authentic engagement and rigor.* Thousand Oaks, CA: Corwin.

Hattie, J. (2015). *What works best in education: The politics of collaborative expertise.* Retrieved from https://www.pearson.com/content/dam/corporate/global/pearson-dot-com/files/hattie/150526_ ExpertiseWEB_V1.pdf

Hattie, J. (2018). *Collective teacher efficacy (CTE).* Retrieved from https://visible-learning.org/2018/03/ collective-teacher-efficacy-hattie/

Helman, L., Rogers, C., Frederick, A., & Struck, M. (2016). *Inclusive literacy teaching: Differentiating approaches in multilingual elementary classrooms.* New York, NY: Teachers College Press.

Heyman, D. (Producer), & Herman, M. (Director). The boy in the striped pajamas. [Motion picture]. United Kingdom: Miramax.

Hirsch, S. (2015). New bill offers a good start on defining PD [Blog post]. Retrieved from https://learningforward .org/publications/blog/learning-forward-blog/2015/12/18/new-bill-offers-a-good-start-on-defining-pd

Honigsfeld, A., & Cohan, A. (2007). The power of two: Lesson study and SIOP help teachers instruct ELLs. *Journal of Staff Development, 29*(1), 24–28.

Honigsfeld, A., & Dove, M. G. (2010). *Collaboration and co-teaching: Strategies for English learners.* Thousand Oaks, CA: Corwin.

Honigsfeld, A., & Dove, M. G. (2015). *Collaboration and co-teaching for English learners: A leader's guide.* Thousand Oaks, CA: Corwin.

Honigsfeld, A., & Dove, M. G. (2017). The coteaching flow inside the classroom. In M. Dantas-Whitney & S. Rilling (Eds.), *TESOL voices: Insider accounts of classroom life, secondary education* (pp. 107–114). Alexandria, VA: TESOL International Association.

Honigsfeld, A., McDermott, C., & Cordeiro, K. (2017). Preparing social studies and ESOL teachers for integrating content and language instruction in support of ELLs. In L. C. de Oliveira & K. M. Obenchain (Eds.), *Teaching history and social studies to English language learners: Preparing pre-service and in-service teachers* (pp. 127–158). New York, NY: Springer.

Howard, E. R., Lindholm-Leary, K. J., Rogers, D., Olague, N., Medina, J., Kennedy, B., Sugarman, J., & Christian, D. (2018). *Guiding principles for dual language education* (3rd ed.). Washington, DC: Center for Applied Linguistics.

Hurd, J., & Lewis, C. (2011). *Lesson study step by step: How teacher learning communities improve instruction.* Portsmouth, NH: Heinemann.

Hurst, D., & Davison, C. (2005) Collaboration on the curriculum: Focus on secondary ESL. In J. Crandall & D. Kaufman (Eds.), *Case studies in TESOL: Teacher education for language and content integration.* Alexandria, VA: TESOL.

Ingersoll, R., & Strong, M. (2011). The impact of induction and mentoring programs for beginning teachers: A critical review of the research. *Review of Educational Research, 81,* 201–233. doi:10.3102/00346543 11403323

Institute of Educational Science, National Center for Educational Statistics. (2018). *Fast facts.* Retrieved from https://nces.ed.gov/fastfacts/display.asp?id=372

Isaacs, W. (1999). *Dialogue and the art of thinking together.* Thousand Oaks, CA: Corwin.

Jacobs, H. H. (1999). *Breaking new ground in high school curriculum.* Reston, VA: NAASP.

Jacobs, H. H. (Ed.). (2011). *Curriculum 21: Essential education for a changing world.* Alexandria, VA: ASCD.

Jacobs, H. H., & Alcock, M. H. (2017). *Bold moves for schools: How we create remarkable learning environments.* Alexandria, VA: ASCD.

Jacobs, H. H., & Johnson, A. (2009). *The curriculum mapping planner: Templates, tools, and resources for effective professional development.* Alexandria, VA: ASCD.

Jensen, B., Sonnemann, J., Hull-Roberts, K., & Hunter, A. (2016). *Beyond PD: Teacher professional learning in high-performing systems.* Washington, DC: National Center on Education and the Economy.

Johnston, W. R., & Tsai, T. (2018). *The prevalence of collaboration among American teachers: National findings from the American Teacher Panel.* Retrieved from https://www.rand.org/content/dam/rand/ pubs/research_reports/RR2200/RR2217/RAND_RR2217.pdf

Kaufman, D., & Crandall, J. A. (Eds.). (2005). *Content-based instruction in elementary and secondary school settings.* Alexandria, VA: TESOL.

Kaufman, R., Guerra, I., & Platt, W. A. (2006). *Practical evaluation for educators: Finding what works and what doesn't.* Thousand Oaks, CA: Corwin.

Killion, J. (2015). High-quality collaboration benefits teachers and students. *Journal of Staff Development, 36*(5), 61–64. Retrieved from https://learningforward.org/docs/default-source/jsd-october-2015/high-quality-collaboration-benefits-teachers-and-students.pdf

Killion, J. (2018). *Assessing impact: Evaluating professional learning* (3rd ed.). Thousand Oaks, CA: Corwin.

Knight, J. (2016). *Better conversations*. Thousand Oaks, CA: Corwin.

Knight, J. (2017, June 2). A close-up look at three approaches to coaching [Blog post]. Retrieved from http://corwin-connect.com/2017/06/close-look-three-approaches-coaching/

Kormákur, B. (Producer & Director). (2015). Everest [Motion picture]. United States: Universal Studios.

Krashen, S. D. (1999). *Condemned without a trial: Bogus arguments against bilingual education*. Portsmouth, NH: Heinemann.

Krownapple, J. (2015). *Equity leaders must work themselves out of a job: What collective efficacy has to do with educational equity*. Retrieved from http://corwin-connect.com/2015/12/equity-leaders-must-work-themselves-out-of-a-job-what-collective-efficacy-has-to-do-with-educational-equity/

Kuhn, D. (2015). Thinking together and alone. *Educational Researcher, 44*(1), 46–53. doi:10.3102/0013189X15569530

Kuusisaari, H. (2014). Teachers at the zone of proximal development—Collaboration promoting or hindering the development process. *Teaching and Teacher Education, 43,* 46–57.

Langer de Ramirez, L. (2009). *Empower English language learners with tools from the Web*. Thousand Oaks, CA: Corwin.

Larmer, J., Mergendoller, J. R., & Boss, S. (2015). *Setting the standards for project-based learning*. Alexandria, VA: ASCD.

Levi, D. (2016). *Group dynamics for teams* (5th ed.). Thousand Oaks, CA: Sage.

Lewis, C. (2002). *Lesson study: A handbook of teacher-led instructional improvement*. Philadelphia, PA: Research for Better Schools.

Lieberman A., & Miller, L. (1984). *Teachers, their world, and their work: Implications for school improvement*. Alexandria, VA: ASCD.

Little, J. W. (1982). Norms of collegiality and experimentation: Workplace conditions of school success. *American Educational Research Journal, 19,* 325–340.

Lortie, D. (1975). *Schoolteacher: A sociological study*. Chicago, IL: University of Chicago Press.

Love, N., Stiles, Mundry, S., & DiRanna, K. (2008). *The data coach's guide to improving learning for all students: Unleashing the power of collaborative inquiry*. Thousand Oaks, CA: Corwin.

Love, N. (2009). *Using data to improve learning for all: A collaborative inquiry approach*. Thousand Oaks, CA: Corwin.

Mann, S., & Walsh, S. (2017). *Reflective practice in English language teaching: Research-based principles and practices*. New York, NY: Routledge.

Mapp, K. L., & Kuttner, P. J. (2013). *Partners in education: A dual capacity-building framework for family–school partnerships*. SEDL. Retrieved from https://www2.ed.gov/documents/family-community/partners-education.pdf

Martin-Beltrán, M., & Madigan Peercy, M. (2012). How can ESOL and mainstream teachers make the best of standards-based curriculum in order to collaborate? *TESOL Journal, 3,* 425–444. doi:10.1002/tesj.23

Martin-Beltrán, M., & Madigan Peercy, M. (2014). Collaboration to teach English language learners: Opportunities for shared teacher learning. *Teachers and Teaching, 20,* 721–737. doi:10.1080/13540602.2014.885704

Marzano, R. J., Waters, T., & McNulty, B. A. (2005). *School leadership that works: From research to results.* Alexandria, VA: ASCD & Aurora, CO: McRel.

Maslow, A. H. (1970). *A theory of human motivation and personality* (2nd ed.). New York, NY: Harper & Row.

Mattos, M., Dufour, R., DuFour, R., Eaker, R., & Many, T. W. (2016). *Concise answers to frequently asked questions about professional learning communities at work.* Bloomington, IN: Solution Tree Press.

McDonald, J. P., Mohr, N., Dichter, A., & McDonald, E. C. (2007). *The power of protocols: An educator's guide to better practice* (2nd ed.). New York, NY: Teachers College Press.

McFarland, J., Hussar, B., Debrey, C., Snyder, T., Wang, X., Wilkinson-Flicker, S., . . . Hinz, S. (2017). *The condition of education 2017* (NCES 2017-144). Washington, DC: U.S. Department of Education.

McFeely, S. (2018). *Why your best teachers are leaving and 4 ways to keep them.* Retrieved from http://news.gallup.com/opinion/gallup/231491/why-best-teachers-leaving-ways-keep.aspx

Mills, G. E. (2017). *Action research: A guide for the teacher researcher* (6th ed.). Upper Saddle River, NJ: Pearson.

Mirel, J., & Goldin, S. (2002, April 17). Alone in the classroom: Why teachers are too isolated. *The Atlantic.*

Murawski, W. W. (2009). *Collaborative teaching in secondary schools: Making the co-teaching marriage work!* Thousand Oaks, CA: Corwin.

Murawski, W. W., & Dieker, L. A. (2013). *Leading the co-teaching dance: Leadership strategies to enhance team outcomes.* Alexandria, VA: Council for Exceptional Children.

Murawski, W. W., & Lochner, W. W. (2017). *Beyond co-teaching basics: A data-driven, no-fail model for continuous improvement.* Alexandria, VA: ASCD.

Nagle, J. F. (Ed.). (2013). *English learner instruction through collaboration and inquiry in teacher education.* Charlotte, NC: Information Age Publishing.

Nair, P. (2014). *Blueprint for tomorrow: Redesigning schools for student-centered learning.* Cambridge, MA: Harvard University Press.

Nair, P., & Fielding, R. (2005). *The language of school design: Design patterns for 21st century schools.* Retrieved from www.DesignShare.com

National Commission on Teaching and America's Future (NCTAF). (2009). *Learning teams: Creating what's next.* Retrieved from https://nctaf.org/wp-content/uploads/2012/01/NCTAFLearningTeams408REG2.pdf

National Education Association. (2015). *How educators can advocate for English language learners (ELLs): All in!* Retrieved from http://www.nea.org/assets/docs/17440_ELL_AdvocacyGuide2015_web.pdf

National Policy Board for Educational Administration. (2015). *Professional standards for educational leaders 2015.* Reston, VA: Author. Retrieved from http://npbea.org/wp-content/uploads/2017/06/Professional-Standards-for-Educational-Leaders_2015.pdf

New York State Education Department. (2018). *Program options for English language learners/multilingual learners.* Retrieved from http://www.nysed.gov/bilingual-ed/program-options-english-language-learners multilingual-learners

Newport, F. (2014). *The new era of communication among Americans.* Retrieved from https://news.gallup.com/poll/179288/new-era-communication-americans.aspx

Nieto, S., & Bode, P. (2012). *Affirming diversity: The sociopolitical context of multicultural education* (6th ed.). New York, NY: Pearson.

Norris, J. M. (2016). Language program evaluation. *Modern Language Journal, 100*(S1), 169–189. Retrieved from https://doi.org/10.1111/modl.12307

Norton, J. (2016). *Successful coteaching: ESL teachers in the mainstream classroom.* Retrieved from http://newsmanager.commpartners.com/tesolc/issues/2016-10-01/3.html

Novak, K. (2014.) *UDL now! A teacher's Monday-morning guide to implementing Common Core Standards using Universal Design for Learning.* Wakefield, MA: CAST Professional Publishing.

Office of English Language Acquisition. (2017). *Fast facts: Languages spoken by English learners (ELs).* https://ncela.ed.gov/files/fast_facts/FastFactsAllLanguagesFebruary2017.pdf

Osterman, K. F., & Kottkamp, R. B. (2015). *Reflective practice for educators: Professional development to improve student learning.* New York, NY: Skyhorse.

Pappamihiel, N. E. (2012). Benefits and challenges of co-teaching English learners in one elementary school in transition. *Tapestry Journal, 4*(1), 1–13.

Pardini, P. (2006). In one voice: Mainstream and ELL teachers work side-by-side in the classroom teaching language through content. *Journal of Staff Development, 27*(4), 20–25.

Peercy, M. M., Ditter, M., & Destefano, M. (2017). "We need more consistency": Negotiating the division of labor in ESOL—Mainstream teacher collaboration. *TESOL Journal, 8,* 215–239. doi:10.1002/tesj.269

Peercy, M. M., & Martin-Beltrán, M. (2011). Envisioning collaboration: Including ESOL students and teachers in the mainstream classroom. *International Journal of Inclusive Education, 16,* 657–673. doi:10.1080/13603116.2010.495791

Perez, K. D. (2012). *The co-teaching book of lists.* San Francisco, CA: Jossey-Bass.

Ponce, J. (2017). The far reaching benefits of co-teaching for ELLs [Blog post]. Retrieved from https://www.teachingchannel.org/blog/2017/01/20/benefits-of-co-teaching-for-ells/

Price, H. B. (2008). *Mobilizing the community to help students succeed.* Alexandria, VA: ASCD.

Quaglia, R. J., & Lande, L. L. (2017). *Teacher voice: Amplifying success.* Thousand Oaks, CA: Corwin.

Reeves, D. (2006). *The learning leader: How to focus school improvement for better results.* Alexandria, VA: ASCD.

Ritchhart, R., Church, M., & Morrison, K. (2011). *Making thinking visible: How to promote engagement, understanding, and independence for all learners.* San Francisco, CA: Jossey-Bass.

Roberts, S. M., & Pruitt, E. Z. (2009). *Schools as professional learning communities* (2nd ed.). Thousand Oaks, CA: Corwin.

Ross, J. A., & Bruce, C. D., (2007). Teacher self-assessment: A mechanism for facilitating professional growth. *Teaching and Teacher Education, 23*(2), 146–159.

Rossell, C. H. (2003). *Policy matters in teaching English language learners: New York and California.* New York, NY: ERIC Clearinghouse on Urban Education.

Ryan, C. (2013). *Language use in the United States: 2011.* Retrieved from https://www.census.gov/library/publications/2013/acs/acs-22.html

Saphier, J. (2005). Masters of motivation. In R. DuFour, R. Eaker, & R. DuFour (Eds.), *On common ground: The power of professional learning communities* (pp. 105–109). Bloomington, IN: Solution Tree Press.

Schön, D. E. (1990). *Educating the reflective practitioner: Toward a new design for teaching and learning in the professions.* San Francisco, CA: Jossey-Bass.

Sergiovanni, T. J. (1994). *Building community in schools.* San Francisco, CA: Jossey-Bass.

Short, D. J., & Boyson, B. A. (2012). *Helping newcomer students succeed in secondary schools and beyond.* Washington, DC: Center for Applied Linguistics.

Shusterman, N. (2009). *Unwind.* New York, NY: Simon & Schuster

Singer, T. W. (2015). *Opening doors to equity: A practical guide to observation-based professional learning.* Thousand Oaks, CA: Corwin.

Singer, T. W. (2018). *EL excellence every day: The flip-to guide for differentiating academic literacy.* Thousand Oaks, CA: Corwin.

Smith, S. C., & Scott, J. L. (1990). *The collaborative school: A work environment for effective instruction* (Report No. ISBN-0–86552–092–5). Eugene: University of Oregon. (ERIC Document Reproduction Service No. ED316918)

Spratt, J., & Florian, L. (2013). Applying the principles of inclusive pedagogy in initial teacher education: From university based course to classroom action. *Revista de Investigación en Educación, 11*(3), 133–140.

Staehr Fenner, D. (2013). *Implementing the Common Core State Standards for English learners: The changing role of the ESL teacher*. Alexandria, VA: TESOL International Association. Retrieved from http://www.tesol.org/docs/default-source/advocacy/ccss_convening_final-8-15-13.pdf?sfvrsn=8

Staehr Fenner, D., & Snyder, S. (2017). *Unlocking English learners' potential: Strategies for making content accessible*. Thousand Oaks, CA: Corwin.

Stein, E. (2016). *Elevating co-teaching through UDL*. Wakefield, MA: CAST Professional Publishing.

Stein, E. (2017). *Two teachers in the room: Strategies for co-teaching success*. New York, NY: Routledge.

Stiggins, R., & DuFour, R. (2009). Maximizing the power of formative assessments. *Phi Delta Kappan, 90*, 640–644.

Stufflebeam, D. L., & Coryn, C. L. S. (2014). *Evaluation theory, models, and applications* (2nd ed.). San Francisco, CA: Jossey-Bass.

TESOL International Association. (2018). *The 6 principles for exemplary teaching of English learners*. Retrieved from http://www.tesol.org/the-6-principles/about

Theoharis, G., & O'Toole, J. (2011). Leading inclusive ELL social justice leadership for English language learners. *Educational Administration Quarterly, 47*, 646–688.

Thomas, W. P., & Collier, V. P. (2002). *A national study of school effectiveness for language minority students' long-term academic achievement. Final report: Project 1.1*. Washington, DC, & Santa Cruz, CA: Center for Research on Education, Diversity, & Excellence.

Tomlinson, C. A. (2017). *How to differentiate instruction in academically diverse classrooms* (3rd ed.). Alexandria, VA: ASCD.

Tremmel, R. (1999). Zen and the art of reflective practice in teacher education. In E. M. Mintz & J. T. Yun (Eds.), *The complex world of teaching: Perspectives from theory and practice* (pp. 87–111). Cambridge, MA: Harvard Educational Review.

Udelhofen, S. (2005). *Keys to curriculum mapping: Strategies and tools to make it work*. Thousand Oaks, CA: Corwin.

Udelhofen, S. (2014). *Building a Common Core based curriculum: Mapping with focus and fidelity*. Bloomington, IN: Solution Tree Press.

Uline, C., Tschannen-Moran, M., & Wolsey, T. D. (2009). The walls still speak: The stories occupants tell. *Journal of Educational Administration, 47*, 400–426.

U.S. Department of Education. (2017). *English learner tool kit*. Washington, DC: Author. Retrieved from https://www2.ed.gov/about/offices/list/oela/english-learner-toolkit/index.html

U.S. Department of Labor, Bureau of Labor Statistics. (2016–2017). Teaching assistants. *Occupational outlook handbook*. Retrieved from https://www.bls.gov/ooh/education-training-and-library/teacher-assistants.htm

Valdés, G., Kibler, A., & Walqui, A. (2014). *Changes in the expertise of ESL professionals: Knowledge and action in an era of new standards*. Alexandria, VA: TESOL International Association. Retrieved from http://www.tesol.org/docs/default-source/papers-and-briefs/professional-paper-26-march-2014.pdf?sfvrsn=4

Valentino, R. A., & Reardon, S. F. (2014, March). *Effectiveness of four instructional programs designed to serve English language learners: Variation by ethnicity and initial English proficiency*. Retrieved from Stanford

Center for Education Policy Analysis website: http://cepa.stanford.edu/sites/default/files/Valentino_Reardon_ELPrograms_14_0326_2.pdf

Van Note Chism, N. (2006). Challenging traditional assumptions and rethinking learning spaces. In D. G. Oblinger (Ed.), *Learning spaces* (pp. 2.1–2.12). Retrieved from https://www.educause.edu/research-and-publications/books/learning-spaces/chapter-2-challenging-traditional-assumptions-and-rethinking-learning-spaces

Vangrieken, K., Dochy, F., Raes, E., & Kyndt, E. (2015). Teacher collaboration: A systematic review. *Educational Research Review, 15*, 17–40.

Vangrieken, K., Grosemans, I., Dochy, F., & Kyndt, E. (2017). Teacher autonomy and collaboration: A paradox? Conceptualising and measuring teachers' autonomy and collaborative attitude. *Teaching and Teacher Education, 67*, 302–315. http://dx.doi.org/10.1016/j.tate.2017.06.021

Villa, R. A., & Thousand, J. S. (2016). *Leading an inclusive school: Access and success for all students.* Alexandria, VA: ASCD.

Villa, R. A., Thousand J. S., & Nevin, A. I. (2008). *A guide to co-teaching: Practical tips for facilitating student learning.* Thousand Oaks, CA: Corwin.

Villa, R. A., Thousand, J. S., & Nevin, A. I. (2013). *A guide to co-teaching: New lessons and strategies to facilitate student learning* (3rd ed.). Thousand Oaks, CA: Corwin.

Villani, S., & Dunne, K. (2012). *Collaborative coaching: Coach's guide.* Naples, FL: National Professional Resources.

Vilorio, D. (2016). *Teaching for a living.* Retrieved from https://www.bls.gov/careeroutlook/2016/article/education-jobs-teaching-for-a-living.htm

Walqui, A., & Van Lier, L. (2010). *Scaffolding the academic success of adolescent English language learners: A pedagogy of promise.* San Francisco, CA: WestEd.

Wang, M., & Degol, J. (2016). School climate: A review of the construct, measurement, and impact on student outcomes. *Educational Psychology Review, 28*, 315–352. doi:10.1007/s10648-015-9319-1

Welborn, B. (2012, March 14). Six keys to successful collaboration [Blog post]. Retrieved from https://www.edweek.org/tm/articles/2012/03/13/tln_collaboration.html

York-Barr, J., Sommers, W. A., Ghere, G. S., & Montie, J. (2016). *Reflective practice for renewing schools: An action guide for educators* (3rd ed.). Thousand Oaks, CA: Corwin.

Zabolio McGrath, M., & Holden Johns, B. (2006). *The teacher's reflective calendar and planning journal: Motivation, inspiration, and affirmation.* Thousand Oaks, CA: Corwin.

Zacarian, D., & Haynes, J. (2012). *The essential guide for educating beginning English learners.* Thousand Oaks, CA: Corwin.

Zeichner, K. M., & Liston, D. P. (1996). *Reflective teaching: An introduction.* Mahwah, NJ: Lawrence Erlbaum.

Zigler, E., & Weiss, C. H. (1985). Family support systems: An ecological approach to child development. In R. N. Rapoport (Ed.), *Children, youth, and families: The action-research relationship* (pp. 166–205). Cambridge, UK: Cambridge University Press.

Name Index

In this index *f* indicates figure and *t* indicates table

Subject Index

In this index *f* indicates figure and *t* indicates table

A SAGE Publishing Company

Helping educators make the greatest impact

CORWIN HAS ONE MISSION: to enhance education through intentional professional learning.

We build long-term relationships with our authors, educators, clients, and associations who partner with us to develop and continuously improve the best evidence-based practices that establish and support lifelong learning.

Solutions YOU WANT | Experts YOU TRUST | Results YOU NEED

EVENTS

>>> **INSTITUTES**

Corwin Institutes provide large regional events where educators collaborate with peers and learn from industry experts. Prepare to be recharged and motivated!

corwin.com/institutes

ON-SITE PD

>>> **ON-SITE PROFESSIONAL LEARNING**

Corwin on-site PD is delivered through high-energy keynotes, practical workshops, and custom coaching services designed to support knowledge development and implementation.

corwin.com/pd

>>> **PROFESSIONAL DEVELOPMENT RESOURCE CENTER**

The PD Resource Center provides school and district PD facilitators with the tools and resources needed to deliver effective PD.

corwin.com/pdrc

ONLINE

>>> **ADVANCE**

Designed for K–12 teachers, Advance offers a range of online learning options that can qualify for graduate-level credit and apply toward license renewal.

corwin.com/advance

Contact a PD Advisor at (800) 831-6640 or visit www.corwin.com for more information